A Bad Day I Fear

The Irish Divisions at the Battle of Langemarck 16 August 1917

Michael James Nugent

Helion & Company

Helion & Company Limited
Unit 8 Amherst Business Centre
Budbrooke Road
Warwick
CV34 5WE
England
Tel. 01926 499 619
Email: info@helion.co.uk
Website: www.helion.co.uk
Twitter: @helionbooks
Visit our blog at blog.helion.co.uk

Published by Helion & Company 2023
Designed and typeset by Mach 3 Solutions (www.mach3solutions.co.uk)
Cover designed by Paul Hewitt, Battlefield Design (www.battlefield-design.co.uk)

Text © Michael James Nugent 2023
Images © as individually credited
Maps drawn by George Anderson © Helion & Company 2023
Cover: Stretcher bearer procession, Ypres 1917. (Open Source). L to R inserts: 16th (Irish) Division and 36th (Ulster) Division formation insignia

Every reasonable effort has been made to trace copyright holders and to obtain their permission for the use of copyright material. The author and publisher apologize for any errors or omissions in this work and would be grateful if notified of any corrections that should be incorporated in future reprints or editions of this book.

ISBN 9-7-81804513-26-2

British Library Cataloguing-in-Publication Data.
A catalogue record for this book is available from the British Library.

All rights reserved. No part of this publication may be reproduced, stored in a retrieval system, or transmitted, in any form, or by any means, electronic, mechanical, photocopying, recording or otherwise, without the express written consent of Helion & Company Limited.

For details of other military history titles published by Helion & Company Limited contact the above address or visit our website: http://www.helion.co.uk.

We always welcome receipt of book proposals from prospective authors.

Contents

List of Images	iv
List of Maps	vi
Acknowledgements	vii
Acronyms	ix
British and German Army Rank Comparison	x
Introduction	xi
1 Strategic Situation on the Western Front, Summer 1917	17
2 Flanders Offensive Planning	29
3 German Defences	45
4 Ground Conditions and Weather	54
5 Opening of the Offensive, 31 July–15 August 1917	59
6 Thursday, 16 August 1917 16th (Irish) Division	100
7 Thursday, 16 August 1917 36th (Ulster) Division	136
8 Aftermath	184
Retrospective	204
Appendices	
I Infantry Battalions of 16th (Irish) and 36th (Ulster) Division	209
II Group Ypres, Fourth Army	211
III Translation of captured order issued by German Fourth Army, dated July 1917	212
IV XIX Corps Operation Order No. 79, 8 August 1917	218
Bibliography	222
Index	229

List of Images

Second Lieutenant John Samuel Carrothers. (*Memoirs of a Young Lieutenant 1898-1917*)	18
Oberst Fritz von Lossberg. (Open source)	48
Messines Ridge Blockhouse at New Zealand Memorial to the Missing. (Author)	49
Ground conditions, August 1917. (Canadian War Museum Archive EO-2249)	58
Captain Chavasse VC gravesite, Brandhoek New Military Cemetery. (Author)	62
Lieutenant Stephen Walter gravesite, Lijssenthoek Military Cemetery. (Author)	67
Pte Stephen Carrigan gravesite, Aeroplane Cemetery. (Author)	73
Frezenberg area and railway. (TNA: WO 95/1977/3 8th battalion Royal Inniskilling Fusiliers war diary)	77
Private Michael Hagan gravesite. (Author)	81
Serjeant John Brophy gravesite. (Author)	82
Second Lieutenant John Witherow. (Great War Ulster Newspaper Archive)	84
Wieltje Farm Cemetery. (Author)	86
German dispositions, 15 August 1917. (TNA: WO158/249)	94
Attacking battalion dispositions schematic.	96
Stretcher bearers struggle through the mud. (Canadian War Museum EO-2202)	99
Lieutenant William Kingston. (Great War Ulster Newspaper Archive)	104
Private Michael Flood. (Will. National Archives Ireland)	107
Captain James Owen William Shine. (Open source)	111
Second Lieutenant Storrar Headstone Potijze Chateau Grounds Cemetery. (Authors Collection)	114
Second Lieutenant George Coombes DCM MM gravesite. (Author)	129
Second Lieutenant Arthur Conway Young gravesite. (Author)	131
Lance Corporal Frederick George Room VC. (Open source)	132
Lance Corporal Frederick George Room VC Wedding. (David & Jennifer Kingscott)	133
Hill 35 from Black Line. (Author)	137
Gallipoli Farm from Hill 35. (Author)	137
Private Edmund Gray. (Christine Tyrell)	143
Lieutenant William Graham Boyd. (Great War Ulster Newspaper Archive)	144
Lieutenant James Matthew Stronge Headstone. (Author)	145
Second Lieutenant Samuel Levis Trinder Headstone. (Author)	146
Captain Thomas Graham Shillington. (Great War Ulster Newspaper Archive)	147

108th Brigade sector. (TNA: WO 95/2505/2 9th Royal Irish Fusiliers war diary)	149
Somme Farm from Pond Farm. (Author)	151
Rifleman William John Watson. (Will. National Archives Ireland)	155
Rifleman James McKinney gravesite. (Author)	157
Haeseler Bunker at Pond Farm. (Author)	159
Second Lieutenant Alexander McCullagh. (Great War Ulster Newspaper Archive)	160
Second Lieutenant Alexander McCullagh gravesite. (Author)	161
Private William Brown. (Peter Johnston)	162
RSM Frederick Jacquest gravesite. (Author)	164
Lieutenant Colonel Audley Pratt gravesite. (Author)	168
Memorial scroll for Lance Corporal Rutledge. (Inniskillings Museum)	172
Second Lieutenant Fred Irwin MM. (Ancestry)	174
Second Lieutenant Fred Irwin MM gravesite. (Author)	175
Corporal John Greenwood MM. (Great War Ulster Newspaper Archive)	182
Aerial photograph, 9 August 1917. (Inniskillings Museum ID 353)	185
Black Line to Hill 35 vista. (Author)	185

List of Maps

1	High ground east of Ypres.	20
2	Flanders offensive plan.	23
3	Fifth Army stages of the offensive.	33
4	German defences, Flanders July 1917.	46
5	Ypres to the Belgian coast.	55
6	Pilckem Ridge: XIX Corps assault, 31 July 1917.	60
7	Westhoek, 10 August 1917.	88
8	16th (Irish) Division area of operations.	101
9	36th (Ulster) Division objectives, 16 August 1917.	139

Acknowledgements

Following the completion of my previous book on the Ulster Division during the German Spring Offensive of March 1918, I took what I believed at the time was going to be a short break, prior to commencing my Langemarck project. That was in January 2019. I was aiming to research and write this book by the end of 2020.

Then COVID struck and threw a large spanner in the works. With research facilities such as The National Archives, Imperial War Museum, Public Records Office Northern Ireland, the Regimental Museums and Libraries all closed for prolonged periods, I had to focus on researching available internet sources and purchasing relevant books, reading and making copious notes. This was no bad thing as I was able to carry out more thorough research into particularly the background to the Third Ypres Offensive, which hopefully is apparent in the narrative.

What pained me most was the inability to travel, and specifically to Belgium to walk the ground. I would not dream of putting pen to paper until I have actually been there to get a feel for the battlefield. As the old Army maxim states, 'Time spent on a recce is seldom wasted.' Taking the opportunity to attend the centenary commemorations for the Ulster Tower at Thiepval, Alison and I swiftly booked an excellent apartment in Ypres and fortuitously taking advantage of a travel window, managed to get there in November 2021. To be able to finally 'walk the ground' after having studied it for two years was cathartic.

As everyone was locked down during the pandemic, I found that friends, colleagues and contacts old and new, were very keen to assist, and spend time in answering queries for which I am eternally grateful. I would like to thank the following who have been of vital assistance in progressing this project to a satisfactory conclusion.

The leading authority on the German Army in the Great War, Dr Jack Sheldon, has been of great support, particularly in identifying the German units facing the Irish Divisions and in providing excerpts from their regimental histories. Jack's altruistic efforts saved me a lot of research time and expense. Having received the German regimental histories, I am once again indebted to Ms Jane Kenny for undertaking the translation of relevant passages in addition to her busy study schedule. The fact that the histories were in *Fraktur*, or Gothic German Font, proved no impediment to Jane and she identified and kindly provided translations of a number of strongpoint names on the battlefield which did not appear in other texts.

The staff of the Regimental Museums of the Royal Inniskilling Fusiliers, Royal Irish Fusiliers and Royal Irish Rifles, have stepped up to the mark yet again. I would particularly like to thank Mrs Pauline McCartney of the Inniskillings Museum for facilitating access to their archives and for the loan of a number of volumes from their extensive collection of Regimental Histories which again, saved a lot of time and expense. Thanks are also due to Mrs Carol Walker MBE and Austin Cheevers of the Somme Heritage Centre for support and in facilitating access to the centre's archives. The Public Records Office Northern Ireland (PRONI) has again been a valuable source of information and I am grateful to the Deputy Keeper of the Records for permission to use material held by them.

In relation to the Royal Inniskilling Fusiliers who put five battalions across the two divisions in the field on that fateful day, I was fortunate in coming into contact via social media with Chris Murphy, an undoubted expert on 7th (Service) Battalion Royal Inniskilling Fusiliers. Chris has been a keen supporter of this project from the outset with advice and material from his research. I would also like to thank my colleague Nigel Henderson for once again granting me access to his excellent Great War Ulster Newspaper Archive.

Without exception, the staff of the various research facilities have been unfailingly helpful and I could not have completed this project without their assistance. I would also like to thank Dr Michael LoCicero, company proprietor Duncan Rogers and all at Helion & Company for once again having faith in my writing ability.

Finally, I would like to thank my family for their support through what has been a long, drawn out process. I am glad finally to see this volume completed, and I know that they are too!

The title of this book, *A Bad Day I Fear*, is a quote by Lieutenant Colonel Claud Potter, Commanding Officer 153rd Brigade Royal Field Artillery who provided support to 36th Division on 16 August. The quotation has been used with the kind permission of his son, Tony.

Acronyms

C-in-C – Commander in Chief
CIGS – Chief of the Imperial General Staff
CQMS – Company Quartermaster Serjeant
CRA – Commander Royal Artillery
DMI – Director of Military Intelligence
FOO – Forward Observation Officers
GHQ – General Headquarters
GOC – General Officer Commanding
HE – High Explosive
MG – Machine Gun
NCO – Non Commissioned Officer
OC – Officer Commanding
OHL – *Oberste Heerseleitung*. The German Supreme Army Command
POW – Prisoner of War
SAA – Small Arms Ammunition
TMB – Trench Mortar Battery

British and German Army Rank Comparison

Field Marshal – Generalfeldmarschall
Lieutenant General – Generalleutnant
General – General der Infanterie
Major General – Generalmajor
Colonel – Oberst
Lieutenant Colonel – Oberstleutnant
Major – Major
Captain – Hauptmann
Lieutenant – Oberleutnant
Second Lieutenant – Leutnant
Serjeant Major – Feldwebel
Staff Serjeant – Vizefeldwebel
Serjeant – Serjeant
Corporal – Unteroffizier
Lance Corporal – Gefreiter
Private – Fusilier/Jager/Soldat

Introduction

Throughout my journey in Great War research, I have constantly been drawn to engagements and battles which have to date not received focused attention in Great War literature. It was this perceived omission which led me to write my first book on the 2nd Battalion Royal Inniskilling Fusiliers at the Battle of Festubert in May 1915, and my second on the Ulster Division during the German Offensive of Spring 1918.

Analysis of this latter battle led me to the conclusion that the lack of a focused account was due to the fact that the British Army experience was perceived as a defeat and something that was better not dwelt on. At that the time of writing that account, similar engagements perceived as defeats or those whose outcome was inconclusive came to mind. This is an issue commented on by Prior and Wilson in their book, *Passchendaele, the Untold Story*, published in 1996:

> There is a dearth of comprehensive accounts of the British Army's struggle in Flanders in the second half of 1917. This seems strange. No Great War campaign excites stronger emotions, and no word better encapsulates the horror and apparent futility of Western Front combat than 'Passchendaele'. Yet the literature on this episode is astonishingly thin.[1]

None more so I would contend than the Battle of Langemarck in August 1917.

In this context, what is particularly striking about this battle is the fact that it came just over ten weeks after the spectacular success of both the 16th (Irish) Division and 36th (Ulster) Divisions in their joint attack at the Battle of Messines on 7 June 1917.

On the day following that battle, the commanding officer of 36th (Ulster) Division, Major General Oliver Nugent in a letter to his wife stated:

> Our men are in great heart. They say they have got their own back at last. They did most extraordinarily well. I have learned that this Division took all its objectives with less loss than any other Division in the Army and we took more prisoners…The Army Comdr was here today to congratulate the Division and he brought the C in C's congratulations as well. In fact we have had congratulations all round and we will feel happy to think that the long weeks of preparation are crowned with success.[2]

---

1 Robin Prior & Trevor Wilson, *Passchendaele: The Untold Story* (New Haven & London, Yale University Press 1996).
2 Public Records Office Northern Ireland (PRONI) D/3835/E/2/13: Farren Connell papers.

This can be contrasted with the mood of the same author writing to his wife on the day of the Battle of Langemarck:

> It has been a truly terrible day. Worse than the 1st of July I am afraid. Our losses have been very heavy indeed and we have failed all along the line so far as this Division is concerned, and the whole Division has been driven back with terrible losses…Our failure has involved the failure of the Divisions on both sides of us and that is so bitter a pill. In July of last year, we did our work but failed because the Divisions on either flank failed us. This time it is the Ulster Division which has failed the Army.[3]

Dramatic words indeed and written when the action on the battlefield was still ongoing. Was this however just the immediate reaction to the events of that day without recourse to time for reflection? The account of one of the official War Correspondents, Philip Gibbs, to all intents and purposes an independent observer is of interest. In an article written for *The Daily Chronicle* five days after the battle on 21 August and titled 'The Irish in the Swamps' he stated;

> It is of the Irish now that I will write, though their story is four days old and not a tale of great victory. It is easier to write of success than of failure, and of great advances than of grim rearguard actions fought by men desperately tried but still heroic…These Irishmen had no luck at all. They gained ground but lost it again. It is up to the Irish to tell this tale, for they were grand men and they fought and fell with simple valour. They were the Southern Irish and the men of Ulster side by side again as they were at Wytschaete, where I met them on the morning of the battle and afterwards, glad because they had taken a great share in one of the finest victories of the war.[4]

From the quotations above, it is evident that a catastrophic series of events must have unfolded in the 10 weeks between Messines and Langemarck to have dealt the Irish divisions such a bitter blow.

The aim of this volume is to examine the factors that impacted so adversely on the two Irish divisions and which led to the disastrous casualties suffered by both in August 1917. Included will be, the strategic position prevailing on the Western Front in the summer of 1917 and the competing aspirations for prosecuting the war between the Prime Minister, the Right Honourable David Lloyd George MP and the Commander in Chief, Field Marshal Sir Douglas Haig. The deterioration of the personal relationship between the two will be shown to have had a detrimental effect on the planning for the continuation of the offensive after Messines.

The British Plans for the offensive which became known as Third Ypres will be analysed along with the personalities involved. The personal relationships between those at command level will be shown to be problematic and to have ultimately played an important negative role in the events from the opening of the offensive on 31 July, onwards.

Whilst the British plans are of great importance, the defensive plans of the Germans are of equal value. The Battle of Messines was disastrous for the Germans and the remarkable efforts

---

3 Public Records Office Northern Ireland (PRONI) D/3836/E/2/14: Farren Connell papers.
4 Philip Gibbs, *From Bapaume to Passchendaele 1917* (London, Heinemann, 1965) p.251.

that they undertook to construct a defensive system to meet the inevitable continuation of the Allied offensive in a limited timespan are studied in detail. This study has been aided greatly by the availability of the regimental histories of the German Regiments in direct opposition to the Irish divisions. A debt of gratitude is owed in this regard to the eminent expert on the German Army, Jack Sheldon, who has been most generous in his support. Integral to the German defensive effort was the construction of myriad bunkers, blockhouses and pillboxes, the sheer number and variety of which astonished me during my research. Numerous accounts from soldiers on the ground recall how these bunkers were impervious to all but the heaviest of artillery shells and the efforts put into the construction of these structures will be examined.

The word 'Passchendaele' is often used to sum up the entirety of the Third Ypres offensive which lasted from 31 July to 10 November 1917. However, whilst the village was an objective, only the final two battles bear its name. The development of the offensive is chronicled by specific battle below:

> Pilckem Ridge 31 July to 2nd August
> Langemarck 16 to 18 August
> Menin Road Ridge 20 to 25 September
> Polygon Wood 26 September to 3 October
> Broodseinde 4 October
> Poelcapelle 9 October
> Passchendaele I 12 October
> Passchendaele II 26 October to 10 November

The name 'Passchendaele' however, often conjures up an image in the mind's eye of men struggling through a sea of mud. It is true that the adverse weather in concert with the preliminary artillery bombardment affected the development of the offensive from the opening day, and the situation around the weather forecasting has provoked debate in other publications on Third Ypres. In this book the weather, and how it affected the Irish divisions both directly and indirectly in the period leading up to the battle and in the battle itself, will be examined.

The Battle of Langemarck opened at 4:45 a.m. on 16 August 1917 and in the official battle nomenclature lasted until 18 August. There is evidence however, that the battle was to all intents and purposes over by the evening of 16 August. The experience of each of the Irish divisions on that fateful day is examined in detail, utilising official histories, war diaries, maps and personal accounts to construct an easily readable narrative which will hopefully assist the reader to understand the importance of that significant day in Irish military history.

Given the events of 16 August, the aftermath is worthy of further scrutiny. The fatalities suffered by each of the Irish divisions are similar and the fatalities suffered by each of the attacking battalions illustrate how the battle unfolded. In other literature on Third Ypres, adverse comments on the performance of the Irish divisions by the Commander of Fifth Army, General Sir Hubert Gough have been highlighted. These comments are investigated in detail and combined with other factors integral to the battle are analysed to see if they bear any semblance of fact.

As highlighted earlier, there has never been a comprehensive account of the Irish divisions at Langemarck written. In the absence of an official history of 16th Division, *Ireland's Unknown Soldiers* by Terence Denman provides an excellent account of the events leading up to and including the Battle of Langemarck, although given that the book covers the entirety of the war, the account is by necessity, brief. Cyril Fall's *The History of the 36th (Ulster) Division* again provides an admirable account of the events leading up to, and the battle itself and extends to 12 pages however, for the same reason as Denman, it covers the basic facts.

There are mentions of both Irish divisions in many other books on Third Ypres, such as Prior and Wilson's *Passchendaele, the Untold Story,* Nick Lloyd's *Passchendaele: A New History* and most recently Paul Ham's *Passchendaele: Requiem for a Doomed Youth* to name but a few. These accounts uniformly provide a sympathetic account of the experience of the Irish Divisions and focus on their losses and the apparent unfeeling comments of General Gough, to illustrate the futility of the continuance of the offensive.

The most comprehensive account to date can be found in Tom Johnstone's 1992 volume *Orange, Green and Khaki.* In this excellent book, Johnstone devotes around 10 pages to the experiences of each of the divisions in the days leading up to the battle and the battle itself.

Whilst carrying out background research for a trip to Belgium to 'walk the ground' and identifying which cemeteries I needed to visit, I was struck by how few of the men I was interested in had a known grave compared to other battles of the conflict. I found it comparable to my previous research on the 2nd Inniskillings at Festubert in 1915 however, there are subtle differences. At Festubert, the dead remained unburied due to the fact that the Germans continued to hold the battlefield until 1918, whereas at Langemarck, the ground conditions were so horrendous that it was impossible to locate and identify remains for burial. This circumstance was remarked upon by Neil Richardson:

> Out of all the descendants of First World War veterans who contacted me, not one had a story to tell about a relative at the Third Battle of Ypres. The simple explanation for this is that, at Ypres in 1917, men were far more likely to die than survive and those that did were often so terribly weakened that they never lived long enough to impart their stories.[5]

In common with Richardson, I found this to be the case. Appeals through social media, military history publications, interest groups, and by word of mouth for accounts in the form of letters and diaries, failed to elicit a positive response.

This situation has given added importance to the accurate recording of the events of August 1917 for two main reasons. Firstly, to provide an accurate account of the battle and secondly, to inform the wider public of the sacrifice of their ancestors.

Given the involvement of the Irish divisions, the issue of political affiliations is never too far from the surface however, it is too simplistic to describe the battle being carried out by the Unionist 36th (Ulster) Division and the Nationalist 16th (Irish) Division. By summer 1917, neither division existed as originally intended. This was partly due to the sacrifices of the 36th Division in July 1916 and the 16th Division in September of that year, and also due to the difficulties of recruiting in Ireland. At the end of September 1916, the Adjutant General Sir Nevil McCready reported that the Irish divisions were 17,194 men understrength.[6] Although

---

5   Neil Richardson, *A Coward if I Return: A Hero if I Fall. Stories of Irishmen in World War I* (Dublin: O'Brien Press, 2010), p.289.
6   Timothy Bowman, *Irish Regiments in the Great War: Discipline and Morale* (Manchester: Manchester University Press, 2003), p.141.

this figure included the 10th Division, the majority of the vacancies were in the two divisions on the Western Front.

Both divisions received reinforcements from unexpected sources. To give two examples, the 7th Leinsters in the 16th Division's 47th Infantry Brigade received 109 men from the Shropshire Light Infantry prior to the battle,[7] whilst at the beginning of July 1917, the 14th Royal Irish Rifles of 36th Division's 109th Infantry Brigade, received one officer and 78 other ranks from the Army Service Corps.[8]

The names of the infantry battalions within each division shows that there was a still an Irish ethos which transcended political affiliations. The 16th Irish Division had two battalions of Royal Inniskilling Fusiliers whilst the 36th had three. The 36th had nine battalions of Royal Irish Rifles whilst the 16th had one. Both divisions had one battalion of Royal Irish Fusiliers, the 7/8th in the 16th and the 9th in the 36th.[9] No matter the composition, the fact remains that both Irish divisions were an integral part of the Fifth Army during the Third Ypres offensive. Hopefully in the following pages, their story can now receive the attention it deserves.

---

7   Bowman, *Irish Regiments in the Great War*, p.143.
8   The National Archives (TNA) WO 95/2511/1: 14th Royal Irish Rifles War Diary.
9   The 1st Royal Irish Fusiliers had been transferred from 4th Division to 36th Division on 3 August 1917 but did not join 107th Brigade until 24th August.

1

Strategic Situation on the Western Front, Summer 1917

Thursday, 7 June 1917 had been a good day for Second Lieutenant John Samuel (Jack) Carrothers, C Company, 8th Battalion Royal Inniskilling Fusiliers. A Farmer from Tamlaght, near Enniskillen, he had joined the battalion in March aged 19, from No 7 officer cadet battalion at Fermoy, County Cork, and it was his first taste of action. He described his elation in a letter to his mother the following day:

> Just a line to let you know that I am quite well and have returned from the biggest push of all without a scratch. Yesterday was a great day for Ireland. Given everything our casualties have been very light, but my platoon lost heavily.[1] We captured an enormous number of prisoners. The part we attacked was a famous ridge just south of Ypres. I went over with the first wave and after all it was the safest place.[2]

Jack Carrothers was right in one regard, it was the biggest push of all, certainly in 1917.

Planning for the 1917 offensives commenced in October of the previous year, even before the Battle of the Somme had drawn to a close. The identities of those involved in the planning process and their relationships are key to how events unfolded.

The plan to make Flanders the main area of effort on the Western Front for 1917 was discussed by the War Committee of the British Cabinet on 26 October 1916. The War Committee was a three-man board delegated to make decisions on war related matters. At the time of this meeting, it was chaired by the Secretary of State for War, the Right Honourable David Lloyd George MP. The Flanders plan was ratified at a further meeting of the committee on 23 November when it was agreed that:

> There was no measure to which the Committee attached greater importance than the expulsion of the enemy from the Belgian coast.[3]

---

1 Commonwealth War Graves Commission data records that the 8th Inniskillings sustained seven fatalities on 7 June 1917.
2 Public Records Office Northern Ireland (PRONI) D/1973/10 Carrothers papers.
3 Brigadier General Sir James Edmonds, *History of the Great War based on Official Documents, Military Operations France and Belgium 1917*, Vol. 2 (London: HMSO, 1948), p.8.

The initial decision for what transpired in Flanders in 1917 therefore, had the signature of Lloyd George. December 1916 was an important month for both David Lloyd George and Douglas Haig. On 6 December, Lloyd George became Prime Minister in succession to Herbert Asquith and on 22 December, Douglas Haig was elevated to Field Marshal by King George V. On the face of it, the two men had a seemingly cordial relationship however, even at that stage, fissures were forming in the relationship which were to adversely impact on events in 1917.

The first indication for Douglas Haig of the nature of Lloyd George's character had come in September 1916. As Secretary of State for War, on 10 September Lloyd George had visited the Headquarters of the French Army Group north (Groupe Provisoire du Nord) at the invitation of its commander, General Ferdinand Foch. The following day, he was due to visit Haig at St Omer however, with his customary lack of punctuality, did not arrive until the next day. On 13 September, Haig wrote to his wife with his impressions of Lloyd George:

Second Lieutenant John Samuel Carrothers. (*Memoirs of a Young Lieutenant 1898-1917*)

> Lloyd George has been with me during the past two days, so I have been able to notice the differences in the two men and to realise how much superior in many ways Mr Asquith is to L.G. I have got on with the latter very well indeed, and he is anxious to help in every way that he can. But he seems to me to be so flighty – makes plans and is always changing them and his mind … The P.M's visit was on business lines. L.G's has been a huge 'joy ride! Breakfasts with newspaper men, and posings for the Cinema shows pleased him more than anything else. No doubt with the ulterior motives of catching votes. From what I have written, you will gather that I have no great opinion of L.G. *as a man or leader*.[4]

Within days, Haig would have a very definite opinion of Lloyd George.

On 17 September, General Foch visited Haig with staff and following a discussion on military matters asked to speak to Haig alone. He then confided that during Lloyd George's visit, he had questioned Foch as to why the British had suffered such heavy casualties at the Somme in comparison to the French. He also asked the opinion of Foch of the abilities of British Generals

---

[4] Robert Blake, *The Private Papers of Douglas Haig 1914-1919* (London: Eyre and Spottiswoode, 1952), p.166.

and divulged that he could not speak with confidence of British Generals as a whole. Foch indicated to Haig that he had been diplomatic and tactful in his replies. Following this visit, Haig noted in his diary:

> Unless I had been told of this conversation personally by General Foch, I would not have believed that a British Minister could have been so ungentlemanly as to go to a foreigner and put such questions regarding his own subordinates.[5]

There is no doubt that this episode coloured Haig's view of the man who was to become Prime Minister within a few months. Whilst correspondence between the two was cordial, Haig remained justifiably wary of Lloyd George's true intentions.

Plans for 1917 initially discussed by the War Committee in October, were further discussed at an Anglo-French conference at Chantilly on 15 and 16 November attended on the British side by the Prime Minister, Secretary of State for War, and the C-in-C, amongst others. The first conclusion reached defined the priorities for 1917:

> That all are unanimously of opinion that the Western Theatre is the main one, and that the resources employed in other theatres should be reduced to the smallest possible.[6]

Following this meeting, the War Committee gathered at 10 Downing Street on 23 November, the meeting being chaired by Lloyd George and attended by Douglas Haig and the Chief of the Imperial General Staff (CIGS) General Sir William Robertson. At that meeting the broad outline of the main 1917 offensive was discussed. Haig's plan was nothing if not bold. The German domination of the high ground around Ypres had been a thorn in the side of the allies since 1914. Haig's intention was not only to drive them off the high ground but to then swing north towards the Belgian coast. As that phase progressed, an amphibious landing was to take place behind German lines with the operations converging on the Belgian coast between Ostend and Zeebrugge, with the intention of liberating these ports.

This plan had a number of strategic benefits to the war effort. Removal of the Germans from the ridge line to the east of Ypres would immediately solve a problem that had bedevilled the British since 1914, namely that the Germans would lose the advantage of being able to command the high ground and observe British movements in the vicinity of the town. Secondly, if the offensive progressed satisfactorily, important railway junctions at Roulers and Thorout would come into British hands, denying the Germans important lines of communication. Thirdly, and perhaps of the greatest importance, was the proposed amphibious landing on the Belgian coast which, if successful would eject the Germans from their submarine bases at Ostend and Zeebrugge, from where they had been waging a ceaseless campaign against British and Allied merchant shipping.

As previously mentioned, the outline plan was approved and was then passed to the main Allied partners, the French, who were enthusiastic in their agreement. With the green light given to the strategic plan, General Sir Herbert Plumer was given the task of coming up with

---

5 Blake, *The Private Papers of Douglas Haig 1914-1919*, p.167.
6 Edmonds, *Military Operations France and Belgium 1917*, Vol. II, p.8.

Map 1 High ground east of Ypres.

tactical plans. As GOC Second Army, Herbert Plumer was a vastly experienced soldier, having 40 years' service at that time. More importantly, he appeared to be the right man at the right time in the right place as his Second Army had been in the Ypres salient since October 1914. Plumer however, had well advanced, existing plans for an attack to capture the Messines–Wytschaete Ridge, Hill 60 and Hill 29 near Pilckem. If successful this would deny the Germans excellent observation of British positions and the plans that he submitted on 12 December 1916, basically reflected these objectives as a first step, and considered using a second army to deal with the more northerly objectives.

This was a key moment and what transpired is evidence of Haig's laissez-faire management style and was the beginning of a slough of confusion which was to characterise the Third Ypres offensive. Instead of confronting Plumer and insisting on a complete plan from him, he ordered General Sir Henry Rawlinson, GOC Fourth Army, to come up with a plan for the northern part of the proposed offensive. His Fourth Army had been in action on the Somme since its inception in February 1916 and Rawlinson had no experience or knowledge of the Ypres salient.

The original plan agreed at the Chantilly conference was subtly changing and this state of affairs was given added impetus by plans being drawn up by the new star in the French Army firmament, General Robert Nivelle. Nivelle had had great success in October 1916, by retaking ground at Verdun which had been lost the previous Spring. Based on that success Nivelle was convinced that momentum was building and that a massive offensive led by the French in the Spring of 1917 would set the Germans on the road to ultimate defeat. Nivelle replaced General Joffre as C-in-C French Armies in the north and north-east in late December 1916 and his ambitious plan for a massive breakthrough by the French on a wide front was approved. This offensive was to be backed by a smaller British attack at Arras.

All however, was not well within the ranks of the French Army. By the end of 1916, French casualties from the outset of the war amounted to nearly one and three quarter million and the Germans still held great swathes of the country. There was general feeling of war-weariness throughout the country, but particularly within the Army. A French Secret Service report on the morale of soldiers in January 1917 was revealing:

> The man in the ranks is no longer aware of why he is fighting. He is completely ignorant of anything happening outside his own sector. He has lost both faith and enthusiasm. He carries out his duties mechanically. He may become the victim of the greatest discouragement, display the worst weakness.[7]

In a country desperate for success, Nivelle's plan was seen as the panacea to all their ills and although he had his detractors within the French Army, Nivelle forged ahead with his plans. Meeting Nivelle for the first time on 20 December, Haig formed a positive opinion of the French General:

> Altogether I was pleased with my first meeting with Nivelle. He is in his 61st year and has had much practical experience in this war as a Gunner, then Divisional Corps then as

---

7   Edward Louis Spears, *Prelude to Victory* (London: Jonathan Cape, 1939), p.102.

Army Commander ... I am sorry for poor old Joffre, but from what I have seen of Nivelle up to date, I think he is the more energetic man.[8]

The attitude of Haig to Nivelle's plan is somewhat puzzling. The normally cautious Scot was aware of the morale situation within the French Army and was concerned as to their long-term capability as a fighting force. In addition, since the Battle of Aubers Ridge in May 1915, Haig had become convinced that the only way to defeat the Germans on the Western Front was by grinding them down through a policy of attrition. Now however, although he had some reservations over Nivelle's plans, he appears to have been enticed by the possibility of breakthrough on a wide front to the extent that the policy of attrition was abandoned. The manifestation of this abandonment was evidenced in a letter from the Chief of the General Staff, Lieutenant General Kiggell, to General Plumer on 6 January 1917, ordering Plumer to redraft his plan:

1. The operation north of the river Lys will not take place until after the subsidiary attacks elsewhere and the main French offensive operations have been carried out. It is therefore to be anticipated that the enemy will have been severely handled and his reserves drawn away from your front before the attacks north of the Lys are launched. Under these circumstances, it is essential that the plan should be based on rapid action and entail the breaking through of the enemy's defences on a wide front without any delay.
2. The plan as submitted by you, indicates a sustained and deliberate offensive such as has recently been carried out on the Somme front. In these circumstances the enemy will have time to bring up fresh reinforcements and construct new lines of defence.
3. The object of these operations is to inflict a decisive defeat on the enemy and free the Belgian coast.[9]

To confuse matters further, two days after this letter was sent, Haig formed another planning team from within his GHQ staff under Lieutenant Colonel Cyril MacMullen to work on a plan for an Ypres offensive.

General Nivelle's plan was for the French to attack in the Soissons-Rheims area with the British attacks to take place in the Arras, Vimy and Ancre sectors. From Nivelle's point of view the British were very much the junior partners in this enterprise, and he believed that if the joint offensive was successful, the Germans, to consolidate their forces would abandon the Belgian coast and render much of Haig's summer offensive unnecessary. Whilst seeing the logic in this theory, Haig continued to plan for a Flanders offensive.

Planning however was not going well. Rawlinson, unfamiliar with the area came up with no plan. Plumer came up with a second plan which envisaged an attack on the high ground at Pilckem, Messines, and Gheluvelt which would suppress German defences and enable Rawlinson's Fourth Army to move northwards towards the Belgian coast with limited opposition. Unsurprisingly, Rawlinson was keen on this plan, emphasising the importance of neutralising the German positions on the Gheluvelt Plateau to enable his advance to proceed

---

8   Blake, *The Private Papers of Douglas Haig 1914-1919*, p.188.
9   Edmonds, *Military Operations France and Belgium 1917*, Vol. II, Appendix V, p.406.

Strategic Situation on the Western Front, Summer 1917 23

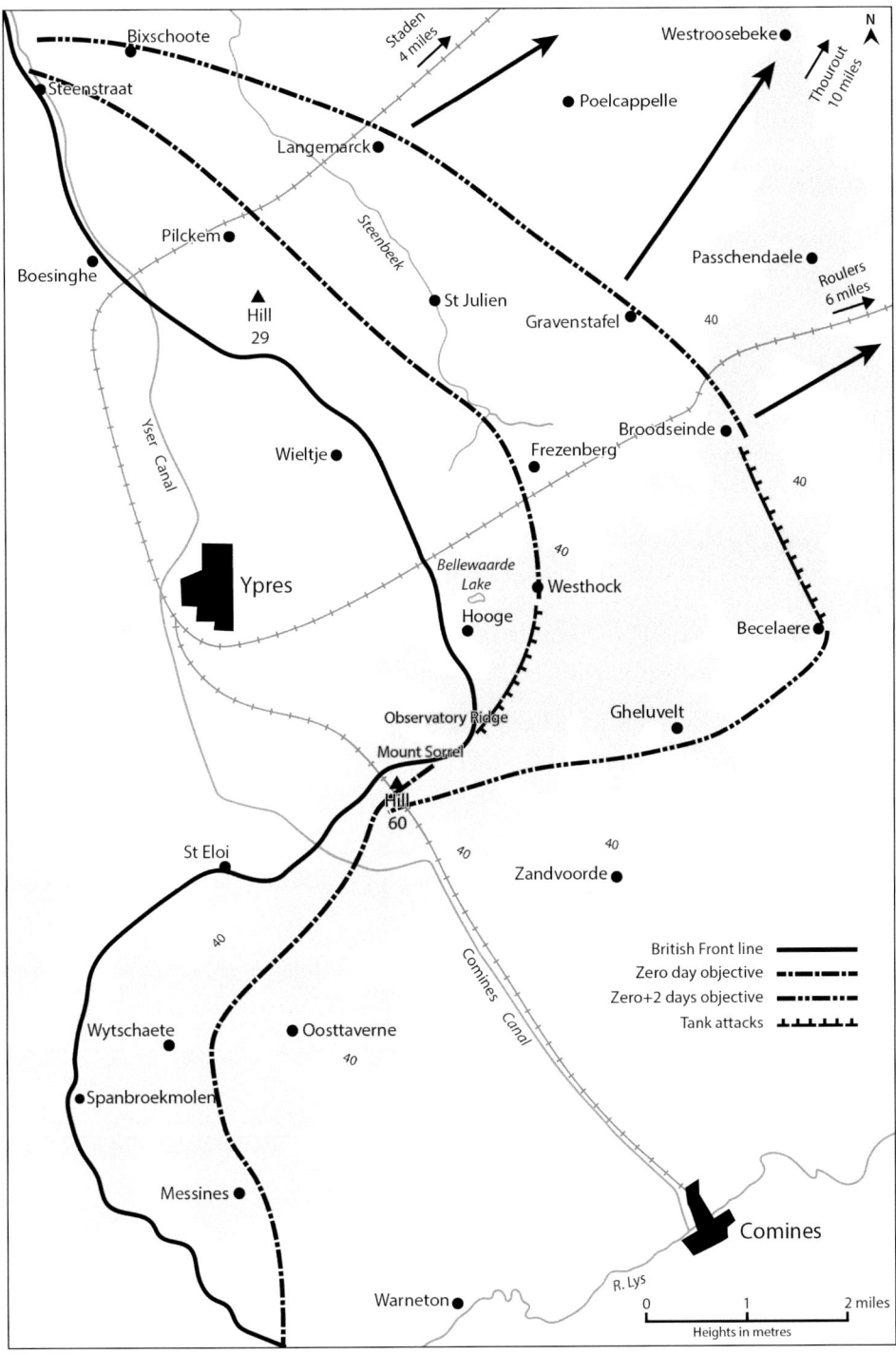

Map 2 Flanders offensive plan.

unhindered. Field Marshal Haig was also impressed by this plan and his internal planning section headed by Lieutenant Colonel MacMullen came up with a novel solution to the lack of Artillery pieces to target all three areas simultaneously. His plan was that the Gheluvelt Plateau should be attacked by tanks without Artillery preparation. This however, was never going to work given the nature of the ground and the fact that as Gheluvelt was the most strongly held position, it would require Artillery to support the tanks' advance.

Nevertheless, by February 1917, this was the plan decided on and an order from Lieutenant Colonel MacMullen's Operations Section was forwarded with the approval of Field Marshal Haig on 14 February:

> The operations proposed take the form of breaking through the enemy's defences on the front from St Yves to Steenstraat (approximately 30,000 yards) the formation of a defensive flank along the Messines-Wytschaete Ridge and on via Gheluvelt, Becelaere and Broodseinde to Moorslede, and an advance north-east via Roulers and Thourout. After a definite stage has been reached in the main advance an attack is proposed at Nieuport and a landing on the Belgian coast.[10]

By March however, Plumer had changed his mind, believing that the three objectives, Pilckem, Messines and Gheluvelt could not be attacked simultaneously and that the Messines attack should be undertaken in advance of the other two objectives. Crucially, he did not specify a time frame between the two attacks. Unwittingly, he was talking himself out of a job.

Field Marshal Haig was still enamoured with Nivelle's plan of a rapid breakthrough on a wide front and he saw Plumer and to a lesser extent Rawlinson's hesitancy to grasp this idea as evidence that Plumer had been in the Ypres area for so long that he had become complacent and had developed a lack of offensive spirit.

Whilst Haig had been concerned with planning for the summer offensive, underhand moves were taking place behind his back. The Prime Minister, Lloyd George, remained unconvinced of Haig's qualities as a military commander, his opinion being hardened by the horrendous casualties sustained on the long, drawn-out campaign on the Somme in 1916. He was deeply uneasy over Haig's plans for 1917 which he envisaged could lead to a repeat of 1916. He gave vent to his feelings at a lunch at 10 Downing Street on 9 February 1917 with the Soldier turned War Correspondent Charles à Court Repington, who later reported that the Prime Minister said that:

> He was not prepared to accept the position of a butcher's boy driving cattle to the slaughter and he would not do it.[11]

As Prime Minister, Lloyd George believed that he was in a position to do something about the situation. As luck would have it, an opportunity arose two weeks later. Like Haig, Lloyd George was extremely impressed with General Nivelle, primarily due to the fact that his successes emanated from an element of surprise, whereas he regarded British attacks as being laborious in their preparation and initiation. He was convinced that the Allied effort would benefit from

---

10 Edmonds, *Military Operations France and Belgium 1917*, Vol. II, Appendix VII, p. 411.
11 John Terraine, *Douglas Haig, the educated soldier*. (London: Hutchinson & Co, 1963), p.242.

a unified command – something that had been first suggested in 1915 and as France were the senior partners in the Alliance, it appeared logical to Lloyd George that to carry this through practically, Field Marshal Haig should subordinate himself and his Armies to the French. To implement this scheme, Lloyd George discussed the matter with the French Prime Minister Aristide Briand, who along with General Nivelle presented it at a joint government and military conference at Calais on 26 February.

Prior to the conference beginning, Lloyd George sat beside Haig at lunch and made no mention of the proposal, which the Field Marshal and the Chief of the Imperial General Staff, General Sir William Robertson, only heard about from the French Prime Minister and General Nivelle in the conference. As could be expected, the British military commanders were stunned by this proposal and rejected it out of hand. Lloyd George could hardly have been surprised at the response and in his memoirs sought to put the blame on Haig and Robertson for being short-sighted:

> This was my first effort to establish Unity of Command. It was resisted so viciously by Haig and Robertson that the delays caused by the time spent in allaying suspicions and adjusting differences destroyed the effectiveness of the plan.[12]

Importantly for Haig, this showed further evidence of the Prime Minister's duplicity. From this point their personal relationship which had started cordially began a downwards spiral which impacted detrimentally on the events of the following months.

In accordance with Nivelle's plan, the British attacked at Arras on 9 April 1917 and the French launched their offensive a week later, on 16 April. Whilst initial results were encouraging for the British, the attack slowed and became an attritional slog before coming to an end in mid-June. The one positive development was the seizure of Vimy Ridge by the Canadians in the initial phase of the offensive.

By contrast, the much lauded French offensive was a calamitous disaster. It opened on 16 April in the same sleet and hail showers which had greeted the British attack the week before. The following day Douglas Haig recorded in his diary:

> I could get no details from the French Mission as to results of today's fighting. This is always a bad sign and I fear that things are going badly with their offensive.[13]

Of the three attacking French Armies only one made any progress at all and fierce German counter-attacks forced them back to their starting positions. In a scenario that was to be repeated against British forces in the Third Ypres offensive, the creeping artillery barrage moved too fast and as the French advanced, they were held up by German strongpoints. The farther they advanced, the weaker they became. At the critical moment, The Germans launched their counter-attack or *Eingreif* Divisions.[14] For the British this should have been a prescient warning.

---

12   The Right Honourable David Lloyd George MP, *War Memoirs of David Lloyd George* (London: Odhams Press Ltd, 1934) Vol I, p.891.
13   Blake, *The Private Papers of Douglas Haig 1914-1919*, p.218.
14   For a description of the role of an *Eingreif* Division, see Jack Sheldon, *The German Army at Passchendaele* (Barnsley: Pen & Sword, 2007), p. xii.

The tragedy of the French attack was witnessed by a British Liaison Officer, Major Edward Louis Spears:[15]

> Everywhere the story was the same. The attack gained ground at most points, then slowed down unable to follow the barrage which, progressing at the rate of a hundred yards in three minutes, was in many cases soon out of sight. As soon as the infantry and the barrage became dissociated, German machine-guns were conjured as if by magic from the most unlikely places and opened fire, in many cases from both front and flanks, and sometimes from the rear as well, filling the air with a whistling sound as of scythes cutting hay. On the steep slopes of the Aisne, the troops even unopposed, could only progress very slowly. The ground, churned up by the shelling, was a series of slimy slides with little or no foothold.[16]

Barely two weeks after the commencement of the Nivelle offensive, discontentment within the French Army boiled over. Whilst initially confined to the singing of revolutionary songs and minor disorder, the mutiny accelerated on 3 May when the 2nd Colonial Infantry Regiment refused to go into the line. This accelerated the protests until the majority of French Infantry Regiments agreed to hold defensive positions, but refused to carry out any offensive action. The agitation spread to major French cities where strikes broke out in support of the Army in major industrial centres.

On 4 May, a meeting was held between senior British and French commanders. In view of the mutiny and of the deteriorating relationship between Haig and Lloyd George, the statement agreed at the conclusion the meeting made interesting reading. The participants agreed:

1. To continue the offensive to the full extent of our power.
2. British will make the main attack and French will support us to the utmost of their power, both by taking over some of our line, and by attacking vigorously to wear out and retain the enemy on their front.
3. Plan to be kept a perfect secret. Governments not to be told any details concerning the place or date of any attack, only the principles.[17]

Time was however, running out for one of the attendees. As the architect of the failed offensive, Nivelle had to go, resigning on 15 May and being replaced by General Philippe Petain. An ardent supporter of Nivelle, Lloyd George, in a brazen volte-face, suddenly became fulsome in his praise of Field Marshal Haig and his Generals for the progress made in the Arras offensive.

For his part, Douglas Haig realised that the French Military had been dealt a devastating blow and were unlikely to be able to play any significant role in the forthcoming Ypres offensive. Not only that, but the other Allies were in decline also. The Italians were facing great difficulties against the Austrians, and the Russian Army was on the verge of collapse. The American Army was still being built up to strength and was unlikely to take the field until well into 1918.

---

15 Spears also served as liaison officer during the Second World War rising to the rank of Major General. He also knighted for his efforts.
16 Spears, *Prelude to Victory*, p.492.
17 Blake, *The Private Papers of Douglas Haig 1914-1919*, p.227.

Haig was acutely aware that the British Army was on its own, and that approval for the Ypres Offensive from the War Committee was dependent on the full cooperation of the French. In those circumstances, he decided to keep the information that the French could not comply with their obligations (confirmed to him by General Petain on 2 June) from the War Committee. Whilst this could be viewed as a dereliction of duty, Haig realised that if no offensive action took place in 1917, the Germans would realise that something was amiss, considering that the Allies had been mounting offensives with regularity since September 1914. As it was, the Germans never found out about the extent of the disintegration of the French Army. It could be argued that if they had, events in 1917 might have turned out differently.

Having made a strategically sound decision in his mind to proceed with the Ypres offensive. He then made what transpired to be a disastrous decision – to appoint General Sir Hubert Gough, GOC Fifth Army to take on the main role in the Ypres offensive.

The appointment was made on 30 April 1917 with Haig recording the appointment in his diary:

> After lunch I explained to Gough that I am preparing for the Ypres operations, and that he would command the northern half of those operations, including the landing force. He must keep this absolutely secret, but is to study the scheme which Col. McMullen (his former Staff Officer) would explain to him.[18]

The decision to appoint Gough has been the subject of much debate in many accounts of Third Ypres and the overwhelming majority of highly respected Military Historians are of the opinion that his appointment was at best a grave error. In the chapter following the conclusion of the battle, I intend to analyse Gough's performance relevant to the Battle of Langemarck in more depth and here, I would like to touch on Haig's rationale for making the appointment.

The first point to note, is that there is no rationale given by Haig in his diaries. The momentous events ongoing at the time however, may give some clues. Since the collapse of the Nivelle offensive and the apparent non-effectiveness of other Allied forces, Haig realised that the British Army was going to have to stand alone for some time until the French again became effective, and the American Army was able to take the field. Neither of these events could be pinned down to a specific date, so Haig was going to have to put what he perceived to be his 'best team' in the field for an indeterminate period of time.

The personalities of both men are I believe key in the reasoning behind this appointment. Haig was a commander who when set upon a course of action, tended not to deviate from it. He gave orders to his subordinates and gave them the latitude to carry them out. Gough on the other hand, was notorious for interfering with the plans of subordinates and kept them under tight control. It is possible that Haig believed that in this crucial period of the war, he could rely on Gough to manage the offensive, especially as Haig recognised that he was renowned as a 'thruster,' someone who could be relied on to get the job done. To counter this are a number of factors. Gough was the youngest by far of any of the army commanders at 47 (Rawlinson was 53 and Plumer 63 at the time of Third Ypres). In addition, Gough had never commanded a major

---

18   Blake, *The Private Papers of Douglas Haig 1914-1919*, p.222 The colonel referred to is Lieutenant Colonel Cyril Norman MacMullen, at that time in charge of Haig's GHQ planning team.

offensive and was a stranger to the Ypres salient having last been there in 1914. To complicate matters, he was still involved in the Arras offensive and would not take up his post until 1 June, which lost a vital month of familiarisation. It is difficult to say if Gough was favoured in Haig's eyes due to the fact that like Haig he was a Cavalryman, and in Haig's opinion would see the opportunity to use cavalry to exploit any advantage, although due to various circumstances which subsequently prevailed, this was never an option. All in all, Haig's decision was a monumental risk. If it had come off, both he and Gough would have been lauded for their perception and offensive spirit. However, with hindsight, the evidence indicates that this was a risk not worth taking and Haig would have been better sticking with General Plumer, methodical, but tried and trusted.

As it was, General Plumer remained in charge of the Messines offensive which took place on 7 June and turned out be spectacularly successful following the explosion of 19 massive mines under German positions. Casualties in the attacking Divisions were very light and many prisoners were taken. Following the mine explosions, the 16th (Irish) and 36th (Ulster) divisions stormed their assigned part of ridge objective and captured what remained of the village of Wytschaete. This success boded well for the continuation of the offensive however, as will be shown, personality clashes, deception and political interference were to plague the planning for the next phase.

2

Flanders Offensive Planning

Released from his commitments at Arras, General Gough and his staff arrived in his new area of operations on 1 June 1917. His French liaison officer, Paul Maze, subsequently recollected:

> Fifth Army arrived in Belgium on June 1st 1917 and made their HQ at La Lovie Chateau, south of Poperinghe ... General Staff were housed in the Chateau and all round under the trees Nissen huts were put up for offices and tents for the officer's sleeping accommodation.[1]

From this time, work started in earnest within Fifth Army in planning for the offensive.

Greatly encouraged by the success at Messines, Field Marshal Haig visited General Plumer on the afternoon of 7 June and congratulated him on his success, some of which he later reflected on himself as he observed in his diary:

> The operations today are probably the most successful I have yet undertaken.[2]

Emboldened by this success, he was understandably keen to push ahead with the next phase of the offensive. General Plumer had planned that II Corps and VIII Corps would continue the offensive by attacking from the area of Bellewaerde Lake to capture positions on the Gheluvelt Plateau to the right of the Ypres-Roulers railway and was of the opinion that it would require three days to relocate Artillery to assist in this operation.

Perhaps Haig saw this as excessive caution on the part of Plumer and he decided to hand over the two Corps to Gough to utilise in his 'northern operation.' This must be regarded as a mistake as the continuation of the offensive at that time would have exerted extreme pressure on the Germans who were shocked by the defeat at Messines and expected daily a continuation of the attack. Creating a delay as we will see, had catastrophic results.

On the day of the Battle of Messines, Haig met with General Petain who had informed him of the perilous state of the French Army due to continued mutinous activities. Petain did however offer six Divisions to assist the continued British efforts under the command of

---

1   Paul Maze, *A Frenchman in Khaki* (London: William Heinemann, 1934), p.227. The Chateau is also known in Flemish as 'Chateau Loewe'.
2   Blake, *The Private Papers of Douglas Haig 1914-1919*, p.236.

General Anthoine. This was a paltry contribution, but all that was available at that time and General Robertson, the Chief of the Imperial General Staff reminded Haig that approval from the War Cabinet for his continued offensive was conditional on the full support of the French – not just six Divisions. With this to ponder, Haig also had the distracting factor of Lloyd George trying to use his influence to support the transfer of men and Artillery to assist the Italians. This was a non-starter for both Haig and Robertson, who firmly believed that all efforts should be concentrated on the Western Front.

On 14 June, an army commanders conference was held at Lillers, near Bethune. At this conference, General Gough outlined that after a study of the ground, he had concluded that the proposed preliminary operation by II Corps and VIII Corps would no longer be carried out and that the attack would be incorporated into the main offensive. Despite his stated wish to proceed as quickly as possible, Haig acceded to this request and in doing so, added to the delay which was daily playing into the hands of the Germans. In addition to Gough's plans which were slowly progressing, the situation with the French support was that it was not going to be ready until 21 July, and a proposed date to recommence the Offensive of 25 July was agreed. This was seven weeks after Messines.

In order to bring Gough's Fifth Army up to strength, four divisions were transferred in June from Plumer's Second Army, 11th (Northern) Division, 16th (Irish) Division, 25th Division and 36th (Ulster) Division. The two Irish divisions became part of XIX Corps, the other two Divisions in the Corps being the 15th (Scottish) Division and the 55th (West Lancashire) Division. The Corps was Commanded by General Herbert Watts, a 59 years old who had been retired in the rank of Colonel at the outbreak of war and in the parlance of the times, had been 'dug out' to command 21st Brigade, 7th Division.

Major General Nugent, 36th Division, recorded his thoughts on the move in a letter to his wife on 18 June:

> 36th Div leaving IX Corps 2nd Army transferred XIX Corps Fifth Army. 'I understand we have been specially asked for.' I shall be sorry to leave our present Army Commander [Plumer] He is such a delightful loyal person to soldier with and one feels all the time that he has no axe to grind. He is always accessible and friendly, and I like him immensely.[3]

The phrase 'specially asked for' is one that was replicated within the 16th Division. On 3 July Major General Hickie attended the 7th Leinster's Battalion Sports and handed out prizes. The following day, he inspected the battalion whilst they were training at Eringhem, northeast of St Omer and in an address congratulated them on their success in the Messines victory and stated that the Division:

> Had been chosen with a few others as 'Storm Troops' an honour earned by the splendid offensive spirit which it had shown since it had come to France.[4]

---

3   PRONI D/3835/E/2/13 Farren Connell Papers.
4   TNA WO 95/1970/4: 7th Leinster War Diary.

A young Captain in the battalion, Max Staniforth, elaborated on this exciting news in a letter home to his parents:

> We are leaving here on the 15th, unless otherwise ordered and shall go into training at a place called Tilkes [Tilques, four miles north-west of St Omer] to be specially trained with a Scottish Division and the Guards as Assaulting Troops for a big push to take a place somewhere to northward. (Assaulting troops simply storm a position and are then taken out at once leaving others to do the dirty work of 'mopping up', consolidating and resisting the counterattack in these times, with such incredible artillery preparations, its usually accounted the best job to have).[5]

It is not known if the two Irish divisions were 'specially asked for' by General Gough however, it is possible that their cooperative attack at Wytschaete on 7 June had drawn attention to their prowess in fighting alongside each other and it was looked upon as a good omen for future engagements. It was certainly however, a good motivational tool to couch their move from Second Army as a special request.

Whilst the Infantry battalions of both Divisions moved to rear areas to undertake training for the forthcoming offensive, there was no respite for the Artillery, Engineers and Pioneer battalions who moved straight from Wytschaete to the area of Poperinghe, west of Ypres, the Artillery of both Divisions coming under the control of the Commander Royal Artillery, 55th Division. With little respite, they went into action on the night of 7/8 July.

Whilst the Irish divisions were being repositioned, planning for the resumption of the offensive was stepping up a gear at Fifth Army HQ. The original plan forwarded to General Gough by Lieutenant Colonel MacMullen had stipulated that the first day's objective was to be an advance to the German second line. This entailed an advance of around a mile and was to be followed by a pause to enable Artillery to be repositioned. At a conference of his commanders on 16 June, a plan was presented which increased the objectives to the German third line. This increased the area of advance by another mile and on top of this, the plan went on to include a further advance of a mile without a break to reposition Artillery, which would hopefully take the advancing troops to the German fourth line and would leave British troops on a line from Langemarck – Gravenstafel – Broodseinde.

This was a wildly ambitious plan and at that stage as overall commander, Field Marshal Haig should have ordered it to be revisited with more modest objectives. As it was, Haig had other matters occupying his mind. He had attended a War Cabinet conference in London from 19-22 June. At this conference, Lloyd George had reiterated his view that there should be no major actions on the Western Front until 1918 and that material support should be given to the Italians. Of more dramatic significance however, was the statement by the First Sea Lord, Admiral Jellicoe, that due to shipping losses from German submarine activity, there was no point in making plans for 1918 as Britain would be unable to continue the war. Given the importance of this intervention, which was news to all those present, Haig recorded Jellicoe's exact words in his diary:

---

5   Richard S Grayson (ed.) *At War with the 16th (Irish) Division. The Staniforth Letters* (Pen & Sword: Barnsley, 2012), p. 144.

There is no good discussing plans for next spring – We cannot go on.[6]

Whilst shipping losses were escalating – 694 ships comprising 2,136,126 tons from January to June 1917, those present were of the opinion that Jellicoe was being overdramatic.[7] The outburst did however impress upon Haig the importance of reaching the Belgian coast and denying the Germans the use of U Boat bases there.

On his return to France, Haig was presented a paper by his Head of Operations at GHQ, Brigadier General John Davidson, which criticised Gough's plan and particularly the advance of up to four miles with limited Artillery support. Instead, Davidson advised that the attack should consist of a series of successive attacks with objectives of around a mile. In essence, this reverted to the original plan. The reasoning contained within it was sound, advancing the view that if the Fifth Army scheme was adopted, the line of advance would be ragged and would not able to withstand German counterattacks and would have insufficient Artillery support.

Davidson's paper was countered by General Gough and in light of what subsequently transpired, the important opening paragraphs of his response are reproduced verbatim as follows:

> In its broad principles, I am in agreement with this paper, insofar as it advocates a continuous succession of organised attacks. The point for discussion is the application of this principle, as regards place and time, and particularly as regards the first day's attack. Should we go as far as we can on the first day, viz. certainly up to the Green Line and possibly the Red Line, or should we confine ourselves to the Black Line on the first day and attack again in three days to gain the Green Line and again to gain the Red Line at a further interval of three days?
>
> It is important to recognize that the results to be looked for from a well-organised attack which has taken weeks and months to prepare are great, much ground can be gained and prisoners and guns captured during the first day or two. After the first attack, long prepared, one cannot hope to gain similar results in one attack as long as the enemy can find fresh reserves, and the depth of ground gained and guns captured usually decline in subsequent attacks.
>
> I think therefore that it would be wasteful, not to reap all the advantages possible from the first attack.[8]

In this response a degree of impetuosity is evident and it easy to see why Gough had gained a reputation as a 'thruster'.

On 28 June, Haig met with General's Gough and Plumer and discussed Gough's plan. Mindful of the newly emphasised importance of reaching the Belgian coast, Gough's version of the plan for an all-out attack was approved however, Haig emphasised the importance of first securing the ridge west of Gheluvelt, as doing so would protect the right of the advance. This was of such importance that Haig stressed that any general advance should be limited until this ridge was secured.

---

6   Blake, *The Private Papers of Douglas Haig 1914-1919*, p.241.
7   Edmonds, *Military Operations France and Belgium 1917*, Vol. II, p.103.
8   Edmonds, *Military Operations France and Belgium 1917*, Appendix XV, p.440.

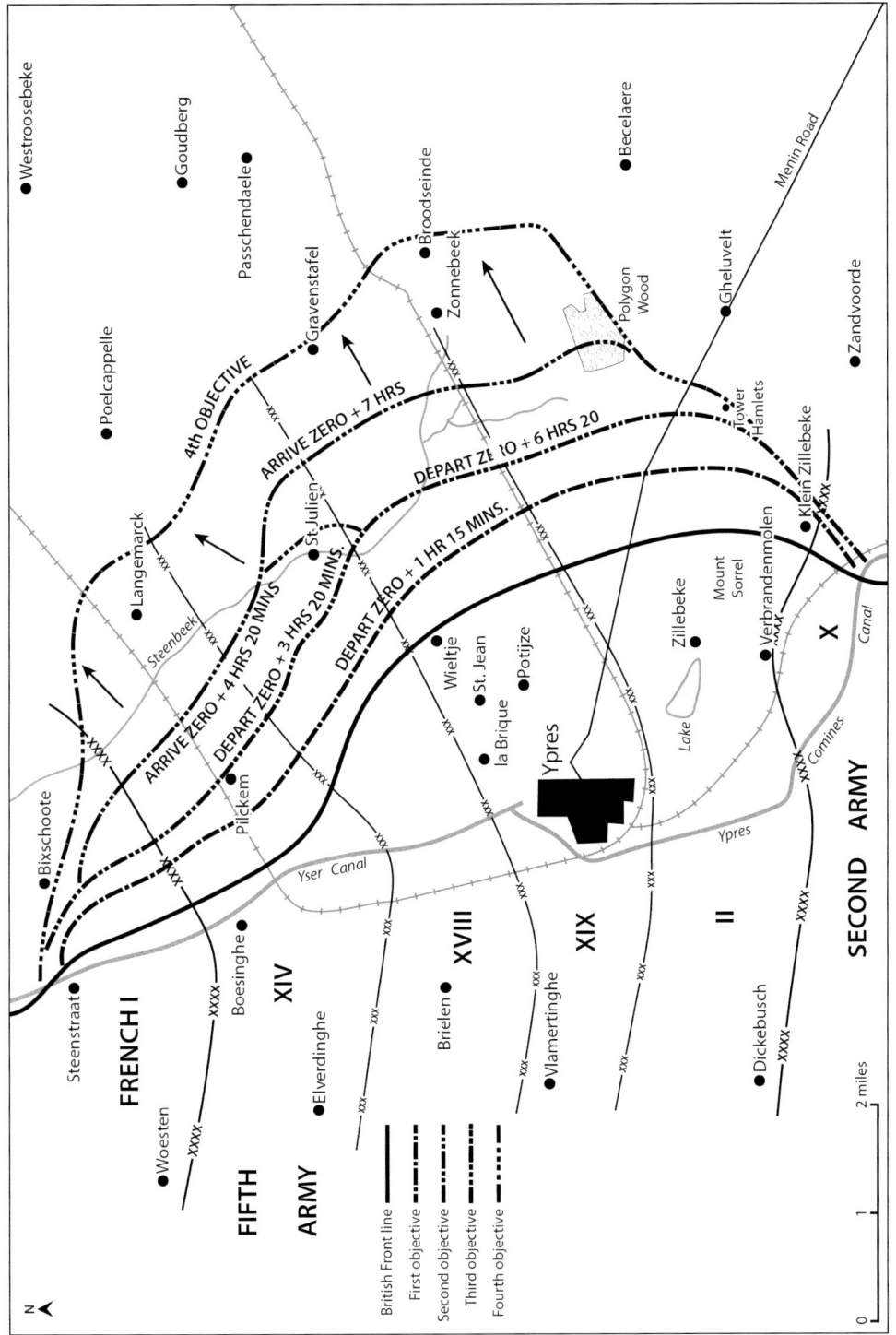

Map 3 Fifth Army stages of the offensive.

Whilst plans for their future were being decided by army commanders, in early July, the officers and men of the Irish divisions were undergoing their specialist training and still had time for recreation in the fine French summer weather. Captain Cyril Falls, a Staff Officer with the 36th Division observed:

> 7 July moved to the training area SW St Omer. Billeting accommodation in the villages was inadequate and had to be augmented by tents. Small hardship this in such weather and such surroundings. Many officers whose accommodation was entirely comfortable chose for preference to sleep in the open air, or in tents in the cherry orchards. The men were soaked in sunshine… In fact the Division never had, during all its service in France and Flanders a pleasanter period than these twelve days of rest and training. They ended with a great gymkhana at Acquin on the 23rd, with horse races, mule races, jumping, transport competitions, wrestling on horseback and sports of all kinds.[9]

As regards the training, it was comprehensive and necessarily repetitive. A scale model of the area of operations extending to around two acres had been constructed in the training areas and the troops were briefed on the topography and obstacles expected, as well as receiving briefings on current tactics. Captain Staniforth of the 7th Leinsters in a letter to his parents, described the intensity of the training:

> Well, as I say, we've rehearsed the thing till we're sick of it, at 4 in the morning and at 2 in the afternoon, and at 11 o'clock at night, with all the additional units to cooperate with us. The same slow moving forward through standing crops and meadows under a blazing July sun, tanks lumbering on ahead, white signal flags stuttering wildly all over the landscape, contact 'planes sweeping down with a sudden roar of engines dropping a message on a white-lettered groundsheet, and rising again, machine-gun teams toiling forwards in little knots with the guns, solitary 'runners' trudging back through the lines with messages for Headquarters, drums thundering far in advance to represent the barrage, bandaged 'casualties' limping, hobbling or borne by the stretcher bearers through the tall corn, long lines of infantry breasting the slope in front, with the sunshine glinting on their bayonets, battalions of the first wave that have done their bit and reached their objective digging in desperate haste against a possible counterattack, or pausing to wipe their faces and look after us as we pass through them and press forward.[10]

Whilst their Infantry colleagues were enjoying the training and the fine weather, the Pioneer battalions – 16th Royal Irish Rifles in 36th Division and 11th Hampshire Regiment in 16th Division, were having a more arduous time near Ypres under the command of 55th Division.

Both battalions were engaged in road construction using beech slabs, and on sinking wells to provide the vast quantities of water that would be required for the men and animals of Fifth Army. Many potential wells had to be abandoned as the Pioneers struck blue clay after around

---

9   Cyril Falls, *The History of the 36th (Ulster) Division* (Belfast: McCaw, Stevenson & Orr, 1922), p.107.
10 Grayson (ed.) *At War with the 16th (Irish) Division*, p.149.

eight feet of digging. The Pioneers were also targeted by accurate German artillery fire as the 11th Hampshire's war diary recorded:

> 1 July. Dull and overcast, fresh NE breeze. Work continued on wells. B Company corduroyed 35 yards of road making a total of 220 yards. Enemy made 3 direct hits with 5.9's on road where they are working, one man slightly wounded, but remained at duty. The light railway on which the material is carried was also damaged and work was delayed 2 hours.[11]

In addition to the Pioneer battalions, another Irish battalion was detailed for this work. Whilst they were not involved in the action on 16 August, it is important that they are included in the narrative.

The 10th (Service) Battalion Royal Dublin Fusiliers had been posted to 48th Infantry Brigade of 16th Division from 190th Brigade, 63rd Royal Naval Division, on 23 June 1917. On 5 July they were attached to 15th (Scottish) Division and provided 5-600 men daily to construct roads and ammunition dumps north-west of Ypres. On 13 July at 2:45 a.m. hostile aircraft dropped several bombs on the Fusiliers camp killing three other ranks and wounding two officers. On this date the Battalion transferred from 16th Division to 15th Division for administration and discipline and to XIX Corps for orders. Indicative of the issues with recruiting in Ireland, of the three men killed, only one was from Ireland.

Private Matthew Taylor, 40733 aged 21 from Bolton, Lancashire. He had previously served with the Loyal North Lancashire Regiment.

Private Edward Rehill, 25215 aged 36 and married with one daughter. From Bolton Street, Dublin, pre-war he was employed as a Civil Servant Messenger.

Corporal Francis Pumford, 40760 from Pontypridd, Glamorgan. Born at Trowbridge, Salop, he had previously served as 43739 Royal Welch Fusiliers.[12]

The following day an order was issued from GHQ indicating that the 10th Dublins were to be regarded as a special case:

> GHQ order OB/1370 14 July. The 10th RDF will be Corps Troops attached to XIX Corps until further notice. The 10th RDF are not to be used during the forthcoming operations. When the question of which Bn's of the 16th Div. are to be amalgamated again arises, it should be borne in mind that the Home Authorities are averse to breaking up or absorbing the 10th RDF. The identity of this Bn should therefore be preserved.[13]

The origins of the battalion indicate that they had friends with influence. The 10th (Service) Battalion Royal Dublin Fusiliers were known as 'the Commercials'. Formed at Dublin in 1915, the initial plan was to provide enough men to form a company for the Fusilier's 5th Battalion from 'commercial men' overseen by a committee of men of stature in the Dublin commercial community. However, initial recruitment was so successful that the initial plan expanded to recruit a full battalion.

---

11 TNA WO 95/1966/2: 11th Hampshire War Diary.
12 All three are buried alongside each other at Poperinghe New Military Cemetery.
13 TNA WO 95/1974/6: 10th Royal Dublin Fusiliers War Diary.

During the Battle of Langemarck, the battalion was tasked with involvement in working parties and on Prisoner of War guard duty at the cage at Ypres, rejoining 48th Infantry Brigade on 20 August.[14]

At the beginning of July, Field Marshal Haig, as BEF C-in-C, was aware that the offensive needed to be underway as soon as possible to maintain the initiative, as the impact of the successful Messines attack began to evaporate. Giving added impetus to his eagerness to proceed were optimistic intelligence updates from his Head of Intelligence, Brigadier General John Charteris. Charteris was Haig's man and had been on his staff in various roles from 1909. When Haig was promoted Field Marshal in December 1915, he promoted and installed his fellow Scot and Presbyterian as Head of Intelligence. The previous incumbent Brigadier General George Macdonogh was promoted to the rank of Major General and posted as Director of Military Intelligence to the War Office. Macdonogh as a rule considered Charteris' intelligence assessments regarding the state of German morale to be excessively optimistic. On 10 July, Haig noted in his diary:

> Charteris, reporting on the situation stated that the political situation in Berlin seemed critical. Confidence in their Army and in the success of the submarine blockade of England seems to be waning.[15]

The relationship between Charteris and Macdonogh was antagonistic and it is of no surprise that Haig focused more heavily and favoured his colleague and friend's assessments, perhaps relying too heavily on them. Haig's view of Macdonogh in a diary entry of 15 October 1917 whilst the offensive was still ongoing, reveals his prejudices:

> Charteris reports on 12 October, 2 Pioneer companies of 233rd Division 'refused to attack'. This is another direct instance of insubordination in German Army and consequent loss of fighting spirit. Yet it is stated in a note by the DMI [Director of Military Intelligence] War Office dated 1 October, 'The moral of the troops in the field gives no cause for anxiety to the German High Command.' I cannot think why the War Office Intelligence Department gives such a wrong picture of the situation except that General Macdonogh (DMI) is a Roman Catholic and is (unconsciously) influenced by information which doubtless reaches him from tainted (i.e Catholic) sources.[16]

Whilst Charteris' assessments enthused Haig, the state of preparedness of the other actors was not encouraging.

In June, Haig had hoped that the offensive would begin in the last week in July and had pencilled in 25 July as a potential date. As early as the beginning of July, General Anthoine in charge of the French Divisions, described this as unrealistic, citing a lack of labour to construct gun emplacements. Conscious of the precarious state of the French Army, Haig generously lent

---

14 The GHQ order was not enough to preserve the 10th RDF. They were disbanded during the reorganisation of February 1918 and the men posted to 19th Entrenching Battalion.
15 Blake, *The Private Papers of Douglas Haig 1914-1919* p.243.
16 Gary Sheffield & John Bourne (eds.) *Douglas Haig. War Diaries and Letters 1914-1918* (London: Weidenfeld & Nicolson, 2005), p.336.

him over 7,000 soldiers to work as Labourers and suggested to General Gough that the French be given less distant objectives. Gough dismissed this suggestion and in keeping with Haig's noninterventionist management style, he did not force the issue.

Gough himself then asked for a delay of a week, quoting the late arrival of heavy artillery pieces which he stated were required to subdue German Artillery positions. Conscious that time was slipping away, Haig agreed to a further delay of three days to 28 July. On 21 July, General Anthoine asked for a further delay of three days as bad weather had reduced the effectiveness of his Artillery preparations. Haig was very much opposed to any further delay as it would impinge on preparations for the assault on the Belgian coast, which was dependant on high tides around 7/8 August. He was also concerned about the weather, as records over many years showed that a period of wet weather was usual for early August. Gough supported Anthoine's request, and Haig, cognisant of giving the French all the support he could, relented again. The date fixed for commencement was now 31 July.

Whilst dealing with the requests of his army commanders, Haig received a startling message from General Robertson, Chief of the Imperial General Staff on 19 July which stated:

> When you left, Cabinet had not definitely approved of your plans. Up to the present no official approval of your plans has been given. I dare say that tomorrow or the next day I shall be told that your plans are approved.[17]

The background to this message centred on Lloyd George's determination to avoid another Somme with its countless casualties, and to remind Haig that he was under scrutiny. This was a bizarre situation, considering that the artillery bombardment for the opening of the offensive had already started, and the Royal Flying Corps had been engaged for a number of weeks in offensive operations to gain control of the skies. Haig was justifiably indignant and penned an immediate reply pointing out that:

> These operations were agreed to at a conference at the War Office as long ago as 23 November 1916 and on 1 January 1917 I was reminded of the great importance attached to this operation by the War Cabinet.[18]

In his diary entry for 21 July, he added the following scathing comment:

> The fact is that the Cabinet does not really understand what preparations for an attack really mean for the forces and Commanders in the field.[19]

The necessary approval arrived with Haig on the evening of 21 July however, the hand of Lloyd George was again evident in that the approval was caveated, that should sufficient progress not be made, arrangements should be progressed to send troops to Italy. In a comment in his diary which confirms that his relationship with the Prime Minister had reached an all-time low, Haig dismissed the suggestion stating:

17 Blake, *The Private Papers of Douglas Haig 1914-1919*, p.245.
18 Blake, *The Private Papers of Douglas Haig 1914-1919*, p.245.
19 Blake, *The Private Papers of Douglas Haig 1914-1919* , p.245.

It would be the act of a lunatic to detach troops from France to any theatre at this stage.[20]

As July progressed, the Irish divisions were coming to the end of their training and were preparing to begin their journey towards the front. A XIX Corps order of 13 July identified locations for each divisional HQ. The 16th Division HQ was to be at 19 Place Berthen, Poperinghe, and the 36th Division HQ was at Winnizeele, just on the French side of the France/Belgium border. Whilst preparations were being made for the move, Major General Nugent had some internal management issues to attend to. A strict disciplinarian, Nugent was always keen to ensure that his battalions had the most competent leaders. In the middle of July and probably with an eye on the forthcoming offensive, he sacked two battalion commanders from 9th and 15th battalions, Royal Irish Rifles. In a letter to his wife Kitty on 20 July he explained:

> I had to inform two of my CO's the other day that I did not think they were up to the mark and must try some other job.[21]

The two officers were, Lieutenant Colonel Philip James Woods DSO, 9th Royal Irish Rifles and Lieutenant Colonel Francis Lewis Rawson Gordon, 15th Royal Irish Rifles. Woods had been a prominent Ulster Volunteer Force member pre-war and post-war became an Independent Loyalist Member of Parliament for West Belfast. Gordon had had previous service at the turn of the century in the Gordon Highlanders. He died at Hove, Sussex, in 1920 aged 42 of illness, aggravated his family claimed by his war service.

As Major General Nugent dealt with disciplinary matters, planning and training continued. Tactics had advanced greatly since the early days of the war, and in place of a straightforward infantry attack supported by artillery, an attack was now an all-arms event. As Captain Staniforth explained in his description of the exercise, infantry, artillery, tanks and aeroplanes were all synchronised in the plan.

The GOC Royal Artillery Fifth Army, was Major General Herbert Crofton Campbell Uniacke. He had an unenviable task, firstly, he had to attempt as far as possible to neutralise the German Artillery. This was easier said than done as the majority of German Artillery pieces were located on the reverse slopes of the ridges surrounding Ypres and they were fed intelligence by Forward Observation Officers who, from vantage points on the ridge could observe British preparations. To facilitate his task, Uniacke required accurate observation from the Royal Flying Corps. This brought into question control of the skies over the battlefield, which was not obtained until late July. His second task was to provide a comprehensive and accurate 'creeping barrage' to protect the troops as they advanced. To do this however, he needed sufficient artillery pieces, the strength of which had to be maintained in the face of accurate German counter-battery fire. An added difficulty was with Gough's plan of a proposed advance of four miles. To provide a creeping barrage to support this, Uniacke had to ensure that artillery pieces could be moved forward at speed once the infantry assault began.

Uniacke issued his plan on 30 June, based on the following principles:

---

20 Blake, *The Private Papers of Douglas Haig 1914-1919*, p.246.
21 PRONI: D/3835/E/2/13 Farren Connell Papers.

Priority was to protect the infantry while consolidating on their objectives.

Enemy batteries which could provide defensive fire were to be bombarded with gas from Zero day minus one to Zero day.

The preliminary bombardment was to last nine days.

Counter-battery fire was to reach a climax on Zero minus four and zero minus one days.

Roads must not be shelled to ease the subsequent move forward of guns.

All wire cutting was to be done by howitzers and mortars to conceal the strength of the field guns.

The creeping barrage which was to include shrapnel, was to start as close as possible to the British trenches and was to move at 100 yards in four minutes.

The protective barrage was to be placed 500 yards beyond each objective and was to search back and forward.

Prompt zone calls were arranged to be called for by air.

Field batteries were to advance beyond no-man's land and heavy batteries into it.

Balloons were to be established well forward.

Counter-battery artillery was to be organized in double groups, each with its own air flight from the Corps Squadron.[22]

Unfortunately, in carrying out research for this book it was discovered the war diaries for the artillery brigades of both Irish divisions, the respective Divisional Commanders Royal Artillery, and XIX Corps Commander Royal Artillery are all absent for the period July to October 1917. To compound matters, General Farndale's otherwise excellent book titled *History of the Royal Regiment of Artillery*, inaccurately records that the Divisional Artillery of the 36th Division was 123rd and 124th brigades Royal Field Artillery, when it was in fact 153rd and 173rd brigades.

Fortunately, there are other sources from which to glean information. Captain Frank Broome was Adjutant for 173rd Brigade Royal Field Artillery. He described his six weeks at Ypres in July and August 1917 as 'six weeks of hell', and elaborated:

> During much of the time I was in a deep tunnelled dug-out where I was unable to leave the telephone, night or day.[23] Cookhouses and lavatories had to be moved underground as nothing could live for long on the surface. For one period – I think it was about eight days, I lost all count of time – I never once saw the light of day. I was busy the whole time receiving orders on the telephone and detailing them to batteries by candle-light. Periodically, my servant would bring me a mug of tea and a biscuit, but there were no mealtimes and no distinction between day and night…It was the worst time of my life, but even so I was much better off than those in the batteries who, being in action continuously for six weeks, suffered more severely than the infantry who were periodically withdrawn.[24]

By the middle of July as British artillery was being positioned on the eastern outskirts of Ypres, the German artillery were having a field day. From their concealed positions they rained down

---

22 General Sir Martin Farndale, *History of the Royal Regiment of Artillery: Western Front 1914-18* (London: Royal Artillery Institution, 1986), p.197.
23 Most likely the Wieltje Dugouts complex.
24 Frank Norman Broome, *Not the Whole Truth* (Pietermaritzburg: University of Natal Press, 1962) p.85.

shells on suspected British Artillery positions. The fact was, there were so many artillery units it was difficult for the Germans to miss. They were however, not having it all their own way. Farndale describes how that when a German battery was located:

> Concentrations of four to six hundred six, eight, and 9.2 inch shells rained down on it. Frequently, this meant total destruction.[25]

This attritional battle continued from 15 July to the commencement of the offensive. Records indicate that in the period 15 July to 2 August 1917, 3091 British artillery pieces fired 4,283,550 rounds at German positions. The greatest concentration of firepower in the war to date. This equates to 225,450 shells per day or 157 shells per minute.[26]

As Major General Uniacke was well aware, control of the skies was vital to the success of the artillery. The efforts of the Royal Flying Corps did not however, start auspiciously. On the day on which the orders to commence the air offensive were issued, 7 July, the War Cabinet ordered two squadrons sent home to protect London from ongoing Gotha bomber raids. Haig regarded this as further interference from ignorant politicians:

> The withdrawal of these squadrons at this time will have a serious effect. Today was the first day of our battle for air supremacy – and the Enemy has also concentrated his fighting machines to oppose us. Our War Cabinet is thus playing the enemy's game in withdrawing aeroplanes from this front.[27]

As it was, bad weather delayed the start of the air offensive, which did not begin until 11 July. In addition to using fighter aircraft to engage German aircraft, the air offensive employed a relatively new tactic of night bombing raids against German aerodromes opposite Second and Fifth Army Fronts. These raids were carried out by 100 Squadron Royal Flying Corps equipped with FE2b aircraft, a two-man fighter which had been converted to a night bombing role as they had proved vulnerable to German fighter aircraft.[28] One of the targets of 100 Squadron was the German ace, Mannfred von Richthofen's 'Circus' whose aerodromes were near Courtrai.

On 12 July, The Royal Flying Corps had one of its busiest days of the war to date, with action concentrated on the Fifth Army front. That evening a 'dogfight' took place involving thirty German aircraft and a joint British and French force of similar size. No Allied planes were lost and it was reported that two German aircraft were downed in this engagement. The scale of the Royal Flying Corps involvement cannot be understated. Daily and weather permitting, flights took place carrying out aerial reconnaissance, artillery cooperation, aerial photography, day and night bombing, as well as offensive patrols targeting German aircraft.

As the month wore on, the Allied pilots gradually began to gain the upper hand, although there were still German night-bombing raids on rear areas where troops were concentrated. Two massive dogfights involving upwards of 90 aircraft took place on 26 and 27 July in which Allied

---

25 Farndale, *History of the Royal Regiment of Artillery*, p.200.
26 Edmonds, *Military Operations France and Belgium 1917*, p.138, fn. 2.
27 Sheffield & Bourne (eds) *Douglas Haig. War Diaries and Letters 1914-1918*, p.302.
28 100 Squadron's FE2b aircraft were replaced in early 1918 with the Handley Page O/400, a larger bomber which enabled crews to strike targets in Germany.

aircraft gained the upper hand and following these there was a marked decrease in German aerial activity.

The following day, the GOC Royal Flying Corps called with Field Marshal Haig who recorded in his diary:

> General Trenchard gave his report on the work of the Flying Corps. Yesterday the fighting was most severe, and the results highly satisfactory. Our aviators, 'drove the enemy out of the air' said Trenchard to me. 'It was a very good day' he added. We crashed 19 machines and drove down out of control 26 = 45. We lost three machines.[29]

Haig corresponded separately to Trenchard with a message to be promulgated to the RFC Squadrons:

> I hope you will convey to all concerned my hearty appreciation of the strenuous efforts which have been made to obtain this grand result, and best congratulations on the success of yesterday's flying.[30]

The success of the Royal Flying Corps had greatly assisted the plans of the Royal Artillery and Major General Uniacke professed himself happy with the progress of his plans. Had he been aware of the German attitude to the bombardment, he may not have been so happy. Captain Kalepky of *Fusilier-Regiment, 'Konigin' Nr. 86* who was on the receiving end of the British Artillery's best efforts noted:

> Whereas here the British Artillery was painfully effective, another feature reduced their effectiveness. In their firing, they followed an exacting pattern with regard to their firing and the targeting, so that it was rather easy for our troops to move in between the imparts of the shells, in particular as the mud absorbed splinters.[31]

Along with the Royal Flying Corps, the use of tanks was a new innovation in warfare. Originally designated as Heavy Section, Machine Gun Corps, and then Heavy Branch Machine Gun Corps, the Tank Corps was renamed on 27 July 1917 in time for the commencement of the offensive.

Impressed by the performance of Tanks and the fear it had engendered following their first use on the Somme in September 1916, and more latterly at Arras in April 1917, it was decided to combine three brigades of tanks in the offensive. Initial reconnaissance reports by Tank Corps Reconnaissance staff were not promising due to the state of the ground however, planning for their use continued regardless.

On 7 July Tank Corps HQ forwarded a detailed plan of the proposed use of tanks to Fifth Army HQ. This plan allotted 156 tanks to Fifth Army with an additional 60 forming the Army

---

29 Sheffield & Bourne (eds) *Douglas Haig. War Dairies and Letters 1914-1918*, p.305.
30 Henry Albert Jones, *The War in the Air: Being the story of the part played in the Great War by the Royal Air Force, Volume IV* (Uckfield: Naval & Military Press reprint of 1934 edition), p.158.
31 University of Leeds (UL): Special Collections: Liddle/WW1/GE09. Papers of Lieutenant Colonel L Kalepky, Das Fusilier Regiment, 'Konigin' Nr.86.

Reserve. The final paragraph of the plan, although only one line, was the most important – 'This project is based on fine weather.'[32]

This view coincided with an instruction paper published by the General Staff in May 1917 titled, *'Notes on the use of Tanks and on the general principles of their employment as an adjunct to an infantry attack.'* Paragraph 2b of these notes stated:

> So long as the bottom is hard, mud or water to a depth of 2 ft. or so is no bar to its progress; but owing to its weight, ground that has been very heavily shelled, or is very sodden to a considerable depth, is unfavourable to its employment.[33]

The warnings were there, but evidence indicates that they were not heeded. It was going to be a risk to employ tanks given the weight of a Mk IV tank was 28 tons and its top speed in favourable conditions was between 4-8 miles per hour. At the time of the offensive, John Charles Fuller was a Lieutenant Colonel on the Tank Corps HQ staff. In January 1958, he forwarded a letter to *The Spectator* magazine to clarify issues raised in an article the previous November regarding the suitability of using tanks in the offensive. Due to the relevance to and impact on the infantry who the tanks were meant to support, the full text of the letter is reproduced as follows:

> On June 15 1917, a report on the eventual battlefield, accompanied with a map was sent to GHQ. The map was marked in four colours: brown, ground suitable for tanks; light green, valleys liable to become flooded; orange, German batteries and dark green; woods impassable for tanks. In the report it was stated that, as the ground then was, tanks could negotiate it in most places; should it rain, the streams (Steenbeck, Reutelbeck and affluents) would become serious obstacles; and should the ground be heavily bombarded, because the drainage system would be destroyed; it would become impassable to tanks and all wheeled transport. On July 16 the initial bombardment was opened and between then and July 31 4,283,000 shells weighing approximately 107,000 tons were fired onto the eventual battlefield. Because ground was the tanks supreme problem, to keep check of the destruction wrought by gunfire, HQ Tank Corps arranged with the RFC to have daily aeroplane photographs taken of the front over which tanks would advance. The information culled from them was transferred to a large-scale map, known as the 'Swamp Map' a copy of which was sent daily to GHQ until HQ Tank Corps were instructed to discontinue sending them. Strange to say, this in no way prevented the maps growing bluer and bluer – blue was the colour used to denote the bogs created by the destruction of drainage dykes. By July 31 from the Polygon de Zonnebeke through St Julien and northwards past Langemarck, the Steenbeck had become a wide moat of liquid mud.[34]

The inference in Fuller's letter is that GHQ didn't wish to hear bad news and the British plans which relied on so many factors gelling were beginning to look unsteady.

32   TNA WO 95/91/6: Tank Corps HQ War Diary.
33   TNA WO 95/91/6: Tank Corps HQ War Diary.
34   *The Spectato r*<http://archive.spectator.co.uk/article/10th-january-1958/19/euston-3221> (accessed 15 February 2022).

Concealing preparations for the offensive from the Germans was exceptionally difficult, given that the British area of operations was overlooked by the Germans, and it was nigh on impossible to conceal the preparations from the local Belgian people. The Parish Priest of Dickebusch, Achiel Van Walleghem, kept a diary throughout the war years. On 27 June 1917 he recorded:

> More and more people are talking about the imminent offensive from the Ypres area to the coast.[35]

An entry two weeks later on 9 July stated:

> There is more and more talk of the imminent offensive. We see the numerous and large-scale preparations here and we hear of those in nearby sectors, railway tracks are being laid on all sides, artillery guns are being brought up and the ammunition dumps are steadily multiplying.[36]

As the Irish divisions prepared to leave their training areas for the journey to the assembly areas at Watou, close to Ypres, last minute reinforcements joined some of the battalions to bring them close to active service strength. Second Lieutenant Jack Carrothers described the complement posted to the 8th Inniskillings in none to flattering terms:

> We are getting some new officers tonight that completes us again after the last show in June. I am sorry to say that the ranks were filled up with English conscripts. They are a poor substitute for the old toughies we fought with at Wytschaete and Messines.[37]

On 30 July, with preparations more or less completed, Field Marshal Haig visited General Gough in his HQ, later recording:

> I saw Gough, in the best of spirits and full of confidence for the results of tomorrow's fight.[38]

Gough may have been putting on a brave face for his commanding officer however, privately, he was more than a little concerned. Despite the cheery optimism of the intelligence reports provided by Brigadier General Charteris, General Gough had less positive news from his own sources, including his liaison officer, Paul Maze:

> Maze returned with the information that British medium guns had blown the camouflage off many concrete pillboxes along the enemy second line, but the shells had scarcely scratched the surface. Prisoners spoke of Eingriff [Eingreif] divisions, completely fresh,

---

35 Dominiek Dendooven (ed.) *1917. The Passchendaele Year. The British Army in Flanders: The Diary of Achiel Van Walleghem* (Brighton: Edward Everett Root Publishers, 2017), p.161.
36 Dendooven (ed) *191*, p. 169.
37 David S Carrothers, *Memoirs of a Young Lieutenant 1898-1917* (Enniskillen: Privately Published, n.d.), p.69.
38 Blake, *The Private Papers of Douglas Haig 1914-1919*, p.248.

waiting in shelters a few thousand yards to the rear to counter-attack. French, British and Belgian pilots, who were able to cross more frequently into German air space from the middle of July onwards, warned that enemy batteries were continually changing their positions and thus escaping much of the allied counter-battery fire.[39]

From the British high command's perspective, all preparations, no matter how comprehensive, had been made.

---

39 Anthony Farrar-Hockley, *Goughie: The Life of General Sir Hubert Gough* (St Albans: Granada Publishing, 1975), p.216.

3

German Defences

> *I find that I can face this offensive in a calm frame of mind, because never before have we had deployed along a front under attack such strong reserve forces, which have been so well trained in their role.*
>
> Crown Prince Rupprecht of Bavaria[1]

Of all the issues open to debate concerning the prosecution of the Third Ypres offensive, there is one certainty – the delay in continuing the offensive rapidly after dealing the Germans such a stunning blow at Messines, greatly assisted the Germans in reorganizing their defences.

Following the Messines offensive Crown Prince Rupprecht of Bavaria, commander of the northern group of German armies and his senior commanders, were immediately aware of British intentions. They recognised that the attack would be followed up and that it would involve an assault on the ridges around Ypres coupled with an advance on the Belgian coast. As a priority, the resources of Fourth Army, which held the ground to the east of Ypres, were supplemented so that seventeen Divisions manned the front line and thirteen and a half were in reserve.[2]

They recognised that following Messines, the initiative was with the British and they fully expected an attack within a short period. Somewhat charitably as it turned out, Crown Prince Rupprecht's Chief of Staff, General der Infanterie Hermann von Kuhl observed:

> It was obvious that the British had imposed an operational pause in order to complete all their preparations with the utmost thoroughness.[3]

Bitter experience had taught the Germans that there was little point in concentrating their defences around a strong front line which would be pounded incessantly by Artillery and they realised that in order to face a major offensive, innovative ideas would be required.

---

1   Jack Sheldon, *The German Army at Passchendaele* (Barnsley: Pen & Sword, 2007), Introduction.
2   Jonathan Boff, *Haig's Enemy: Crown Prince Rupprecht and Germany's War on the Western Front* (Oxford: Oxford University Press, 2020), p.173.
3   Sheldon, *The German Army at Passchendaele*, p.31.

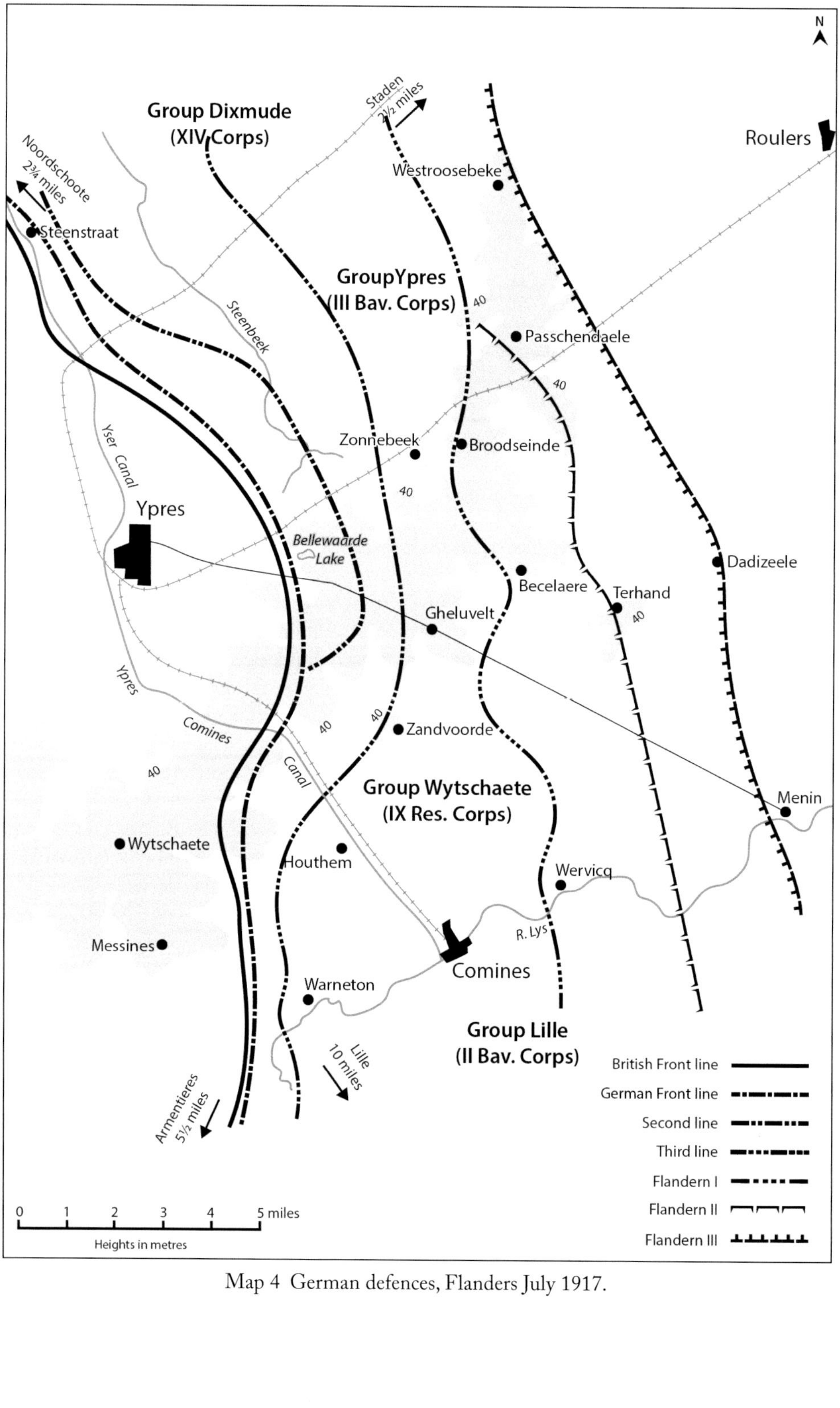

Map 4 German defences, Flanders July 1917.

Opposite the ground held by General Gough's Fifth Army was the German Fourth Army, commanded by General Friedrich Sixt von Armin, a 66-year-old Prussian who had first fought in the Franco-Prussian War of 1870–71. Within the Fourth Army were a number of Army 'Groups,' each similar to a British Corps. Opposite the area which was to be attacked by the British XIX Corps on 31 July and then by the Irish Divisions on 16 August 1917, was Army Group Ypres.

On 13 June 1917, a German defensive expert, Oberst [Colonel] Fritz von Lossberg was posted to Fourth Army as its Chief of Staff. The original plan had been to interchange the entire staffs of Fourth and Sixth armies however, this move had been vetoed by the Kaiser.

Aged 49 at the time of the offensive, Friedrich Karl (Fritz) von Lossberg had been a soldier since 1888 and before the war had been an Instructor at the *Kriegsakademie*. Regarded as an expert defensive tactician, he had had previous success against both the British and the French. He arrived at the Headquarters of General Sixt von Armin on the morning of 13 June and following a long meeting with the General, was given a free hand in creating an effective defensive system. Later that day he visited the various Army Group and Divisional Headquarters to get a feel for the battlefield. The situation he found himself in was a Godsend. He commented later in his memoirs:

> During the Champagne, the Somme and the Arras battles I assumed duties as the Army Chief of Staff in those sectors only after the enemy break-ins had already occurred. For the battle of Flanders, I had sufficient time from 13 June to 31 July to organize in detail the defence for large scale attack.[4]

Cognisant of the urgency of the situation, he worked through the night during which:

> I calculated the number of trench divisions (*Stellungsdivisionen*) and attack Divisions (*Eingreifdivisionen*) needed for the defence of the enemy's anticipated large-scale attack as well as the additional artillery, aviation and other combat assets (*Kampfmittel*) that would be needed. My requests were quickly approved by OHL.[5]

What Lossberg came up with as a defensive plan was simple, but effective. He believed that the offensive would be carried out as similar offensives had been, a prolonged artillery bombardment followed by an all-out infantry offensive on a wide front. The geography lent itself to the defenders, with the valley of the Steenbeek to be crossed by the attackers who would be under observation by the Germans who held the ridges beyond. Counterattacks by infantry could be directed from the ridges and supported by accurate artillery fire from the batteries on the reverse side of the ridges.

In developing his plan, von Lossberg came up with a system that was ingenious. The front line, situated in the boggy ground was to be lightly held and protected by barbed wire

---

4   Major General David Zabecki & Lieutenant Colonel Dieter Biedekarken (eds.) *Lossberg's War: The World War 1 Memoirs of a German Chief of Staff.* (Lexington, Kentucky: The University Press of Kentucky, 2017), p.287.
5   Zabecki & Biedekarken (eds.) *Lossberg's War*, p.288. The OHL was the *Oberste Heerseleitung*, the German Supreme Army Command.

defences and teams of men in foxholes. Just over a mile behind this came the *Albrecht Stellung*.[6] Between the front line and the *Albrecht Stellung* were mutually supporting machine gun posts constructed of reinforced concrete and holding one or two machine guns. These strongpoints became known generically as 'pillboxes' to the British as they resembled one. To the Germans, they were known as MEBUS, (*Mannschafts-Eisenbeton-Unterstände*) and they stretched back another mile to the next line of defence known as the *Wilhelm Stellung*.[7] It was here that the counterattack divisions were located with shelter in large reinforced bunkers, and behind them at further intervals of a mile were lines of defence, Flanders 1, Flanders 2 and Flanders 3, each garrisoned by infantry units. In all, the defensive system stretched seven miles and the premise was that the concrete machine gun posts would slow the advance and thin the attackers out and when this occurred, the counterattack divisions would engage them supported by the artillery from over the ridges and push the attackers back to their start point or beyond.

Oberst Fritz von Lossberg. (Open source)

Eingreif Divisions were only to be deployed in an organised fashion if the local defensive counterattacks had failed. In implementing this system, responsibility was given to relatively junior officers to mount local counterattacks without waiting for authority from those at Headquarters–trusting the man on the ground to act on his initiative.

What was unique about this system was the widespread employment of ferro concrete pillboxes, although this was not the first time that the Irish Divisions had come across them. At the Battle of Messines, 15th Royal Irish Rifles had encountered a farmhouse that been reinforced with concrete and had supporting smaller concrete bunkers located close by. Captain Miller of the 15th Rifles chronicled its capture:

> Ordered Lieut. Falkiner to take his platoon less Lewis-gun team, and put out of action the strongpoint which I had spotted on my right. Got the Lewis gun into action to spray the place ... then I went to the left of the line and got B Company to attack another strongpoint which was plugging at our left. Then I went back to the right of the line and found that

---

6 Named after Albrecht Duke of Wurttemberg commander of German Fourth Army until 1917. *Stellung* translates to position.
7 Named after the Kaiser and also known as the *Artillerie Schutzstellung*.

Messines Ridge Blockhouse at New Zealand Memorial to the Missing. (Author)

Lieut. Falkiner had got Lumm Farm. The Huns put up a fight here. However, one of the concrete places was bombed by Riflemen Aicken and Cochrane.[8]

Under the direction of Oberst von Lossberg, the Germans utilised the time afforded to them by the delay in the continuation of the offensive, to massively step up the construction of strongpoints of various sizes. According to Vancoillie and Blieck, during this period the Germans erected approximately 9,000 reinforced structures on the Ypres front. A testament to their construction is that many still exist today.[9]

Given the importance of these structures to the experiences of the Irish Divisions on 16 August, it is of value to investigate further how these strongpoints were constructed.

First, the Germans looked at trying to reinforce buildings which already existed:

> Shelter could also be provided by making use of damaged civilian buildings close to the front, these were adapted for a more warlike use. Windows and damaged walls were sealed

---

8   Cyril Falls. *The History of the 36th (Ulster) Division* (Belfast: McCaw, Stevenson & Orr, 1922), p.96.
9   Jan Vancoillie & Kristof Blieck. *Defending the Ypres Front 1914-1918. Trenches, Shelters and Bunkers of the German Army* (Barnsley: Pen & Sword, 2018), p.59.

up and the interior of the building and its roof reinforced, with sandbags at first but in due course complete concrete structures were built within a house. Cellars were especially prized and these were later often covered with an extra layer of concrete to transform them into a dugout.[10]

Where this was not possible, bunkers were constructed from scratch. As this was being done on a massive scale, an industry existed to support it as Thurlow described:

At the start, sand and road material for the manufacture of the concrete was requisitioned locally, but later the gravel for the best quality concrete was brought from the Rhine, through Holland via the Meuse and Scheldt in barges and by rail. It consisted of water worn gravel of flintstone and quartz broken to about half inch gauge. The sand was mostly coarse, sharp and clean.[11]

There were not sufficient German Pioneers to construct all the bunkers required and these were supplemented by Belgian forced labour and Prisoners of War, the use of the latter for labour in connection with the operations of war being contrary to the provisions of the Geneva Convention of 1906 and the Hague Convention of 1907.

There were two main methods of constructing bunkers, firstly by the use of prefabricated concrete blocks which were manufactured in vast quantities in factories in rear areas and brought to the front by train. Without any reinforcement in the structure, these proved susceptible to Artillery fire. By far the best method was by using poured concrete, which obviously proved logistically difficult close to the front line. The method of construction of these was well planned:

The building process of a bunker was phased and often several teams each with their own specialisation, worked on a bunker. First one team dug out soil to create an excavated site. Often civilian labourers and POWs were used for this work, under German supervision. As soon as the ground was suitably excavated, a team twined iron rods into a mesh. Another team started pouring cement to create the floor plate, which served as a foundation. While the floor plate was being poured, iron workers started connecting the rods to the mesh where the walls were to be built. All the rods were connected to ensure the greatest possible strength. Wood workers then arrived to build the formwork. If necessary, this process continued around the clock… A standard bunker measuring approximately 5 x 10 metres required the following – 92 cubic metres concrete (Approx 830 bags of cement) 110 cubic metres of sand with gravel and 1200 litres uncontaminated water. Sixteen tonnes of iron rods were required. The minimum thickness of the roof and walls was set at 1.5 metres in 1917. This thickness was proved through experience to withstand the impact of several medium calibre shells or one heavy calibre shell.[12]

---

10 Vancoillie & Blieck. *Defending the Ypres Front 1914-1918*, p.40.
11 Colonel Edward Thurlow DSO. *The Pill-Boxes of Flanders* (Uckfield: Naval & Military Press reprint of 1932 edition), p.11.
12 Vancoillie & Blieck. *Defending the Ypres Front 1914-1918*, p.59.

Not all bunkers were of this size. The figures provided above give some idea of the extent of the effort required to construct up to 9,000 of them.

The reinforcement of the concrete with iron rods made them exceptionally durable and impervious to all but the heaviest artillery. When constructed, the pillboxes were camouflaged with earth and sods however, as the British bombardment gathered intensity, this camouflage was swept away and they stood out clearly on the landscape, the white concrete reflecting any sunlight there was.

The British therefore knew that the pillboxes were there, as Paul Maze described whilst observing the Gheluvelt Plateau:

> Although our heavy shells landed on Stirling Castle with clockwork regularity, parties of Germans could be seen sneaking round its ruins, some work was obviously going on.[13] Every morning as I looked up the slope with fresh eyes I detected an increase of white patches amidst the piled up brick dust. Our aerial photographs soon revealed the enemy's new scheme of defence, which took the form of pill boxes made of concrete, a new and unexpected obstacle. Our artillery had to deal with them one by one.[14]

The problem was that artillery assets could not deal with them effectively. With the walls and roof over four feet thick, the vast majority of British shells caused no lasting damage. The most effective artillery against these structures was a direct hit from nothing less than an eight-inch Howitzer. Unfortunately, howitzers of eight inches and above were very much in the minority in the British arsenal.

Whilst the pillboxes were a formidable defensive means, they were not without their vulnerabilities as Captain Kalepky of *Fusilier-Regiment, 'Konigin' Nr. 86* recalled.

> The bunkers were reasonably strong and could withstand even direct hits from some of the heavy enemy shells, but owing to the ground conditions in the Flanders area they could not be erected over a strong foundation. When a couple of heavy shells opened up a crater close to them, they would lean over, sometimes with the entrance down, with the soldiers trapped inside…There was no way of rescuing them of course and we suffered a rather heavy number of fatalities in this way-and the thought of the painfully slow death of those entombed haunted us all.[15]

For the British attack though, the pillboxes and bunkers brought an extra dimension into the attack which had not been factored into the plans. As each of the reinforced structures contained, or had the potential to contain multiple machine guns, each of these had to be dealt with before the advance could continue. The British creeping barrage, as previously mentioned, was to advance at a rate of 100 yards every four minutes. Once the belt of pillboxes was reached, it would appear obvious that considerable time would be taken dealing with each individual pillbox, and therefore the protection of the creeping barrage would be lost.

---

13 Stirling Castle was a strongpoint situated near the hamlet of Westhoek on the Gheluvelt Plateau.
14 Maze, *A Frenchman in Khaki*, p.228.
15 UL: Liddle/WW1/GE09, Lieutenant Colonel L Kalepky Papers.

The existence of the pillboxes themselves struck a note of trepidation into British troops who had never encountered them before. Second Lieutenant Edwin Campion Vaughan was attached to the 1/8th Warwickshire Regiment, 143rd Infantry Brigade, 48th (South Midland) Division. He was to attack alongside the 36th (Ulster) Division on 16 August and later recalled being briefed by his company commander:

> A Company Commander's conference was held during the morning…we heard the Coy Commander on his return say, 'and those red squares are concrete pillboxes, reinforced with iron and absolutely shellproof.' At a briefing it was confirmed that the German defences consisted of enormous concrete blockhouses so situated that the guns mutually enfiladed each other. I felt a terrible sinking inside when I heard this, for it appeared that any attack must be unsuccessful, but when we discussed it exhaustively, we came to the conclusion that the reports must be exaggerated, and we decided not to worry about them.[16]

Unfortunately, the reports were not exaggerated.

Clearly, the British were aware of these defensive structures and following raids and interrogation of prisoners, were aware of the Germans defensive plans and those for carrying out counterattacks. Documents detailing these tactics had been captured and were promulgated to battalions before the opening of the offensive on 31 July. Copies of these documents are contained within the papers of Lieutenant Colonel Kenneth Charles Weldon DSO commanding officer 7/8th Royal Irish Fusiliers and are enclosed at Appendix 1 for reference.[17]

Whilst the Germans were preparing intensely by building numerous pillboxes, they also adhered to the old maxim that attack was the best form of defence. In the days prior to the opening of the offensive and aware that the British rear areas were crammed with troops and supplies, they intensified their artillery bombardment, day and night, confident that they were bound to hit something. This tactic was complemented on a nightly basis by German bomber aircraft which targeted areas where billets were thought to be. The Pioneer battalion of 16th (Irish) Division, the 11th Hampshires reported on 21 July at 9.45 pm:

> Enemy Aircraft dropped four bombs near the camp, one of which was a dud. No casualties.[18]

Captain Douglas Browne MC of the Tank Corps recalled that 5th Army Headquarters, far behind the front line was not immune from being targeted either:

> Poperinghe, two miles to the south was shelled for half an hour or so every morning, often in the evening and at odd hours during the day. The shells passed almost over our camp and while one was dressing or preparing to turn in for the night one used to hear the whistle overhead and the distant crash and echo in the unfortunate town. And once we were genuinely entertained by a crisis nearer at hand. An enterprising 15-inch gun,

---

16 Edwin Campion Vaughan, *Some Desperate Glory: The Diary of a Young Officer 1917* (Barnsley: Pen & Sword, 2017), p.183.
17 Imperial War Museum (IWM) Doc. 7190 Colonel Kenneth Charles Weldon Papers.
18 TNA WO 95/1966/2: 11th Hampshire Regiment War Diary.

probably travelling in luxury on a train took a few pot-shots at the 5th Army Headquarters in the chateau itself.[19]

Prior to the opening of the campaign, all preparations, both offensive and defensive were completed in the heat of a Belgian summer, where shell fire on both sides raised clouds of dust on detonation. The assumption was that the offensive would be carried out when it was dry and the ground was firm. What would happen if the weather changed?

---

19   Captain Douglas Gordon Browne MC, *The Tank in Action* (Uckfield: Naval & Military Press reprint of 1920 edition), p.119.

4

Ground Conditions and Weather

> *Under the most favourable conditions, an attack against such a position as confronted us would have been a task of great difficulty and risk. As things actually were, it was nothing but rank folly.*
> Brigadier General Christopher Baker-Carr
> 1st Brigade, Tank Corps[1]

Whilst the British and Germans meticulously prepared their offensive and defensive plans, there were connected elements which were to impact greatly on the prosecution of the forthcoming campaign.

Shown on the map overleaf, the ground around Ypres had long been contested, with the high ground, known as the West Flemish Ridge forming a natural boundary in the shape of a semi-circle around the historic Belgian town. In Roman times, the ridge acted as a divider between warring tribes and its importance continued, being the scene of military engagements throughout the middle-ages and the European wars of the late 17th and early 18th centuries, with Ypres itself changing hands many times, as the eminent historian, Richard Holmes noted:

> Ypres became French by the treaty of Nijmegen and was fortified by Vauban.[2] Captured by the Dutch in 1713, it was held by them until the French recovered it in 1744. It changed hands several times in 1792-4 and during the Waterloo campaign of 1815 its fortifications were hastily patched up by a British garrison. Ypres was Dutch after Waterloo and became Belgian when Belgium gained her independence in 1833.[3]

It was of no surprise when it again became the fault line between the British and Germans at the advent of trench warfare in October 1914. From the map it is obvious that whoever controlled this feature had a commanding position to view the defences of Ypres and could also control the land behind the ridge which afforded access to the coast.

---

1   Christopher D'Arcy Baker-Carr, *From Chauffeur to Brigadier* (Driffield: Oakpast Ltd reprint of 1930 edition), p.187.
2   Sebastien le Prestre de Vauban, a legendary French Military Engineer employed by Louis XIV.
3   Richard Holmes, *Fatal Avenue: A Traveller's History of the Battlefields of Northern France and Flanders 1346-1945* (London: Random House, 2008), p.155.

Ground Conditions and Weather 55

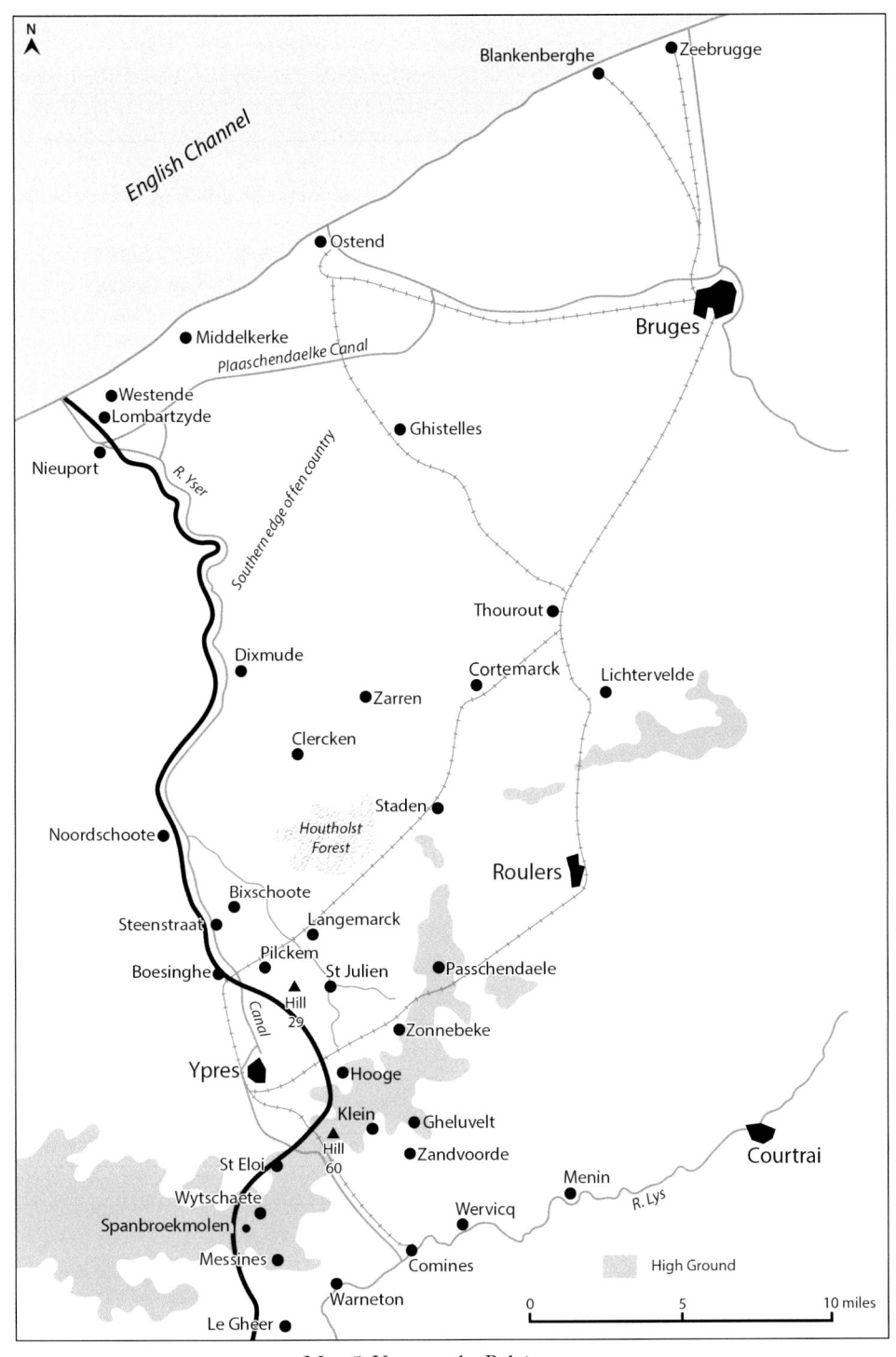

Map 5 Ypres to the Belgian coast.

The ridge was strategically important however, at its highest point near the village of Gheluvelt, it was just short of 70 metres above sea level. As the ridge continues and sweeps around Ypres, its height diminishes slightly so that by Passchendaele village it had dropped to 53 metres. On 31 July therefore, the British were to attack uphill and on 16 August, the Irish Divisions were to attack from the low-lying ground between the ridge and Ypres, with the two Divisions occupying positions between St Julien and Frezenberg. St Julien is 15 metres above sea level and Frezenberg double that at 30 metres.

Bisecting this area were a number of small streams, the Steenbeek, the Zonnebeke and the Hanebeke.[4] These had been managed over centuries by farmers as part of an intricate drainage system which was a necessity in such low-lying ground which was a mixture of sand and clay.

As can be imagined, the 4,283,550 shells fired by British Artillery between 16-31 July, totally destroyed this drainage system to the extent that even before the offensive began, the effects were disastrous for the prospects of the British:

> After our preliminary bombardment which lasted for 16 days with ever growing intensity and the German retaliation thereto, the whole surface of the ground consisted of nothing but a series of overlapping shell craters, half full of yellow, slimy water. Through falling into these ponds hundreds upon hundreds of unwounded men whilst advancing to the attack, lost their lives by drowning…The original roads had almost ceased to exist and in order to enable wheel traffic to move at all, even in the area behind the line it was necessary to lay down corduroy tracks which were constantly destroyed by shell fire.[5]

This was the state of the ground on the morning of 31 July 1917 and in the afternoon, it began to rain. The weather changed, with drizzle starting around 1:00 p.m. By 4:00 p.m. the drizzle had turned to heavy rain which persisted for the rest of the day and into the following day. Major General Nugent of 36th Division, whilst not involved in the initial phase of the offensive, described the situation on 1 August:

> It has been raining continuously for nearly 24 hours. The whole of this country is a vast bog and it is impossible to move men or guns or stores so the day has been quiet. Neither the Germans or ourselves have been able to do anything and there has been very little shelling. All over the country guns and wagons are stuck in the mud and there is no prospect of moving them till the ground dries. It looks like raining for days…we thought that we were going in at once this evening, having got orders to be ready, but these were afterwards cancelled. I suspect we shall move very soon.[6]

The very worst of luck for the British, but could this deluge have been foreseen? This has been the subject of much debate over the intervening years however, with the crucial importance of the offensive weighing heavily on the shoulders of Field Marshal Haig, would he have been so reckless as to forge ahead knowing that the weather was against him?

---

4 The spelling of these stream names varies considerably. The version employed here is that of the British Official History.
5 Baker-Carr, *From Chauffeur to Brigadier*, p.186.
6 PRONI D/3835/E/2/14 Farren Connell papers.

The man who did much to court controversy surrounding the weather was Haig's Intelligence Chief, Brigadier General Charteris. In his biography of Field Marshal Haig, he states:

> Haig was already anxious about the weather conditions that were to be anticipated. Careful investigation of the records of more than eighty years showed that in Flanders the weather broke early each August with the regularity of the Indian monsoon, once the autumn rains set in difficulties would be greatly enhanced.[7]

This statement is fundamentally wrong and over the years has been seized upon by Haig's detractors as evidence that Haig had continued with the offensive whilst ignoring sound advice.

The man responsible for providing weather forecasting for the British was Ernest Gold, by the time of the Armistice holding the rank of Lieutenant Colonel and in charge of the GHQ Royal Engineers Meteorological Section based at St Omer. He and his team had been responsible for accurate weather forecasting at Messines and continued their work throughout the offensive. Some forty years after the event in November 1957, an article by the eminent historian Sir Basil Liddell Hart appeared in *The Spectator* concerning Passchendaele which prompted a number of letters to the Editor which backed the claims of Brigadier General Charteris. Having kept his powder dry for 40 years, Ernest Gold was keen to set the record straight and in his reply to one correspondent, stated the facts whilst deriding any counter argument:

> In his letter about Passchendaele (*Spectator*, December 27) Brigadier Desmond Young states: 'In fact the monsoon conditions of August 1917, were no worse than in the previous three years.' This statement needs correction; it is quite contrary to the evidence of the actual records which show that the weather in August 1917 in and behind the battle area was exceptionally bad. The rainfall directly affecting the first month of the offensive was more than double the average; *it was over five times the amount for the same period in 1915 and in 1916* … Brigadier Young may have been misled by an unconsidered statement of Charteris that in Flanders the weather broke early in *August* with the regularity of an Indian monsoon. This statement is so contrary to recorded facts that, to a meteorologist, it seems too ridiculous to need formal refutation.[8]

By all accounts the rain which began on 31 July and continued well into August was indeed exceptional and was commented on as such by the locals, as the local priest observed in his diary on the eve of the Battle of Langemarck:

> Rain and thunder almost all day. Even in the winter, I hardly saw so much water and mud as there is now. No-one has ever known such weather in August. The bad weather is a calamity for the harvest and also for the fighting.[9]

---

7 Brigadier General John Charteris, *Field Marshal Earl Haig* (London: Cassell & Company Ltd, 1929), p.272.
8 *The Spectator* <http://archive.spectator.co.uk/article/17th-january-1958/14/sirin-his-letter-about-passchendaele-spectator-dec accessed 9 March 2022> (accessed 11 September 2002).
9 Dendooven (ed.) *1917*, p.201.

The delays which had plagued the previous weeks from a variety of sources, had ensured that the offensive had been postponed on a number of occasions and was now set for 3:50 a.m. on 31 July 1917. Had Haig been more forceful with his subordinates and French allies and insisted on attacking on 28 July, it is conceivable that the outcome would have been much different, as it would have afforded the attackers the luxury of three days of dry weather with which to establish a foothold, move artillery and bring up reserves. As it was, the die was cast.

Ground conditions, August 1917. (Canadian War Museum Archive EO-2249)

5

Opening of the Offensive, 31 July–15 August 1917

An understanding of the initial phase of the offensive so far as it affected the attacking infantry divisions of XIX Corps, 55th (West Lancashire) Division and 15th (Scottish) Division, is of crucial importance in comprehending how the following days before the opening of the Battle of Langemarck detrimentally impacted on the 16th (Irish) and 36th (Ulster) Divisions. It is not intended to re-examine the opening of the offensive, but rather to set the scene.

The operational order for the attack was issued to 55th Division on 23 July 1917 and stated:

> It is the intention, with the object of preparing for a further advance, to capture and occupy as a line of resistance, the enemy's GHELUVELT – LANGEMARCK Line and to throw out strong outposts to obtain a footing on the GRAVENSTAFEL Spur and to occupy enemy works to the east of the GHELUVELT – LANGEMARCK Line as far as about the line TORONTO – AVIATIK Farm…The 55th Division will attack with 165th Infantry Brigade on the right, 166th Infantry Brigade on the left and the 164th Infantry Brigade in Reserve. The 15th Division will be on the right and the 39th Division will be on the left of 55th Division.[1]

To attain the objective, the 55th and 15th divisions would have had to successfully advance 4000 yards or just over two and a quarter miles, an ambitious target by any stretch of the imagination. The 16th Division was designated as Reserve for this operation.

The advance commenced with a massive Artillery barrage at 3:50 a.m. 31 July, described articulately in the history of the 55th Division:

> Not since the war began had so intense a barrage been put down, and of its wonderful effectiveness all ranks in the line bore eloquent testimony.[2]

---

1   TNA: WO 95/2903/2: 55th Division War Diary.
2   Reverend James Ogden Coop, *The Story of the 55th (West Lancashire) Division* (Liverpool: Daily Post Printers, 1919) p.49.

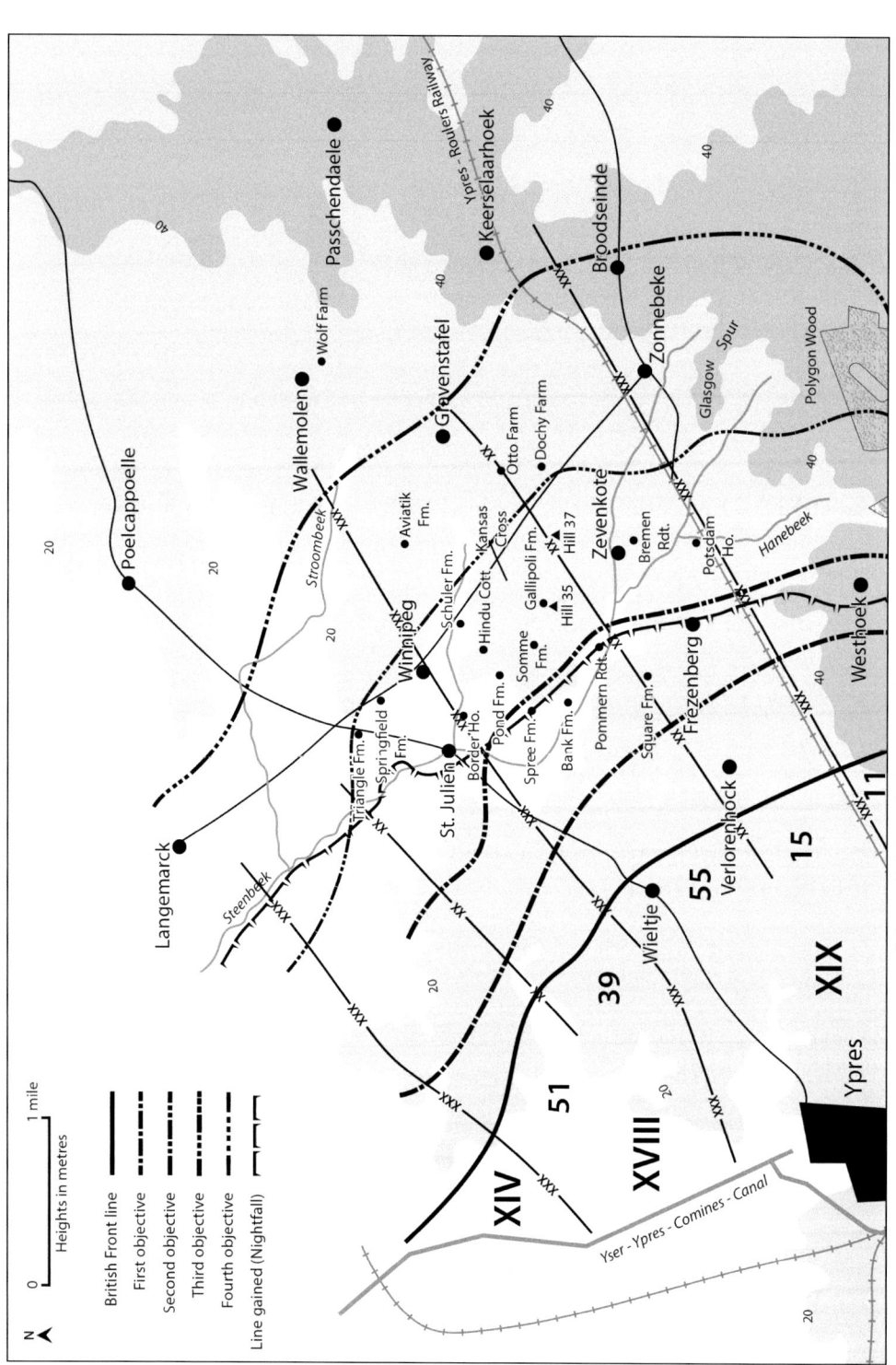

Map 6 Pilckem Ridge: XIX Corps assault, 31 July 1917.

The initial infantry advance was rapid and successful for 55th Division and the second objective (also known as the Black Line) was captured by 9:00 a.m. although there was still considerable resistance from Spree Farm and Bank Farm which were eventually captured with the assistance of a tank. The right of the 55th Division's attack was held up by enfilading fire from Square Farm, which was in 15th Division's area and had not yet been captured by them. This strongpoint was eventually captured by 1/7th King's Liverpool Regiment and the divisional history gives some idea of the strength with which the strongpoint was held:

> The garrison of 130 men surrendered and threw down their arms. They afterwards ran off to the right with their hands up and were all taken prisoner by 46th Infantry Brigade.[3]

The advance continued and a third objective (also known as the Green Line) was captured. This was in the area of Schuler Farm. A patrol was seen to be as far forward as Aviatik Farm however, this unit was isolated and returned to consolidate on the third objective. The fact that the 39th Division on the left had had to fall back to Border Farm, left the 55th Division troops open to enfilading fire from the Germans on the left. Two Victoria Crosses were awarded for actions during 55th Division's advance. Corporal Tom Mayson 1/4th King's Own Royal (Lancaster) Regiment, received the award for twice destroying machine gun positions and Lieutenant Colonel Bertram Best-Dunkley, commanding officer of 2/5th Lancashire Fusiliers, for determined leadership of his men to achieve their objective.[4] For his actions on that date and on the following two days Captain Noel Godfrey Chavasse VC MC Royal Army Medical Corps, attached 1/10th King's (Liverpool Regiment) of the 55th Divison's 166th Infantry Brigade was awarded a bar to his Victoria Cross which he had received in 1916, the only man in the Great War to achieve such an honour.[5]

Meantime, to the right of 55th Division, the advance of 15th (Scottish) Division also initially progressed well, and the attacking troops found that through the heavy shelling, the German front line had ceased to exist, although a number of concrete pill boxes remained intact. The first objective was taken by 5:00 a.m. and the attackers swept on towards Frezenberg village which was captured by 44th Infantry Brigade with the assistance of a Tank, 'Challenger'.

The advance continued against stiff opposition from fortified strongpoints which had to be dealt with individually before progress could be made. However, the second objective (Black Line) was captured by 10:00 a.m. although the troops there continued to come under sustained machine gun fire from German positions on Hill 35 and Gallipoli Farm. Reinforcements in the form of 45th Infantry Brigade were brought up to push through the consolidated line to attack the third objective (Green Line). The advance proceeded under a creeping barrage until the attacking troops came upon a belt of uncut wire ten yards thick and two feet high just east of Bremen Redoubt. Displaying considerable bravery, a path was cut through the obstacle whilst the troops were under constant fire from Hill 37. The strongpoint on the hill was eventually

---

3   Coop, *The Story of the 55th (West Lancashire) Division* p.50.
4   Lieutenant Colonel Best-Dunkley led his men to capture Spree Farm and then recapture it following a German counterattack. Severely wounded in the action, he died of wounds aged 27 on 5 August 1917.
5   Captain Chavasse subsequently succumbed to wounds. He received the bar to his Victoria Cross for actions on 4 August 1917.

Captain Chavasse VC gravesite, Brandhoek New Military Cemetery. (Author)

captured and 150 prisoners taken there as the 46th Brigade reached the third objective and consolidated there at 11:25 a.m.

In common with the position then facing 55th Division, the attacking troops of 8th Division who were on 15th Division's right on the other side of the Ypres-Roulers railway, had not been able to progress beyond the second objective, leaving the right flank of the Scotsmen open to enfilading fire from the direction of Zonnebeke.

By late morning, both attacking divisions of XIX Corps had achieved their objectives and were consolidating their positions. For the British, this was a remarkable success although the extent of the XIX Corps advance was not immediately realized due to communication problems and led General Gough to order consolidation on the third objective, a wholly unrealistic proposition as 55th and 15th divisions were open to attack from either side as well as frontally.

The manner and extent of the British advance was exactly what the Germans had been expecting and was proof that von Lossberg's tactics were working. Drizzle commenced to fall around 1:00 p.m. and this coincided with the beginning of the German response as the 15th Division experienced:

> Between noon and 1pm three enemy 'planes flew very low over the Divisional front, carrying out a thorough reconnaissance of the position without receiving any attention on the part of the RFC.[6]

The absence of the Royal Flying Corps was as a result of the poor weather conditions. A programme of offensive flying that had been planned for 31 July had to be severely curtailed:

> As a result of the bad weather with low clouds all day and rain in the afternoon, the extensive prearranged programme for the co-operation of the squadrons of the Royal Flying Corps could not be put into force.[7]

This reconnaissance precipitated the beginning of a massive counterattack by the Germans utilising the *Eingreif* divisions, specially trained for the task. In increasingly heavy rain, the fresh German troops swept forward and gradually across the XIX Corps front, pushed the depleted and exhausted troops of 55th and 15th divisions back. To compound matters, with the lack of aerial support, communication could not be maintained with the Artillery who were therefore unaware where the British forward positions were.

The speed of the German counterattack caused great difficulties for the British. The 55th Division's 164th Brigade were ordered to retire and form a defensive line from Hill 35 to Border House but on attempting this discovered that the Germans had beaten them to it. A further rapid withdrawal had to be made to avoid the remnants of the Brigade being surrounded. To their right, the 15th Division's 45th Brigade were forced out of Otto and Dochy Farms and had to retire to Iberian Farm. Despite a courageous counterattack by a composite unit of 45th Infantry Brigade in the evening of 31 July, by nightfall, the British front line in the XIX Corps area ran roughly

---

6   Lieutenant-Colonel J Stewart DSO and John Buchan, *The Fifteenth (Scottish) Division 1914-1919*. (Edinburgh: Blackwood & Sons, 1926) p.166.
7   Henry Albert Jones, *The War in the Air. Being the story of the part played in the Great War by the Royal Air Force. Volume IV* (Uckfield: Naval & Military Press, 1934, Reprint) p.161.

along the second objective or Black line between St Julian and Frezenberg. The Germans made a number of attempts over the next few days to recoup their lost ground but were thwarted by a combination of strong resistance from XIX Corps troops and the appalling ground conditions.

Given their positions alongside each other on the battlefield and the strength of the opposition it is of no surprise that the casualties of 55th and 15th divisions sustained are remarkably similar. In the period 31 July-3 August, 55th Division had 3,447 officers and men, killed, wounded and missing. The 15th Division had just four less at 3,443.[8]

In the afternoon of 31 July, Field Marshal Haig visited General Gough at his Headquarters along with the Chief of the Imperial General Staff General Robertson, to obtain an update on progress. Gough presented a optimistic view of the day's fighting at that point, claiming that his forces had taken 5,000 prisoners and 60 guns. Haig was briefed that fighting had been most severe and progress slowest to the right of Fifth Army front. This was the Gheluvelt plateau and Haig had expected this to be the case. Haig recorded the visit in his diary and gave instructions to Gough as to future actions:

> As regards future operations, I told Gough to continue to carry out the original plan; to consolidate ground gained, and to improve his position as he may deem necessary for facilitating the next advance, the next advance will be made as soon as possible, *but only after adequate bombardment and after dominating the hostile artillery.*[9]

The final line is italicised for emphasis in any copy of Haig's diaries I have come across. This view was reinforced the following day when Haig met the Corps Commanders at Fifth Army HQ. On being briefed by General Watts commander XIX Corps, he noted the following:

> XIX Corps. General Watts explained how his divisions got right forward to the extreme limit, viz. Green line, but were obliged to retire owing to artillery fire from the main ridge on the east. This confirms my view that progress cannot be made by an advance towards the Fôret de Houthoulst until the *main* Broodseinde – Staden ridge is taken. His troops are now on the Black line.[10]

On 2 August, Haig again visited General Gough to reiterate his instructions:

> At 10 am I saw Gough and N. Malcolm with Kiggell. I showed him on my relief map the importance of the Broodseinde-Passchendaele ridge and gave it as my opinion that his main effort must be devoted to capturing that. Not until it was in our possession could he hope to advance his centre. He quite agreed. I also told him to have patience, and not to put in his infantry attack until after 2 or 3 days fine weather, to enable our guns to get the upper hand and to dry the ground.[11]

---

8   Edmonds, *History of the Great War based on Official Documents, Military Operations France and Belgium 1917* p.178, footnote 1.
9   Blake, *The Private Papers of Douglas Haig 1914-1919* p.250.
10 Sheffield & Bourne (eds) *Douglas Haig. War Diaries and Letters 1914-1918.* p.309.
11 Gary Sheffield & John Bourne (eds) *Douglas Haig. War Diaries and Letters 1914-1918.* (London: Weidenfeld & Nicolson, 2005) p.309-10.

Haig's instructions were clear. There was to be no advance until the German Artillery on the right of the battlefield was dealt with and the ground was firmer, although Gough was permitted to improve his position. This instruction is of crucial importance in understanding what subsequently transpired.

On the evening of 31 July, Gough met with his Corps Commanders at his Headquarters to consider the position after the day's fighting, and in accordance with Haig's instructions agreed that several adjustments needed to be made before a general attack with Fifth Army could be made. Gough later recorded:

> On the 4th, the II, XIX and the right of the XVIII Corps were to complete the capture of the third objective (the green line) … We arranged to make preparations to carry out the attacks on these dates, but it was recognised that bad weather might cause a postponement.[12]

Whilst not directly involved in the combat operations of 31 July, the day was however a day of preparation and hard labour for both Irish divisions.

The 16th Division's 47th Infantry Brigade had been training up until 30 July and that night were billeted at Brandhoek, between Ypres and Poperinghe. At 4:10 a.m. on 31 July the 7th Leinsters travelled by train to Potijze, east of Ypres where a working party of 21 Officers and 500 other ranks were detailed to dig trenches near Potijze Chateau to bury cable. As the offensive had just begun, German Artillery were shelling British rear positions heavily to prevent reinforcements and supplies being moved up. This made the Leinster's task exceptionally difficult as the regimental history recollected:

> The neighbourhood of the chateau was unhealthy, the enemy's guns paying it great attention. Proceeding along the Potijze road the party came under heavy shrapnel fire and a number of casualties occurred including 2nd Lt Wilkie whose thigh was broken by a shell splinter. CSM Byrne A Coy, a most efficient Warrant Officer was killed with a number of men of A Coy on the road. It seemed impossible to proceed to dig a trench under those conditions but, encouraged by Colonel Buckley who showed a fine example and the company officers, the men fell to with a will and soon provided themselves with shelter in the trench they were digging. The work took several hours to complete but after the first couple the shelling subsided, and the work was only occasionally interfered with. Rain began to fall heavily in the afternoon…The working party returned to the grounds of Goldfish Chateau late in the afternoon but the only shelter from the pouring rain was the men's groundsheets and a very dismal night was spent in the open.[13]

The senior NCO referred to, A/Company Serjeant Major Patrick Byrne, was a single man from Arklow, County Wicklow. In his Will he left all his property and possessions to his mother, Margaret Fitzanson, residing at Lower Main Street, Arklow. He is buried alongside nine of his comrades at Potijze Chateau Lawn Cemetery.

---

12 General Sir Hubert Gough, *The Fifth Army* (London: Hodder and Stoughton, 1931) p.201-2.
13 Lieutenant Colonel Frederick Ernest Whitton, *The History of the Prince of Wales's Leinster Regiment (Royal Canadians) Part II* (Uckfield: Naval & Military Press, 1924, Reprint) p.424.

66 A Bad Day I Fear

A sister battalion in 47th Brigade, the 1st Royal Munster Fusiliers, were tasked on 31 July with a similar cable laying operation near Frezenberg involving 12 officers and 700 other ranks. They also were shelled heavily and sustained over 50 casualties including eight killed.

The 48th Infantry Brigade of 16th Division were designated as reserve to the attacking Divisions. As the opening day progressed, Major General Thuillier, Commanding Officer of 15th (Scottish) Division became increasingly concerned at the heavy casualties incurred and requested assistance from 16th Division. In response, 7th Royal Irish Rifles and 9th Royal Dublin Fusiliers were placed at his disposal. The 7th Royal Irish Rifles were attached to 44th Brigade and the 9th Dublins to the 45th Brigade to be used only in an emergency. Both these battalions were moved up to the original British front line, but took no part in the fighting.

In the early evening of 31 July, the 8th Royal Dublin Fusiliers were attached to 55th Division's 164th Infantry Brigade and marched through the Menin Gate at Ypres to positions in the original British front line. The battalion had been on standby all day and the battalion's Chaplain Father Willie Doyle SJ MC, observed a tragic incident which showed that long range German Artillery was not the only danger:

> We were to be held in reserve for the opening stages of the battle so we lay all that day in the open fields, ready to march at a moment's notice should things go bad at the front…A curious incident happened close by while we were waiting. One of our aeroplanes, flying rather low, dashed into the cable which was holding an observation balloon overhead. The steel wire snapped like a thread, the balloon with its two occupants shot up in the air disappearing in the clouds, while the aeroplane crashed to the ground, both pilot and observer were killed. A few minutes later we saw the two ballooners come dropping down attached to their parachutes and land safely, none the worse for their trying experience.[14]

Research indicates that only one person was killed in this accident. A native of Maidstone, Kent, Lieutenant Stephen Reginald Park Walter was aged 20 and was attached to 32 Squadron Royal Flying Corps. He had transferred to the RFC from 2nd Battalion Queens (Royal West Surrey) Regiment in 1916 and was wounded whilst an Observer on a patrol on 23 June 1916.[15] He had six 'kills' to his name and was on his second patrol of the morning when the accident occurred, most likely in poor visibility which blanketed the Ypres area. Lieutenant Walter is buried at Lijssenthoek Military Cemetery. His parents arranged for the inscription, 'Pass friend – All's well' to be placed on his headstone.

On 31 July, the 49th Infantry Brigade remained in reserve at Vlamertinghe, three miles west of Ypres, although still out of danger as the war diary of the 7th Royal Inniskilling Fusiliers recorded:

> Moved to assembly camp at Vlamertinghe under 1 hour's notice to move. A very wet and uncomfortable night was spent in a barren and muddy field. During the night a German inflammatory shell was reported to have struck the field. No damage or casualties were

14 Carol Hope, *Worshipper and Worshipped. Across the Divide – an Irish Padre of the Great War. Fr. Willie Doyle, Chaplain to the Forces, 1915-1917* (Brighton: Reveille Press, 2013) p.569.
15 Trevor Henshaw, *The Sky their Battlefield* (London: Grub Street, 1995) p.88.

Lieutenant Stephen Walter gravesite, Lijssenthoek Military Cemetery. (Author)

caused by the unexpected visit of this shell. Trench strength on 31 July–30 Officers and 823 Other Ranks.[16]

The strength of the battalion at that time is of interest. At full active service strength, a battalion would have numbered around 1,000 officers and men, so the 7th Inniskillings were slightly below that but still an effective fighting force. Throughout this chapter, I intend to show how the strength of the infantry battalions of the Irish divisions was gradually degraded through enemy actions and the appalling weather conditions to such an extent that they were no longer capable of carrying out an effective attack on 16 August.

By 31 July, 36th Division had moved to the XIX Corps reserve area between Watou and Poperinghe around six miles to the west of Ypres. Accommodation was in tents and the infantry battalions spent the day preparing kit and cleaning weapons as the rain increased in strength. Analysis of battalion war diaries indicates that the strength of the battalions averaged just over 900 officers and men. Some officers of the infantry battalions took the opportunity to travel the short distance to Ypres to carry out reconnaissance of the area, as did Sergeant Robert McKay of the Division's 109th Field Ambulance, who found it an ominous experience:

> All the roads leading to Ypres are under observation and the German Gunners have the range of them to perfection. The nearer one approaches the town, the wreckage and desolate appearance gets worse. Before the war, Ypres had a population of 17,480 and was a beautiful place. Now it is a scene of destruction baffling description. The gardens in the suburbs are covered with weeds and all kinds of rubbish, whilst many of the principal buildings are only mounds of rubble. The culminating point of destruction appears as soon as one arrives at the Cloth Hall, all that is left of this historic building is one bit of a square tower and a few pieces of walls. Not a roof is on any of the buildings in the vicinity…After visiting the relay post we returned as quickly as possible to the unit. Here, I was asked what it was like up the line. I told them, but some of the men laughed and said it could not be worse than the Somme. I said that if the Infantry get away as they did at Messines it would be alright. If they are held up, God help us.[17]

Evidence that the offensive was not going well came later in the day with 109th Field Ambulance being tasked to provide an officer and 64 men as Stretcher Bearers to assist 55th Division.

Both Pioneer battalions of the Irish divisions were having an arduous time in support of the 55th Division advance. No. 1 Company of 16th Royal Irish Rifles were tasked with repairing the Wieltje-Spree Farm road. When they commenced work at 5:30 a.m. they found the road virtually non-existent due to shellfire with only the outline being discernable. As they were directly behind the front line, the work was regularly interrupted due to heavy German shellfire. Nonetheless, they stuck to their task enduring constant shelling and heavy rain, until relieved by No. 3 Company at 5:30 p.m. By that time 350 yards of the road had been repaired with beech slabs and rubble. No further work by No. 3 Company was possible due to continued heavy shelling. Whilst carrying out their work on 31 July they sustained 23 casualties of whom

---

16   TNA WO 95/1977/2: 7th Battalion Royal Inniskilling Fusiliers War Diary.
17   IWM Doc. 22065 Sergeant Robert McKay 109th Field Ambulance RAMC.

10 were killed. One of those killed was 23 years old Corporal James (Jim) Alexander Weir, a native of Castlewellan, County Down. In France since October 1915, he had fought at the Somme and Messines. His platoon commander Lieutenant David Dawson later wrote to his father, William:

> It is with deep regret that I write to tell you of the death of your son on July 31st. He was a Corporal in my platoon and our work had to be done under very heavy shell fire in the German front trenches. He was one of a party who were acting as Stretcher Bearers to one of the wounded who had to be carried through shell fire to the Dressing Station. The shell burst among the party and your son and three others were killed. I don't think that he suffered any pain, and it will be perhaps some consolation to you to know that he died when trying to help another. As his Platoon Commander, I feel the loss very keenly; he was one of the very best NCOs and a very popular soldier.[18]

The 11th Hampshires were engaged in similar work near Potijze and had a similar experience, being heavily shelled. They sustained 17 casualties including three killed, one of whom was forty years old Major Gawain Murdoch Bell, a native of York. He is buried at Brandhoek New Military Cemetery.

The rain continued incessantly on 1 August causing General Gough to cancel a planned operation due for 2 August by II Corps to capture the original second objective (Black Line) on Gheluvelt plateau. The cancellation of this operation due to the weather left the German artillery with a free hand to continue shelling the positions held by 55th and 15th Divisions.

The rain which had begun on the afternoon of 31 July, continued without ceasing for three days. As the 55th and 15th divisions had made modest gains, the new front line had moved forward. An unintended consequence of this is that the area which had been the focus of heavy shelling was now a swamp of liquid mud over two miles wide which had to be traversed to reach the new front line. Access routes across the swamp were created by the Royal Engineers with Infantry working party support, utilising duckboards to create a path. Whilst these were adequate, they were also in full view of German Artillery spotters and it was not long before these came under close attention from German Artillery.

The battalions of 16th (Irish) Division however, were already in the old British front line in support of the attacking divisions and were having a torrid time. The 6th Connaught Rangers, comprising many of John Redmond's Irish National Volunteers from Belfast, had moved on 1 August at an hour's notice to relieve the 2nd Royal Dublin Fusiliers in the old British reserve line on the St Jean-Wieltje Road. There, they remained in what passed for trenches in pouring rain for the evening until at 2:00 a.m. on 2 August, 150 men under the command of Second Lieutenant Justin John Pope,[19] were tasked to find and retrieve the wounded of 55th Division and a further 50 to retrieve the wounded of 15th Division, who lay between the old British

---

18 Andrew Henry, *From Hilltop to Over the Top* (Rathfriland: Drumlough &District Historical Society, 2018) p.146.
19 Second Lieutenant Pope later transferred to the Royal Irish Rifles and was awarded the Military Cross. He survived the war, being discharged due to wounds with the Silver War Badge. A son, Second Lieutenant Basil Holland Pope was killed in action whilst serving with the Royal Tank Regiment in Egypt in 1941.

front line and the German front line. In the conditions, the task was arduous in the extreme, requiring six men to each stretcher. They carried out this work for nine trying hours successfully retrieving many wounded men. The commander of 55th Division Major General Jeudwine, acknowledged their assistance in writing on 6 August:

> We are very much indebted to you for the brave and devoted work of 150 men of 6th Connaught Rangers who were lent to us as stretcher bearers. They had about the hardest task that any stretcher bearers have had in this war – a very long carry under severe fire over ground which was difficult beyond description. From all I hear that they performed their task most gallantly – not I am afraid without severe casualties to themselves. I should be grateful if you could convey the thanks of all ranks of the 55th Division to their OC and to the men themselves and tell them how much their services are appreciated.[20]

At 11.55 pm on 1 August, XIX Corps issued an operational order as follows:

> 36th Division will move on 2nd inst. 1 Infantry Brigade by train to Goldfish Chateau and thence to the 55th Division area east of Ypres, where it will come under orders of GOC 55th Division, *but will not be used except in case of emergency.* [Author's italics]
> The following reliefs will take place on the night of August 3rd/4th
> The 16th Division will relieve 15th Division in the Right Sector
> The 36th Division will relieve 55th Division in the Left Sector. Reliefs to be complete by 4 a.m. August 4th.[21]

The plan therefore to keep the Irish divisions in reserve and fresh until the next phase of the offensive proposed for mid-August had fallen apart after less than two days of action. A further surprise was to follow however for 36th Division. The 107th Infantry Brigade was identified as the Brigade to be held in reserve by 55th Division and travelled as arranged to 55th Division's sector where they were ordered to relieve the 55th Division's 164th Infantry Brigade. As this was being effected, to his great surprise 45 minutes later Brigadier General Withycombe, commanding 107th Brigade received a further message from 55th Division, ordering him to relieve 165th and 166th brigades as well.

There is no doubt that 55th Division had suffered grievously and it could be said that 107th Brigade were being used in an emergency however, on the afternoon of 2 August, the entire 55th Division was relieved by a single brigade of 36th Division, certainly not what was envisaged when the operational order was issued. Major General Nugent moved quickly to support 107th Brigade and in effect the relief stipulated in the operational order for the night 3rd/4th August was carried out twenty-four hours earlier. Even carrying out the relief was problematic as Falls recounted:

> It was carried out in continuous rain through mud 18 inches deep, under heavy fire from howitzers of heavy calibre and in the midst of bombing attacks launched against the

---

20   TNA WO 95/1970/2: 6th Battalion Connaught Rangers War Diary.
21   TNA WO 95/960/1: XIX Corps War Diary App. 34.

right flank of 55th Division. Not till 6 o'clock in morning of August 3rd was its completion announced. The Brigade had heavy casualties, particularly the 10th and 15th Rifles which had taken over the Black line…That night two battalions of the 108th Bde, the 13th Royal Irish Rifles and the 9th Royal Irish Fusiliers relieved the 165th Bde which had moved back to the old British front and support lines and two battalions of 109th Bde, the 11th Inniskillings and 14th Royal Irish Rifles the 166th Bde, the whole force under the command of BG Withycombe GOC 107th Bde who had his HQ in the mined dugouts at Wieltje.[22]

When the relief as completed, Major General Nugent went forward to observe the battlefield and was aghast at what he found:

We have all moved up and taken the place of the Division which was in front of us (55th) so we are now in the front and the next move falls to us. The weather conditions are simply indescribable…It is knee-deep in mud in some places and the mud in camp is only surpassed by the mud in front. I went up this morning to the front, not right up to the new line as that is unapproachable by day and it was really pitiful to see the conditions in which these unlucky men were living. The whole country has been ploughed up by shellfire, all drains stopped and there is nothing but water and mud everywhere.[23]

As a result of the horrendous conditions, Nugent believed that the threat of an imminent attack from the Germans was remote, and cognisant that the Division would be making an attack in the near future, removed two of the battalions out of the front line, relieving them with a company from one of the 107th Brigade battalions on a rotational basis.

By 4 August, elements of 16th Division had already been in what passed for the front line for 36 hours. In carrying out their relief, the 6th Royal Irish Regiment had difficulty finding where the front line was as their war diary recorded:

2nd August about 9.00 pm relieved the Royal Scots Fusiliers and the Argyll & Sutherland Highlanders in the front line facing Frezenberg ridge. About midnight they were ordered to proceed to the north of Frezenberg and fill a gap in the front line which was hard pressed there. They moved up in the dark and at early dawn had arrived at the Frezenberg crossroads without finding any formed body of our troops. Fortunately the morning was dull and misty, as the first indication that the battalion had reached the most forward area held by the enemy was HQ which was leading being fired on by an enemy machine gun at a range of about 150 yards. Two companies were rapidly extended to form a front line and the other two were placed in support. As it was then daylight, the men just took cover in shell holes where they were and lay there for the day. Towards evening the battalion Headquarters of three battalions of 15th Division were located at Square Farm. The remains of these battalions, some 250 men were holding the shell holes in front of Square Farm. The battalion

---

22 Falls, *The History of the 36th (Ulster) Division* p.112.
23 Nicholas Perry (Ed) *Major General Oliver Nugent and the Ulster Division 1915-1918* (Stroud: Sutton Publishing, 2007) p.158.

relieved these units after dark and held this position until the night of 5/6th in a continuous downpour and heavily shelled day and night.[24]

The battalion were relieved at midnight on 5 August by the 8th Inniskillings, and did not reach their billets, soaking wet and exhausted, until 6:00 a.m. on 6 August. In their short stay in the front line, the battalion war diary records that they sustained 139 casualties, nearly 25 per cent of the total fighting strength of the battalion.[25] Of these, 32 were killed in action or died of wounds. On 2 August, two men from opposite ends of the country fell. Thirty-six years old Second Lieutenant Robert Adair Dickson, from Stranmillis Road, Belfast, was killed. He had emigrated to Canada and had returned to enlist as a Private in the Royal Fusiliers before being commissioned, joining the Royal Irish Regiment in August 1916.[26] He has no known grave and is commemorated on the Menin Gate, panel 33.

Private Stephen Carrigan 6394, was attached to the battalion's C Company. Aged 21 and from Pump Lane, Waterford, he had married a local girl, Mary Corr, only nine months earlier. He is buried at Aeroplane Cemetery, near Ypres, grave I.A.3A.

The 8th Inniskillings had suffered a grievous loss on 4 August when their CO, Lieutenant Colonel Thomas Henry Boardman DSO, died of wounds from shellfire as the Battalion made its way forward.[27] With a replacement CO, the battalion continued on its task its war diarist noting:

> The Frezenberg Ridge was very heavily shelled by enemy 4.2's and 5.9's during advance to this position and a number of casualties were inflicted on us.[28]

The Commonwealth War Graves Commission records that 14 men were killed in carrying out this relief, Many more were wounded.

Captain Staniforth of the 7th Leinsters described the nightmare he and his men had to endure when attempting to relieve the remnants of the Gordon Highlanders of 15th Division:

> Moving up to relieve the Gordons on 2 August. I collected my 30 men and in straggling Indian file we struck out across the battlefield. The rain was still coming down and the heavily laden men sank to the base rock at every step. They were nothing but stumbling figures of mud, every now and then they would slip and fall full length in the sludge, rifle and all, so time after time we had to stop and pull one man or another out who had sunk up to his thighs and was helpless. And all the time, German shells whizzed and tore into the ground, burying themselves in the swamp and throwing up fountains of water over us. My signalling sergeant, whom I had known and trained since he enlisted in my platoon at

---

24 Brigadier General Stannus Geoghegan, *Royal Irish Regiment 1900-1922* (Uckfield: Naval & Military Press, undated, reprint) p.116.
25 TNA WO 95/1970/3: 6th Battalion Royal Irish Regiment war diary.
26 Private PS/2360 21st (Service) Battalion Royal Fusiliers (4th Public Schools) In France from 4 November 1915.
27 From Cheshire and a Schoolmaster before the war. He had been married four months before his death. Buried at Brandhoek New Military Cemetery (Plot III.F.I).
28 TNA WO 95/1977/3: 8th Royal Inniskilling Fusiliers war diary.

Pte Stephen Carrigan gravesite, Aeroplane Cemetery. (Author)

Fermoy before Christmas 1914, was blown to pieces as he struggled to release himself from the mud, the corporal had both his legs mangled and lay in a foot of slime until he died. Another shell buried two men beside me and tore a gash in the palm of my hand.[29]

Ten men of the 7th Leinsters were killed in effecting this relief.[30]

Whilst the infantry were struggling through the mud, the Artillery were having an equally trying time. Lieutenant Colonel Claud Potter was posted to command 153rd Brigade Royal Field Artillery on 3 August, its previous commanding officer having been wounded that day. Immediately on arrival, he set out to find his Brigade which had been attached to 55th Division since early July. He found them in exposed positions 750 yards north-east of Wieltje. The positions that they were in were constantly under German counter battery fire and were subject to close attention from enemy aircraft who were pinpointing their position. Due to the inherent dangers, he ordered them to move the following day to a new position amidst the ruins of St Jean. Effecting this move through the thick, cloying mud was easier said than done. By the time the move was completed 20 men had become casualties including 35 years old Second Lieutenant Maurice Cane from Celbridge, County Kildare, who was killed.[31]

With so many men being wounded it was imperative that proper arrangements were put in place by the Irish divisions to manage not just the steady stream of casualties that were occurring daily, but also preparing for those likely to occur when the main advance took place. As part of the XIX Corps medical plan, 109th Field Ambulance of 36th Division took over Red Farm on 4 August as the Main Dressing Station. The Farm was around three miles west of Ypres, towards Poperinghe. They too faced difficulties due to the ground conditions:

Unit took over Red Farm. 109th Field Ambulance now in charge of the collection of all sick and wounded from the line and billets and the evacuation. As the Motor Ambulance cars of the unit are on account of the low chassis unsuitable for the bad roads east of Ypres, arrangements made with 6 Motor Ambulance convoy to evacuate the wounded from St Jean and the Canal Bank to Red Farm. The cars of the unit and attached cars from 108th and 110th Field Ambulance to evacuate to the Casualty Clearing Station. Two Bearer sub-divisions each from 108th and 110th Field Ambulance attached and also 89 OR from Tunnelling Coy. The heavy rain of the last week having rendered the ground over which the wounded have to be carried unsuitable for vehicles, a large number of bearers will be required for the Company carriers. At present, Motor Ambulance cars are unable to proceed farther than St Jean as there is no turning place farther forward and as the road between St Jean and Wieltje is not suitable for wheeled stretchers an additional carry of 800 yards is imposed on the bearers.[32]

---

29 Grayson (ed.) *At War with the 16th (Irish) Division. The Staniforth Letters.* p.157.
30 It has not been possible to positively identify the sergeant or corporal as two of each rank were killed in this action.
31 Second Lieutenant Cane is commemorated on the War Memorial at Christ Church, Celbridge There is also a stained glass window dedicated to him there.
32 TNA WO 95/2499/2: 109th Field Ambulance RAMC War Diary. Red Farm Commonwealth War Graves Commission Cemetery currently stands beside where Red Farm once was.

Their comrades in the 112th Field Ambulance of 16th Division set up their Main Dressing Station a short distance away at The Mill, Vlamertinghe on the same day, their war diary providing a clear insight into casualty management preparations:

> Reorganised duties in Dressing Station. Elements of 36th Division working alongside. System – patients conveyed by motor lorries or char-a-bancs and dropped on the east side of the mill where they pass through four marquees fitted with forms, the last having a YMCA bar open day and night. Thence they pass to two waiting room tents and thence across the lane to the Mill Base reaching the south entrance of the Clerks room, where AFB 210 is made out at separate tables according to Divisions. Thence across the Mill Yard and into a hall where AT service is given by special nurses. Then into the Dressing Room which accommodates six Dressers. Passing out after dressing to another door they wait either in another hall or upstairs in a large waiting room above the Dressing room and are sorted out by a special NCO i/c evacuation who dispatches them to their proper Casualty Clearing Station as per Corps orders. Admissions – Wounded 171 Sick 190.[33]

It is of interest to note that on that date [4 August] sick cases in all probability precipitated by the conditions, exceeded the numbers wounded.

The relief of the 55th and 15th divisions by the Irish divisions was completed by 10:00 a.m. 4 August.[34] In the original Fifth Army plan, they were still meant to be in reserve, training and resting for the next phase of the offensive.

The brigades of 16th Division that had been supporting 55th and 15th Divisions since 1 August were finally relieved on the evening of 5 August. The 6th Connaught Rangers marched to what were described as 'very comfortable' billets near Brandhoek where a warm welcome of hot food, rum and tea were awaiting them. Lieutenant Colonel George Buckley of the 7th Leinsters was acutely aware of the stress that his men had been through, and along with the orders detailing their relief, he included an emotionally charged motivational letter copied to each of the company commanders to be read to the men:

> As we are going out tonight, right back for a real rest, I want to put before you one or two facts which in turn I want you to put before the officers and men of your companies. I consider this the greatest trial that the old 7th Leinsters have ever gone through and I am proud to say that in the eyes of our Brigadier and GOC we have come through it with flying colours and high honour. On Friday last when two battalions were detailed to hold the present front line I was asked to join in a general protest in account of the exhaustion of our men. I reported our men to be in a greater state of exhaustion than I had ever seen the battalion before. But realizing that this was a fight to the finish, I was loth to say anything that would tarnish our well-earned reputation in the GOC's eyes as the 'Fighting Leinsters', so I closed my written report with these words – 'Although I feel it my duty to report that the men of my battalion are really genuinely exhausted, *at the same time I know that we are living in exceptional days and we shall make an exceptional*

---

33 TNA WO 95/1967/2: 112th Field Ambulance RAMC War Diary.
34 The 36th Division officially assumed sector command from 55th Division at 4:00 am; from 15th Division by 10.00 am.

effort if called upon to do so.' I felt I was speaking for my officers and men and I am proud to see how magnificently you have all – Officers and men – backed me up. As a result, General Hickie decided to give the Leinsters pride of place, *he left us to hold the whole front single handed, the same front as he originally detailed to be held by two battalions.* No greater compliment, no greater honour has ever befallen the 7th Leinsters. Generals Pereira and Hickie have written me words which make me thrill with pride for the honour of commanding a battalion with so grand a fighting spirit. Both Generals will personally speak to thank the men as soon as we get out. Tell all your officers, NCO's and men of what I am telling you. We are not yet out of the wood, let us see to it that at the eleventh hour nothing is done to detract from the high honour that has come to us. I appeal to you once again – Officers and men let us pull ourselves together for the last lap. Let us carry out the relief in silence, cheerfulness and order. No stragglers, no missing men, no rifles or packs abandoned. Let us march out up to the Leinster standard on which the 7th has always prided itself. As for me, my heart has bled for you all during these days and nights of trial. I shall thank God when I see you all safely out, and there is no prouder colonel in the whole British Army than I am today.[35]

In their four days at the front, the 7th Leinsters had suffered greatly. Captain Max Staniforth described the bliss of uninterrupted sleep and the physical effects of the sodden battlefield:

We woke to rest and peace, the first hot food for eight days, the first wash or shave, and the first dry clothes – but these things are too sacred to write of! Our casualties totted over 300 and many sick – mainly trench feet from being waterlogged for a week and wrinkled like crocodile skin. We could not have put 50 effectives on parade out of the battalion.[36]

In the following days. The systematic degradation of the Irish divisions continued unabated. Both Divisions minimised the exposure to the horrors of the front line by holding their sectors with half of a brigade and rotating the battalions through to enable men to dry their clothes and get some rest however, the casualty toll continued to climb inexorably. Whilst it is not possible to tell the story of each and every casualty, hopefully what follows can give a flavour of the torment suffered by those holding the front line and those supporting them.

The 8th Royal Dublin Fusiliers had relieved the 1st Battalion Royal Munster Fusiliers in the front line on 5 August, the relief being impeded by heavy shelling. The Dublin's right Company boundary was on the Ypres-Roulers railway line in the vicinity of Wilde Wood.

The war diary recorded how the battalion was heavily shelled throughout 6 August. On the morning of 7 August at 9.00 a.m. a German shell struck and ignited a box of Verey lights at battalion HQ, asphyxiating the commanding officer and his command team and causing them to be evacuated to hospital. The battalion was relieved by 9th Royal Dublin Fusiliers at 3.30 a.m. on 8 August. During this relief there was a German counterattack supported by gas shells

---

[35] Lieutenant Colonel Frederick Ernest Whitton, *The History of the Prince of Wales's Leinster Regiment (Royal Canadians) Part II* (Uckfield: Naval & Military Press reprint of 1924 edition), p.428.

[36] Grayson (ed.) *At War with the 16th (Irish) Division. The Staniforth Letters.* p.162. In their tour of the front line, the battalion had had 19 men killed.

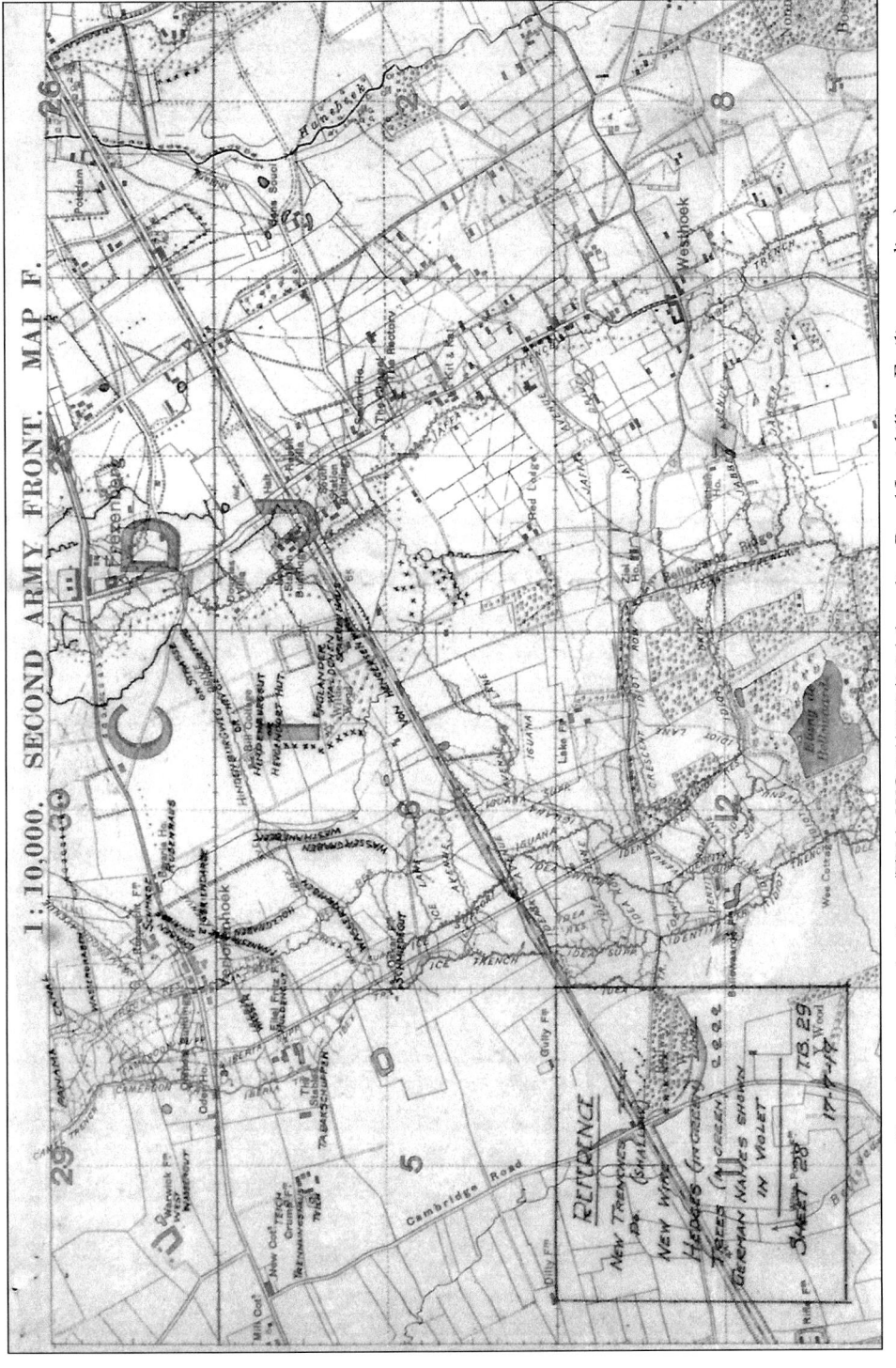

Frezenberg area and railway. (TNA: WO 95/1977/3 8th battalion Royal Inniskilling Fusiliers war diary)

which was repulsed. In this tour of the line, the battalion suffered 61 casualties from enemy action, including 15 killed.[37]

Remarkably, and an indication of the character of the man, the battalion Chaplain, Father Willie Doyle volunteered to remain with the 9th Dublins instead of moving with the rest of 8th battalion to the relative safety of the rear. It was not long before his services were required:

> Word reached me about Midnight that a party of men had been caught by shellfire nearly a mile away. I dashed off in the darkness, this time hugging my helmet as the Boche was firing gas shells. A moment's pause to absolve a couple of dying men and then I reached the group of smashed and bleeding bodies, most of them still breathing. The first thing I see almost unnerved me, a young soldier lying on his back, his face and hands a mass of blue phosphorous flame, smoking horribly in the darkness. He was the first victim I had seen of the new gas which the Germans are using, a fresh horror in this awful war. The poor lad recognized me as I anointed him on a little spot of unburnt flesh, not a little nervously, as the place was reeking with gas, gave him a drink which he begged for so earnestly and then hastened to the others.[38]

The 9th Dublins held the line until the night of 10 August under near constant shellfire which impacted particularly heavily on C Company, whose officers all became casualties save for Second Lieutenant John McGrath who the war diary recorded:

> Did valuable work in keeping the Company together under the most distressing circumstances.[39]

Born and raised at St John's, Newfoundland, Canada, where his father was a Customs Official, John McGrath had enlisted in the Newfoundland regiment and had been a Corporal in this regiment when he attended Officer Cadet School at Fermoy, County Cork, in April 1917. His service record indicates that he failed his exams, but was recommended for a commission, only joining 9th Royal Dublin Fusiliers in the field on 29 June 1917.[40] Two other officers who joined the battalion with him on that date, Second Lieutenants Wilfred Anthony Harty and Frederick Dowling, were both killed in the first eight days of August.

The 7th Royal Inniskilling Fusiliers of 49th Infantry Brigade had moved to the front line on 7 August on the left of 16th Division's area of operations and relieving their sister battalion, 8th Inniskillings. Their headquarters was situated in the recently captured Square Farm and the war diary described the battlefield:

> Beck House about 150 yards in front of the left centre of the front line was held by the Germans who had a MG there. Bn HQ at Square Farm. This farm had been strongly concreted and had about five feet of reinforced concrete on top. It had apparently originally

---

37　TNA WO 95/1974/3: 8th Royal Dublin Fusiliers War Diary.
38　Carol Hope, *Worshipper and Worshipped. Across the Divide – an Irish Padre of the Great War. Fr. Willie Doyle, Chaplain to the Forces, 1915-1917* (Brighton: Reveille Press, 2013) p.589.
39　TNA WO 95/1974/4: 9th Battalion Royal Dublin Fusiliers war diary.
40　TNA WO 339/83495: Major John McGrath service record.

been made as an aid post by the Germans. On its southern front was a veranda about 8 foot broad running its entire length with about 1 foot of concrete overhead cover, only the ends were open. The accommodation was not suitable for more than 100 men at a pinch…There was a good supply of well water about 10 yards away. From this farm there was a very fine view of the country all round excepting our own front line which was in a dip. Iberia Farm, Delva Farm, Zevencote, Coffee Farm and Hill 37 all being visible as was Pommern Castle in the north and Frezenberg on the south… the ground was remarkably open and free from natural obstructions, hedges, trees, etc. Ulster Div. were about 100 yards on our left. Intense Artillery fire from Germans from 8:55 p.m. and 9:45 p.m. A/Lt TH Shaw and Sgt Carroll both of B Coy during this bombardment in moving forward to their front line of old trenches and shell holes, presumably lost their bearings and wandered into the German positions where presumably they were captured.[41]

Unfortunately, both men named above were killed and have no known grave, being commemorated on the Menin Gate at Ypres. Second Lieutenant Thomas Herbert Shaw was 21 years old and had been born at Strandtown, Belfast. Employed in the Linen trade pre-war, he had enlisted in the Black Watch in September 1914, regimental number 2116. He had served in France from May 1915 and having applied for a commission, had been appointed Second Lieutenant in 7th Inniskillings on 12 June 1916. In addition to being commemorated on the Menin Gate, he is also commemorated on the Bangor and District War Memorial, County Down.[42]

Serjeant Samuel Carroll was aged 20 and from Liverpool. He had previously been wounded in 1915 at Gallipoli whilst serving with the Inniskilling's 1st battalion. His was the second fatality the family suffered in the Great War, his elder brother William having been killed in August 1914, serving with 2nd Battalion South Lancashire Regiment.

Square Farm was certainly a hotspot. Having being forced out of it in the advance of 31 July, the Germans obviously had its location pinpointed with considerable accuracy as any battalion based there was subject to constant bombardment. The 49th Infantry Brigade war diary recorded that on 8 August:

Heavy shelling continues. Square Farm the forward Bn HQ comes in for a great amount of shelling. 1500 5.9's fell in the vicinity today.[43]

Having been relieved by 7th Inniskillings, 8th Inniskillings made their weary way to bivouacs at Vlamertinghe where they arrived in an exhausted condition, all ranks soaked through having spent two days holding the front line with no shelter in torrential rain. In a letter home to his mother, Second Lieutenant Jack Carrothers glossed over the experience but hinted at the ordeal which he had come through:

Dear Mother, Have just got your letter. You need not worry about me now as we are out. It is a great relief and makes one enjoy life. I am not a bit the worse. Some of the other officers

---

41   TNA WO 95/1977/2: 7th Royal Inniskilling Fusiliers War Diary.
42   TNA WO 339/65237: Second Lieutenant Thomas Herbert Shaw service record.
43   TNA WO 95/1976/6: 49th Infantry Brigade War Diary.

are badly shook … I am second in command of a company. These changes were caused by casualties. This day is rather dark and dull. I hope tomorrow will be fine.[44]

In the period from 3-8 August, the battalion had had two officers and 20 men killed, 77 wounded and four missing.[45]

One of those killed was Private Michael Hagan 30698, aged 34 from Megargy townland near Magherafelt, County Londonderry. A Farm Labourer prior to enlisting, Michael was also married with a four year old son. He enlisted in the 8th Inniskillings at Omagh early in 1915 and embarked for the Western Front with the battalion in February 1916. Michael was killed by shellfire on 5 August as the battalion moved to the front line. He was initially buried on the battlefield in a grave marked with a cross however, in a graves consolidation process in July 1919, his remains were exhumed and reburied at Potijze Chateau Grounds Cemetery, Plot II.A.5.[46]

Buried in the next row to Private Hagan is Serjeant John Murphy 4501, 2nd Battalion Royal Irish Regiment. His battalion had taken over the front line from the 6th Connaught Rangers on 5 August, coming under a heavy barrage along the Potijze Road as they effected the relief. The battalion war diary records that Captain Philip James Gordon Gordon-Ralph, a 27 year career officer who had been born at Bengal, India, had returned from leave that day. Unfortunately, he was killed the following day by shellfire. The battalion war diary recorded on 6 August:

Heavy enemy shelling, mostly 5.9's and 4.2's. Also, many cases of trench feet.

and the following day:

Enemy aircraft and artillery very active. Enemy aircraft appear to do as they like.[47]

Serjeant John Brophy was killed on 7 August, as was Second Lieutenant James Wilson Mark, a 28-year-old from Newry, County Down. Serjeant Brophy was a native of Kilkenny, where his widowed mother lived at Upper Walkin Street. She later received a dependant's pension of eight shillings and sixpence per week for the loss of her son. In their time in the front line, the battalion sustained 70 casualties from enemy action, including 14 killed. They also had 50 cases of men with trench foot. Serjeant Brophy is also buried at Potijze Chateau Grounds Cemetery, Plot I.B.11.

The battalion were relieved in the line close to Frezenberg by 7/8th Royal Irish Fusiliers, the relief being completed in the early hours of 8 August. When daylight came, they became aware of German planes paying close attention to their positions. This was followed closely by an accurate artillery bombardment which reached a crescendo at 10:00 p.m. for 30 minutes. This pattern continued for the three days that the battalion held the line. In that tour the battalion suffered 108 casualties including 20 killed.

---

44 Carrothers, *Memoirs of a Young Lieutenant 1898-1917*. p.73.
45 TNA WO 95/1977/3: 8th Royal Inniskilling Fusiliers War Diary.
46 Michael's widow Agnes requested the inscription, 'In fond remembrance of my dearest husband' to be placed on her husband's CWGC headstone.
47 TNA WO 95/1979/1: 2nd Royal Irish Regiment War Diary.

Private Michael Hagan gravesite. (Author)

Serjeant John Brophy gravesite. (Author)

Amongst those killed was 33 years old Serjeant Edward Aspell 7396, a native of Kilkenny. A career soldier, Edward had enlisted in the Royal Irish Fusiliers in 1902 and had served in India. He had fallen foul of military discipline on a number of occasions, mostly caused by intoxication through alcohol. The most notable transgression being in 1906 when he was sentenced to 84 days imprisonment for striking a superior officer whilst drunk. Transferred to the Army reserve in 1909, he continued to fall foul of the law and served time at Kilkenny Prison on a number of occasions for being drunk and disorderly. He was mobilised in August 1914 and went to France with 1st battalion, being wounded in November of that year. In January 1915 he was court-martialled for being drunk in the trenches. At that time in the rank of Corporal, he was reduced in rank to Private and sentenced to three months Field Punishment No 1.[48] Following this, Edward became a reformed character. He was wounded again in July 1915 and by January 1916 had been promoted to the rank of Serjeant. He transferred to 7/8th battalion in May 1917. Sergeant Aspell has no known grave and is commemorated on the Menin Gate at Ypres and on the Kilkenny World War 1 Memorial. His mother, Bridget, at Garden Row, Kilkenny, received a Dependant's Pension of 15 shillings per week.

Even behind the line, there was no respite from enemy shellfire. A Labour Camp was located next to the Mill at Vlamertinghe, home to 112 Field Ambulance. At 7:45 p.m. on the evening of 9 August, the camp came under shellfire, killing five and wounding eight. The casualties were fortunate in their location as they were immediately treated by the Field Ambulance and passed onto the evacuation chain. On that day, the Field Ambulance treated 156 wounded and 106 sick.[49]

Nevertheless, 16th Division did not have a monopoly on misery and mounting casualties.

The experience of 14th Royal Irish Rifles of the 36th (Ulster) Division's 109th Brigade in moving up to relieve 55th Division units, did not inspire them with confidence in the organisational planning of Fifth Army, an issue which was to become a common complaint in both Irish divisions:

> 3 Aug The battalion left camp at 4 pm and entrained at Vlamertinghe at 6 pm, detrained 20 mins later and marched to Ypres. The whole place is just a picture of desolation, and the roads are in a terrible state with mud. We relieved the 55th Division, 5th North Lancs and King's Own in an old front line with our HQ in a deep mine shaft which is a seething mass of men of every description. The arrangements about relief and information of this location are at present NIL and companies must at first ferret round and find water, shelter and anything else they require. One cannot help comparing the handing over of the 36th Div after the capture of Messines with this handing over. The weather is against us, but a little system would save the troops much hardship.[50]

The 9th Royal Irish Rifles of the 36th Division's 107th Brigade at the beginning of August, had a strength of 39 officers and 846 other ranks. On the night of 2/3 August, they relieved 55th Division units in the old British front line, the battalion HQ being at Uhlan Farm. On the

---

48 Field Punishment No 1 was an archaic penalty whereby the subject soldier was chained to a large object such as a wagon wheel for two hour periods every day in full view of his comrades.
49 TNA WO 95/1967/2: 112th Field Ambulance War Diary.
50 TNA WO 95/2511/2: 14th Royal Irish Rifles War Diary.

evening of 5 August, they moved forward to take over the front line from 10th Royal Irish Rifles and located their HQ at Plum Farm. Between 3 and 5 August, they had already had five men killed by shellfire. One of those who fell was 19 years old Private Alfred Cecil Callow from Balham, London, who had joined the 9th battalion as a reinforcement, having been transferred from the King's Royal Rifle Corps. Second Lieutenant John Witherow aged 24 from Kincull House, Straidarran, Claudy, Co. Londonderry, died of wounds on 5 August. He had been commissioned from the Officer Cadet Battalion at The Curragh in May 1916. His younger brother Alexander had died of wounds a year previously on the Somme whilst serving with 8th Royal Irish Rifles. The battalion's Presbyterian Chaplain, the Reverend John Wright, wrote to John's family outlining the circumstances of his death:

> He had gone out with his company to hold ground recently taken and was wounded in the arms and body and died on the way to hospital in the motor ambulance. I can testify to the fine sterling qualities of your boy in his battalion. He was so cheerful and willing and so anxious to be just in all his ways with the men under his command. His example was a stimulus to so many and he did much to consolidate the position.[51]

Second-Lieutenant John Thomas Witherow

Royal Irish Rifles, killed in action, 5th August, 1917. Son of Alex. & Margaret Witherow, Kincull House, Straidarran, Londonderry.

Second Lieutenant John Witherow. (Great War Ulster Newspaper Archive)

Patrols from the battalion were sent out on 6 August and found the enemy front line occupied. When relieved on 9 August, the strength of the battalion was 39 officers and 766 other ranks. In their short spell in the front line, the battalion had had 83 officers and men killed, wounded or missing, just under 10 per cent of their strength.

Staff Officers occasionally got justifiable criticism for being out of touch in cushy billets to the rear however, this wasn't always an accurate reflection and Captain Edwin Godson of 108th Brigade described the difficulties faced in visiting the battalion Headquarters at Plum and Uhlan farms:

---

51 Correspondence published in *The Northern Whig*, 11 August 1917.

Spent quiet morning observing. Afternoon ditto as visibility was exceptional. Boche has plenty of guns and strafes the lost ground unmercifully, but his concrete dugouts are strong. How furious he must be to see us safely ensconced in them. SOS went up for strafe at night. 11th [Royal Irish Rifles] had 65 casualties. Pretty hot. Went round all Bn. Hq's with Duke in evening. (Bde Major). First Woolly bears right by us [Slang term for any large calibre high explosive shell], then 4.2's and whizz bangs [small calibre German shells] at Plum farm which he saw us enter. Then the same at Uhlan farm. The Bns. are showing the wear and tear a bit.[52]

The men of 107th Brigade Machine Gun Company having taken over their positions from 55th Division on 2 August were called into action on 6 August when it was believed that the enemy were attempting a raid. Having been sat in shell holes open to the elements for four days, the gun teams were glad of the break in the monotony. The company diary records that when the SOS rocket was sent up, they fired 50,000 rounds in 35 minutes.[53] Having fired this immense amount of ammunition, it was noted that it was difficult to get fresh ammunition up owing to the state of the ground, and when relieved on 7 August, the gun teams were completely exhausted from exposure.

With the battalions holding the front line mostly devoid of cover and exposed to the constant rain, the issue of rations provided a timely morale boost as well as much needed sustenance. On 5 August, 15th Royal Irish Rifles were relieved in the front line and moved to reserve in the old British front line. The following day, whilst collecting rations for their companies, two Company Sergeant Majors from the battalion were killed together, as described in a letter by a colleague, Regimental Quartermaster Sergeant Thornton:

> Bob Toye has been killed. He was up with rations on the night of 6th August and whilst at the ration dump a shell exploded close to him and killed him instantaneously along with another Company Sergeant Major from Belfast. These two were my best friends. Bob joined with me and was in the stores with me almost all the time, so I can feel a little of the sorrow that his mother will feel.[54]

CQMS Robert Ernest Toye was one of four sons of Mr and Mrs John Toye from Garvagh, County Londonderry, to serve in the Great War. Aged 26, Robert was an Accountant with the Ulster Bank pre-war. Killed with him was CQMS George Frank Newell. George's parents Henry and Helen were in the clothing trade and owned a popular department store under the family name at Royal Avenue, Belfast. Aged 26, George was the third son of the family to die. His elder brother Walter had died serving with the Black Watch on 10 July 1915 and his younger brother David was killed serving with the Royal Fusiliers on 13 March 1916.[55] Both men are buried at Wieltje Farm Cemetery which was close to where they fell. Their graves

---

52 IWM Doc. 10995. Edwin Albert Godson papers.
53 TNA WO 95/2503/6: 107th Brigade Machine Gun Company War Diary.
54 Correspondence published in *The Northern Whig*, 24 August 1917.
55 The Newell brothers are commemorated on an impressive family headstone shaped like a cenotaph at Belfast City Cemetery (Plot K 289).

Wieltje Farm Cemetery. (Author)

however were disturbed in subsequent shelling, and they grouped with four others, 'known to be buried in this cemetery.'

The steady drip of casualties was a source of frustration for Major General Nugent who was aware that scarce resources were being steadily squandered, and he vented his irritation in a letter to his wife on 6 August:

> It looks like more rain I am afraid. There was heavy artillery fighting yesterday and we are having a number of casualties I am sorry to say. It is always the most unsatisfactory way of all that one can lose men, because it goes on day after day gradually frittering the men away and shaking their morale with no tangible results in the shape of ground gained or visible dead Boche. We are I daresay inflicting a lot of loss on him but we don't see it… Where our front line is now is very much overlooked, in fact no one can show a nose on it by day and we shall continue to be overlooked until we can gain more ground.[56]

Major General Nugent's frustration was well founded. The 8th Royal Irish Rifles took over the front line on 5 August. When relieved by the 9th Inniskillings on 7 August, they had

---

56 Perry (ed.) *Major General Oliver Nugent and the Ulster Division 1915-1918*, p.163.

sustained 174 casualties. In their tour, the 9th Inniskillings had 106 casualties including 20 killed. The 10th Royal Irish Rifles sustained 113 casualties in two days in the front line between 5-7 August. All the battalions suffered similarly. Casualties such as this were not sustainable for any length of time.

For those wounded, being evacuated for treatment was another trying ordeal. Sergeant McKay of 109th Field Ambulance visited the location at St Jean where an Advanced Dressing Station was located beside a graveyard. Due to heavy enemy shelling of the road rendering it impassable to vehicles, Motor Ambulances were not able to take the casualties, who had to be carried back to the Field Ambulance at Red Farm by already exhausted Stretcher Bearers. He described the scenes he witnessed:

> The sights at St Jean were most pitiful, the second day I was at this post, five died within an hour. The walking wounded made their own way down as best they could, trusting to be lifted by motor lorries farther down the road. St Jean was a regular death trap. Even the graves behind the house where we were were blown open in all directions and bits of bodies were lying everywhere.[57]

Having spent 4-6 August at St Jean, he was glad to leave on 7 August:

> As a rule, I am not very nervous, but I don't wish to spend another night at St Jean… Bringing the wounded down from the front line today. Conditions terrible. The ground between Wieltje and where the infantry are is simply a quagmire, and shell holes filled with water. Every place is in full view of the enemy who are on the ridge. There is neither the appearance of a road or path and it requires six men to every stretcher, two of them being constantly employed helping the others out of the holes, the mud in some cases is up to our waists. A couple of journeys to and from the Mine Shaft [at Wieltje] to the line and the strongest men are ready to collapse. All the regimental Aid Posts are in pill-boxes which have been wrested from the enemy and they are of great strength. Some of them have had as many as five direct hits from 5.9's and are nothing the worse. Unfortunately, all of them have a serious fault, their door being towards the German line. It is a job getting into them as they are all under enemy observation, and once in it is worse getting out as he puts a barrage round them when he sees anyone about.[58]

As Sergeant McKay had noted, all the British positions were under constant observation by the Germans from Gheluvelt Plateau, a situation that had existed since the failure to capture the Plateau on 31 July. It will be remembered that Field Marshal Haig had specifically ordered General Gough not to implement a further attack until the enemy artillery in this location had been dominated. Having been delayed by the poor weather, General Gough ordered an attack to seize this feature on 9 August. Once again however, the weather was to intervene. On the evening of 8 August, there was a thunderstorm and torrential downpour which necessitated the postponement of the attack by 24 hours.

---

57 IWM: Doc. 22065 Sergeant Robert McKay 109th Field Ambulance RAMC.
58 IWM: Doc. 22065 Sergeant Robert McKay 109th Field Ambulance RAMC.

88   A Bad Day I Fear

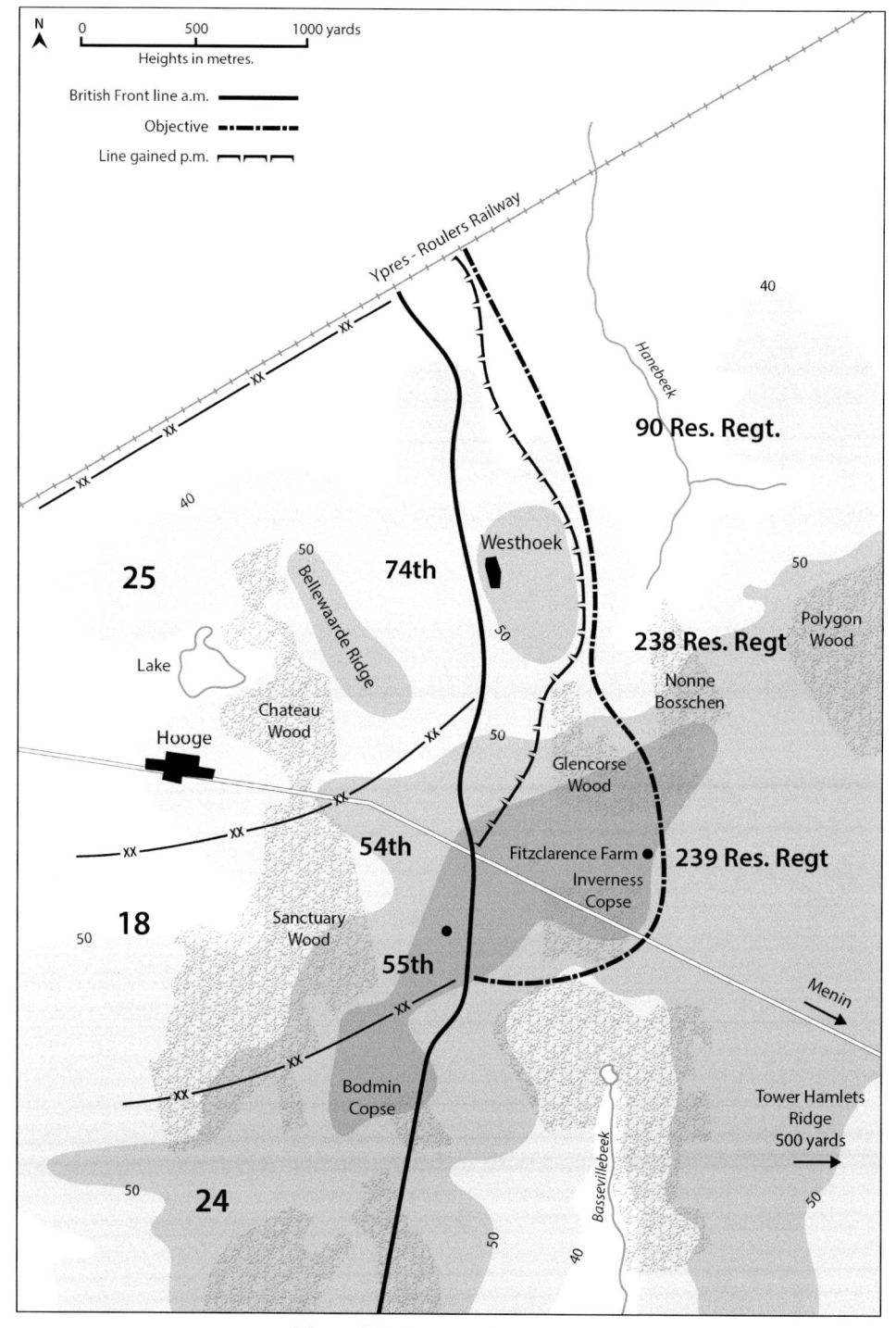

Map 7 Westhoek, 10 August 1917.

Ground Conditions and Weather 89

The attack on 10 August is of interest from an Irish perspective due to the involvement of 2nd Royal Irish Rifles, of 74th Brigade, 25th Division, who attacked on the opposite side of the Ypres-Roulers railway line from where their Irish colleagues of 16th Division were holding the line

The battalion war diary details the heroic efforts of 2nd Royal Irish Rifles on 10 and 11 August in attacking the strategically important village of Westhoek:

> The battalion led by Major Rose was formed up in its assembly position by 3.05 am. At Zero, the Rifles advance to the attack. Two strong concrete dugouts at Westhoek were quickly rushed by special parties detailed by C Company and the enemy holding them, taken completely unawares, offered little resistance. The waves rushed forward to Jabber Support, most of the enemy who were holding this line fled, making no attempt to fight. Rushing blindly back, they were caught in the British barrage and annihilated…At 10 am the enemy were seen coming over Anzac Ridge and down the forward slope towards Hannebeeke Valley presumably with the intention of massing for a counter attack. This concentration continued throughout the day and at 3.30 am a feeble effort was made by the Germans to move forward but broke down under machine gun and rifle fire with the help of Artillery support which came later. At 7.30 pm, a more determined effort was made under cover of a smoke barrage and a heavy bombardment of the front line and Westhoek Ridge. The SOS signal was sent up but the British Artillery did not respond. Shortly thereafter a British aeroplane appeared and dropped an SOS signal, whereby the artillery immediately opened a heavy bombardment that completely broke up the attack and almost wiped out the enemy whose remnants could be seen running in all directions. Many casualties were also inflicted by small arms fire.[59]

The attack by 2nd Royal Irish Rifles was the pinnacle of success for the attack of 10 August as strong German counterattacks drove most of the other attacking formations back, particularly in the area of Inverness Copse and Glencorse Wood, the strength of the German counterattacks were indicative of the importance of the Gheluvelt Plateau to them. General Gough ordered a further attack to take place at 11:55 p.m. that night however, this was postponed when it was realized that it would be impossible to get the attacking troops into position by that time. This proposed attack was then cancelled altogether.

The Royal Irish Rifles' success came however at great cost. When they took over the line on 5 August, the strength of the battalion was 15 officers and 479 other ranks – evidence of the fact that it was not only the Irish divisions who were being seriously depleted. Their casualties between 5-11 August numbered 351.[60] Following relief, battalion strength amounted to 10 officers and 148 men or not even the active service strength of a company. Despite these horrendous casualties, they managed to capture four officers and 150 men of *Reserve Infantrie Regiment Nr.90*, a 77 mm gun and five machine guns.

Two of those killed highlight the range of service within the battalion. Private Patrick Maguire 9697, from Clonroche, County Wexford, was 17 years and four months when he was

---

59   TNA: WO 95/2247/1: 2nd Royal Irish Rifles war diary.
60   The battalion war diary indicates that 34 men were killed, however, this was compiled shortly after the event, Commonwealth War Graves Commission data base records 66 officers and men fatalities.

killed, having been with the battalion less than a year. His mother Rose Anne later received a Dependant's Pension of five shillings per week. Records indicate that Patrick's service medals were returned.

Captain Samuel Valentine Morgan had been with the Royal Irish Rifles since enlistment as a Boy Bugler aged 15 in 1896. From Newtownards, County Down and the son of a musketry instructor in the Regiment, he had steadily risen through the ranks, obtaining a commission on 1 October 1914. He had been Adjutant at Portobello Barracks, Dublin during the Easter Rising when Captain Bowen-Colthurst ordered the execution of pacifist Francis Sheehy-Skeffington. No blame was attached to him for his actions on that day.[61] He joined the 2nd battalion in May 1917 and was in charge of D Company.[62] Neither have a known grave and both are commemorated on the Menin Gate.

The failure of the attack of 10 August to subjugate the German defences on Gheluvelt Plateau, was to have dire consequences for the Irish divisions. The attack in which they were scheduled to be involved was planned for 14 August however, this attack was based on the premise that the attack of 10 August would have achieved its objectives, which it clearly had not. The order from Field Marshal Haig of the afternoon of 31 July is worth reiterating here:

> I told Gough to continue to carry out the original plan: to consolidate ground gained, and to improve his position as he may deem necessary for facilitating the next advance: *the next advance will be made as soon as possible, but only after adequate bombardment and after dominating the hostile artillery.*[63]

Clearly, these conditions had not been met. General Gough should have realised this and paused the offensive until the Gheluvelt Plateau was seized, as any future advance was still going to be vulnerable to Artillery fire from this position. As noted earlier however, Gough was chosen for the role due to the fact that he was a 'thruster' and his impetuosity was always going to drive his decision making. It is at this point that Douglas Haig should have exerted control and ordered a halt to the offensive until the conditions on the battlefield were more favourable and a concerted, well planned and resourced effort could be made to seize Gheluvelt. Haig as we have seen however, was loathe to interfere in the operational planning of subordinates, and let Gough continue.

At least one person in command recognised the dangers. Lieutenant General Claud Jacob, commanding II Corps who had made the abortive attack of 10 August, asked for a delay in any further attacks until the objectives of 10 August had been achieved. On receipt of this request at Fifth Army, a postponement of 24 hours was agreed – not to achieve the objectives as requested by Lieutenant General Jacobs, but to effect reliefs.

The issue of the Gheluvelt Plateau aside, Gough should have been aware through his chain of command of the unacceptable losses being suffered in the front line and of the horrendous

---

61 James Taylor, *Guilty but Insane. J.C. Bowen-Colthurst: Villain or Victim?* (Dublin: Mercier Press, 2016) p.127.
62 TNA WO 339/21471: Captain Samuel Valentine Morgan service record. Captain Morgan's younger brother John, had been killed in action on 16 May 1915, serving with 2nd battalion Royal Inniskilling Fusiliers at Festubert, France.
63 Blake, *The Private Papers of Douglas Haig 1914-1919* p.250.

state of the battlefield. There is evidence however, that those in command were ignorant of the conditions on the battlefield. Brigadier General Baker-Carr of the Tank Corps attended GHQ at St Omer on 10 August to give a lecture on the use of tanks. As he had come from the front, at lunch he was questioned concerning the progress of the offensive and gave his views with candour. Before leaving, he was called to see Field Marshal Haig's Director of Operations, Brigadier General (later Major General) Sir John Davidson who expressed his disappointment in Baker-Carr's opinions. The following exchange then took place:

> B-C: 'You asked me how things were and I told you frankly.'
> D: 'But what you say is impossible.'
> B-C: 'It isn't. Nobody has any idea of the conditions up there.'
> D: 'But they can't be as bad as you make out.'
> B-C: 'Have you been there yourself?'
> D: 'No.'
> B-C: 'Has anyone in Operations Branch been there?'
> D: 'No.'
> B-C: 'Well then, if you don't believe me, it would be as well to send someone up to find out. I'm sorry I've upset you, but you asked me what I thought and I told you.'[64]

This exchange is indicatative of a fundamental disconnect between the troops on the ground and those planning the offensive and will be examined in more detail in a later chapter.

Whilst the abortive attack on Gheluvelt Plateau took place, the Irish divisions continued to hold their positions whilst the shellfire continued, and actually increased, as the attack was taking place. Major General Nugent described the extent of the shelling in a letter to his wife:

> The shelling is extremely heavy, far heavier than anything we have had to endure before and it is all over the front, not alone on the front line. Even at my Hdqrs shells are continually dropping around. However, that is a trifle compared to what Battns are getting up the line and our casualties are getting very heavy. It is a horrible wearing form of fighting having to sit still and be shelled night and day.[65]

Someone who was up the line and had had a very close shave was the indefatigable Father Willie Doyle who recorded:

> I had finished breakfast and had ventured a bit down the trench to find a spot to bury some bodies left lying there. I had reached a sheltered corner when I heard the scream of a shell coming towards me rapidly and judging by the sound, straight for the spot where I stood. Instinctively I crouched down and well I did so, for the shell whizzed past my head – I felt my hair blown about by the hot air, and burst in front of me with a deafening crash. It seemed to me as if a heavy wooden hammer had hit me on the top of the head and I reeled like a drunken man, my ears ringing with the explosion. For a minute I stood wondering

---

64   Christopher D'Arcy Baker-Carr, *From Chauffeur to Brigadier* (Driffield: Oakpast Ltd, 2014) p.199.
65   Perry (Ed) *Major General Oliver Nugent and the Ulster Division 1915-1918* p.165.

how many pieces of shrapnel had hit me, or how many arms and legs I had left and then dashed through the thick smoke to save myself from being buried alive by the shower of falling clay which was rapidly covering me. I hardly knew how I reached the dugout for I was speechless and so badly shaken that it was only by a tremendous effort I was able to protect myself from collapsing utterly as I had seen so many others do from shell-shock.[66]

Following the noticeable increase in German shelling on 10 August, the officers and men of 7/8th Royal Irish Fusiliers of 49th Brigade, 16th Division observed a definite decrease on 11 August, and a welcome increase in British aerial activity which provided some cover from German aircraft which had made a point of strafing the front line during low altitude passes. The battalion was relieved at 11:00 p.m. however, the relief was not completed until 3:30 a.m. as the guides got lost in the dark. In their tour of the front from 7-11 August, the battalion war diary recorded 108 casualties, dead, wounded and missing.[67]

As preparations continued towards the resumption of the offensive, 36th Division continued to rotate those holding the front. On the evening of 12 August, 107th Brigade relieved 108th and 109th brigades in order that these units, tasked with spearheading the attack, could get some much needed rest and time to prepare. On the morning of 13 August, the Division were handed a timely intelligence boost when a deserter from the German *Bavarian Infanterie Regiment Nr.19* gave himself up and was able to confirm that the 36th Division were opposite 5th Bavarian Division.

Part of Group Ypres of General Sixt von Armin's Fourth Army, 5th Bavarian Division at that stage of the war comprised three Regiments, the 7th, 19th and 21st Bavarian Infantry Regiments, each with a strength of around 4,000 men. Unlike the Irish divisions, they were well rested. They had fought in the latter stages of the Battle of Arras and from the beginning of July had been resting and training at the Brasschaet training area in the vicinity of Antwerp. It had taken over the front around St Julien on 10 August. By 14 August, 21st and 19th regiments held the front line, with 7th Regiment in reserve. The conditions that the Germans were facing on the front line were similar to those facing the Irish divisions as the Regimental History of 21st Regiment recorded:

> The position was formed of narrow trenches and shell holes with waterlogged soil and sticky walls, which didn't make for particularly pleasant dwelling. The battery positions and concrete dugouts served as accommodation. The main point of defence was the *Wilhelm-Stellung* on the undulating terrain about 1 km east of the Steenbeeke. The line was formed of trenches shielded by zones of barbed wire and equipped with concrete dugouts, which, having received the special attention of enemy artillery, was now potted with large shell holes. The second position, the *Flandern-Stellung* [Flanders Position] lay 2 to 3 km behind, running westward to the reasonably well-preserved town, Passchendaele, on similarly undulating terrain.[68]

---

66   Hope, *Worshipper and Worshipped. Across the Divide – an Irish Padre of the Great War. Fr. Willie Doyle, Chaplain to the Forces, 1915-1917* p.593.
67   The Commonwealth War Graves Commission database records 20 men as having been killed during this period.
68   Generalmajor Karl Reber, *Das K.B. 21. Infanterie Regiment* (Munchen: Berlag Mar Schid, 1929), p.209.

There was evidence also that despite having a better geographical position than the Irish troops, the German defenders were also suffering from the effects of the British Artillery as the regimental history continued:

> The companies had little peace due to the enemy artillery fire and was unable to change position throughout the following days. Lt. Lothar Weiß was wounded. The 12th Company received a direct hit on the 13th and the 11th Company on the 14th, killing 18 men, the 7th Company lost seven men and suffered eight wounded on the 15th.[69]

Of interest is the fact that within the Regimental Histories of both *Bavarian Infanterie Regiment Nr. 19* and *Nr.21*, the belief was that the main attack would fall on 15 August. When it did not, the men of *Infanterie Regiment Nr.19* continued their observation of British positions:

> On the 15th August the enemy shelled the battalions' positions according to plan. Rear areas also came under heavy artillery fire. Throughout the day, the usual activity was observed behind enemy lines, primarily pioneers.[70]

Next to this Division at this time and opposite 16th (Irish) Division was 3rd Reserve Division, comprising *Reserve Infantrie Regiments Nr. 2* and *Nr. 49* and *Fusilier Regiment Nr.34*. They had been based around Frezenberg since 4 August.[71]

Heavy rain which occurred again on 14 August caused a further postponement to that requested by Lieutenant General Jacobs, with the attack now timed for 4:45 a.m. 16 August.

For both Irish divisions 14 August was moving day. Orders were issued from Division to Brigade and down to the battalions, and those identified as spearheading the attack were moved into forward positions, relieving those who had held the front line, who then moved to reserve positions.

The 48th Infantry Brigade of 16th (Irish) Division were on the right of the divisional line with their boundary being the Ypres-Roulers railway. On the other side of the railway were 2nd Middlesex Regiment, 23rd Brigade, 8th Division. The 7th Royal Irish Rifles were on the right of the brigade front with the 9th Royal Dublin Fusiliers to their left. In close support were the 2nd Royal Dublin Fusiliers with the 8th Royal Dublin Fusiliers in reserve. The ordeal that the battalions had been through in the previous 10 days is typified by the 2nd Royal Dublin Fusiliers battalion strength on moving into position as the war diary recorded:

> Owing to casualties suffered on 7/8th, battalion went into line with three companies. One Coy 8th RDF under Captain Cowley attached, one section 48th TMB under 2nd Lt. Storrar attached. Assaulting strength 2 RDF – 14 Officers and 293 OR, Coy of 8 RDF 6 Officers 85 OR. Total – 20 Officers 368 OR.[72]

---

69 Reber, *Das K.B. 21*, p.209.
70 Hauptmann Otto Schaidler, *Das K.B. 7. Infanterie-Regiment Prinz Leopold* (Munchen: Selbstverlag Bayerischen Kriegsarchivs, 1922), p.374.
71 Intelligence Section of the General Staff, American Expeditionary Forces, *Histories of Two Hundred and Fifty-One Divisions of the German Army Which Participated in the War 1914-1918* <http://www.gwpda.org/1918p/USintel_germanarmy14-18.pdf.> (accessed 21 January 2023).
72 TNA WO 95/1974/2: 2nd Royal Dublin Fusiliers War Diary.

94 A Bad Day I Fear

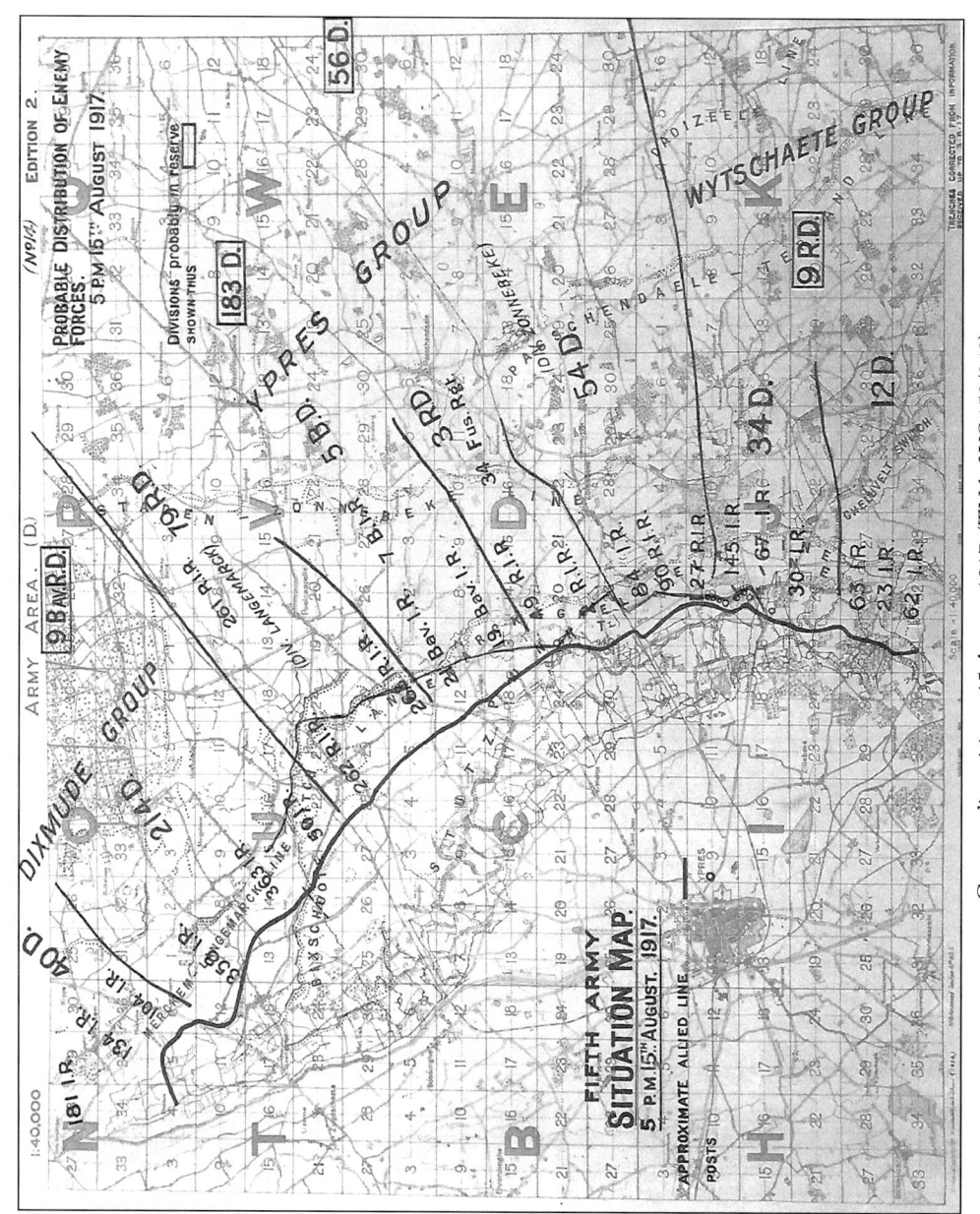

German dispositions, 15 August 1917. (TNA: WO158/249)

The relief was not without incident either, as the attached company from 8th Royal Dublin Fusiliers were strafed by enemy aeroplanes as it was being carried out. This composite battalion was just over a third of active service strength.

The 49th Infantry Brigade was to the left of 48th. They lined up for the attack with 7th Royal Inniskilling Fusiliers on the left and 8th Royal Inniskilling Fusiliers on the right. The 2nd Royal Irish Regiment was in reserve. This brigade was in a similar parlous state as regards battalion strengths. The 7th Inniskillings took over the line with 19 officers and 472 other ranks. As was the practice, 5 officers and 100 other ranks were left out of the battle, in order to provide a nucleus to reconstitute the battalion should they be decimated. This gave an attacking strength of 14 officers and 372 other ranks.

On the 36th (Ulster) Division front, 108th Infantry Brigade were on the right, bordering with 49th Infantry Brigade. Their attacking battalions were 13th Royal Irish Rifles on the left and 9th Royal Irish Fusiliers on the right, next to 7th Inniskillings.[73] Behind these two battalions and in support were the 12th Royal Irish Rifles, with 11th Royal Irish Rifles in reserve. The Brigade Headquarters moved to the dugouts at Wieltje and 13th Royal Irish Rifles established their HQ at Bank Farm with 9th Royal Irish Fusiliers HQ at Plum Farm.

To the left of 108th was 109th Infantry Brigade. The attacking battalions on this frontage were to be 14th Royal Irish Rifles, with their HQ at Spree Farm, and on their left, and on the left of the divisional front were 11th Royal Inniskilling Fusiliers. In immediate support were 9th Royal Inniskilling Fusiliers with 10th Royal Inniskilling Fusiliers in reserve. The long trek to the front line was begun by the 14th Rifles at 6:15 p.m. in pouring rain and no sooner had the rear of the column reached Wieltje, when they were targeted by enemy artillery. Fortunately, there were no fatalities, but the relief was not completed until 11:00 p.m. The battalion HQ at Spree Farm came in for special attention by German Artillery that night and all through 15 August. Despite numerous direct hits, the German engineering proved up to the task and the structure remained intact.

To the left of the 11th Inniskillings were 1/8th Warwickshire Regiment of 143rd Infantry Brigade, 48th (South Midland) Division. This battalion were nearly opposite the village of St Julien and were also in the first wave of the advance. Second Lieutenant Edwin Campion Vaughan of the Warwickshires was aged 19 and recalled his trepidation when the orders were given:

> On 16th we will be in support of the Irish Rifles at St Julien. The imminence of the attack made me very frightened and I trembled so much that I could not take part in the discussion at first. But after poring over the map for a bit and passing on all information to my platoon, I grew calmer.[74]

The anxiety returned however, when he went to bed:

> I could not sleep, but lay awake thinking and wondering about the attack, fancying myself blown to bits, or lying out on the wire with a terrible wound. It was not until dawn that I dozed off.[75]

---

73 D and B companies of 7th Royal Inniskilling Fusiliers lined up in 9th Royal Irish Fusiliers positions due to the topography of the area.
74 Vaughan, *Some Desperate Glory*, p.191.
75 Vaughan, *Some Desperate Glory*, p.193.

5th Bavarian Division

7th Bavarian Infantry Regiment   21st Bavarian Infantry Regiment   19th Bavarian Infantry Regiment

36th (Ulster) Division

109th Inf Bde	108th Inf Bde		
11th InnisFus	14th RIRifles	13th RIRifles	9th RIFus
1 Coy 9th InnisFus	2 Platoons 12th RIRifles		
(Moppers Up)	(Moppers Up)		
9th InnisFus	12th RIRifles		
10th InnisFus	11th Royal Irish Rifles		

107th Inf Bde
8th RIRifles
9th RIRifles
10th RIRifles
15th RIRifles

16th (Irish) Division

49th Inf Bde		48th Inf Bde	
7th InnisFus	8th InnisFus	9th RDubFus	7th RIRifles
7/8th RIFus		2nd RDubFus	
2nd RIRegt		8th RDubFus	

47th Inf Bde
7th Leinsters
1st RMunFus
6th RIRegt
6th Connaughts

Attacking battalion dispositions schematic.

Whilst the Infantry battalions were moving into position, those in support were also putting the final touches to their preparations. The Trench Mortar Batteries of 36th Division were busy carrying out wire-cutting barrages, with X battery launching 88 rounds of 6 inch mortars at barbed wire entanglements around Pond Farm. The Pioneers of 16th Royal Irish Rifles were toiling under enemy shellfire to construct duckboard tracks through the swamp that was the approaches to the front line, to enable mule trains to bring up much needed supplies. The officers and men of the Royal Engineers were equally as busy however, 122nd Field Company RE questioned some of the orders they had been given:

> Received orders that crossings of the Steenbeek had to be reconnoitred and if any necessary, extra bridges provided for reserves to cross by during attack. Infantry holding line nearby could give us definite information about these crossings. 2 Officers and a party went up and put in a new bridge. They were heavily shelled and both these officers were wounded. One man KIA. It seems very curious that with a well known obstacle such as Steenbeek running behind our line, which all supports must cross, that this had never been reconnoitred by infantry holding line in front of it and that it should be necessary to send up RE officers at the last moment to reconnoitre this.[76]

The 150th Field Company Royal Engineers were engaged in similar work to the Pioneers, constructing tracks to bring up supplies, all the while under shellfire. On 14 August, two men from the company were killed. Thirty-six years old John Frazer Lemon was a single man who lived with his widowed mother at Cheviot Avenue, East Belfast. He is buried at Brandhoek New Military Cemetery.[77] Also killed on that date was 28 years old Second Lieutenant James Daintith, a married man from Warrington, Cheshire. He had been appointed Second Lieutenant on a Temporary Commission on 16 May 1917 and had only joined 150th Field Company on 1 August 1917. Initially buried close to where he fell, his remains were exhumed in July 1919 and reburied at White House cemetery, St Jean-les-Ypres.[78]

The Field Ambulances of the Royal Army Medical Corps of both divisions were still dealing with sick and wounded however, all lightly wounded cases were moved out as preparations were made for the anticipated influx of casualties. It is of interest to note that as the date of the attack approached due to the conditions, the medics of both divisions were dealing with roughly equal numbers of cases of sick and wounded. Additional numbers of men seconded from the Pioneers and Divisional Salvage Company were drafted in to assist as Stretcher Bearers when the attack commenced. There was certainly a need for them as Sergeant McKay of 109th Field Ambulance graphically recalled:

> One morning we volunteered to go up at 4.00 am and take 48 men along to bring six seriously wounded fom a pillbox known as Scottish Post. The Germans had a barrage on round

---

76 TNA WO 95/2497/2: 122nd Field Company RE War Diary. A search of the Commonwealth War Graves Commission data base failed to identify fatalities for this unit.
77 He is also commemorated on the Queens Island Unionist Club Memorial at St Anne's Cathedral, Belfast.
78 The company war diary records his death as occurring on 14 August, whilst the CWGC records his date of death as 13 August.

the house when we got up, but we got in through it and got the wounded out, seven cases altogether. As soon as we got out through the barrage, the gunners followed us with shells the whole way down. We were well scattered out, each stretcher party with its patient separated as far as possible from the next one. However, we were all obliged to follow one path along duckboards and alongside at one point, two tanks were stuck in a hole. I saw the stretcher party in front of mine all blown down by a bursting shell; my five men and I all lay down in over twelve inches of mud. None of the party in front appeared to be much injured as one after the other, they picked themselves up, lifted their patient and ran for it as quickly as possible. My party was next on the list to receive attention. From where we were lying we could hear the gun firing at us, then came the drone of the shell which immediately developed into a wild screech (resembling an express train flying through a station at full speed) all ending up in a deafening explosion … The German gun had fired ten or twelve 5.9's at us when he placed one just to the left of our stretcher. Mud was flying everywhere when we heard the gun go again and I could have sworn the next shell was coming down fair on my back. Luckily it missed the stretcher and only covered us with more mud … Had the ground been hard or had the shelling been done with shrapnel, I believe not a single man would have escaped that morning. As conditions were, the shells only buried themselves in the soft mud before they burst. As things were only two of the party were slightly wounded, but all the remainder were badly shaken.[79]

The eve of the battle, 15 August, was a day of making final preparations and of waiting. Due to the conditions, some of the battalions did not reach their assembly positions until close to zero hour, the 7th Royal Irish Rifles not being in position until 2:30 a.m. on 16 August – two hours and 15 minutes before the attack was due to commence. There appears to have been some confusion in the distribution of orders as Lieutenant Arthur Glanville, 2nd Royal Dublin Fusiliers recorded:

Day of misery for all and anxiety for officers who do not know what time attack starts until late at night. Impossible to get into position in dark under hellish shelling.[80]

The portents were not good. Superiority over the German Artillery had not been established, the ground conditions meant that the infantry attack keeping up with the creeping barrage was always a risky strategy, for the same reason, tanks could not be used to their full potential and the attacking troops, at least on the XIX Corps front, were exhausted and understrength.

Always soaked through, with little shelter, under persistent German shellfire, and seriously understrength, the officers and men of the Irish divisions passed the final hours before the attack as best they could. Even the locals had a feeling of foreboding as the Parish Priest, Achiel van Walleghem recorded in his diary:

In the night there are constant flashes of light, hundreds per minute which suggests to us that there is a terrible amount of shelling going on, even if we hear little noise with the wind in the wrong direction. Rain and thunder almost all day.[81]

79 IWM Doc. 22065 Sergeant Robert McKay 109th Field Ambulance RAMC.
80 IWM: Doc 21037 Arthur Evanson Glanville Papers.
81 Dendooven (ed.) *1917,*. p.201.

Stretcher bearers struggle through the mud. (Canadian War Museum EO-2202)

6

Thursday, 16 August 1917 16th (Irish) Division

As the most important chapters, particularly from an Irish perspective, I had to put some thought into how to proceed in telling the story of the Irish divisions on 16 August 1917. My primary concern remains, 'what would the reader want?' and to that end I have decided to outline the orders from Corps level and then tell of the experiences of each battalion working from right to left on the XIX Corps frontage. The story of each battalion will be based on war diaries, published works and, where they still exist, personal accounts. Maps, photographs and details of some men who fell, or performed exceptional acts will be included as will be the accounts of the German defenders. Hopefully, this will construct a picture of the valiant efforts of Irishmen in the face of extraordinary circumstances on 16 August 1917.

A point worthy of note at the outset was that both the British and the Germans were operating on summer time, meaning that German times are one hour ahead of those of the British. Where German names exist for specific features such as fortified structures and pillboxes, these appear after the British spelling in brackets.

The second major attempt by Fifth Army to break the German stranglehold around Ypres commenced at 4:45 a.m. on Thursday 16 August. At the centre of Fifth Army front was XIX Corps, the two attack formations 36th (Ulster) Divison on the left and 16th (Irish) Division on the right. In reserve were the 15th (Scottish) Division and the 61st (2nd South Midland) Division. A second line Territorial Division, the 61st had been in Fifth Army reserve and were attached to XIX Corps on 7 August as replacement for 55th (West Lancashire) Division which had suffered heavily during the opening phase of the offensive.

To the right of 16th Division on the other side of the Ypres–Roulers railway were 8th Division who were back attacking the same positions they had attacked in the abortive attack of 31 July. In that attack they had suffered over 3,000 casualties and had less than two weeks to recover and reorganise. To the left of 36th Division from the village of St Julien were 48th (South Midland) Division, another Territorial Division.

XIX Corps was under the command of Lieutenant General Herbert Henry Watts, an officer who had done well out of the war, having been a Colonel in 1914. The Operations Order for the attack by XIX Corps was issued by his staff on 8 August 1917. For reference, the relevant operational order is reproduced as Appendix II. The attack was to be carried out in two phases, with the ultimate objective being the dotted line depicted on the map on page 101 and known

Map 8 16th (Irish) Division area of operations.

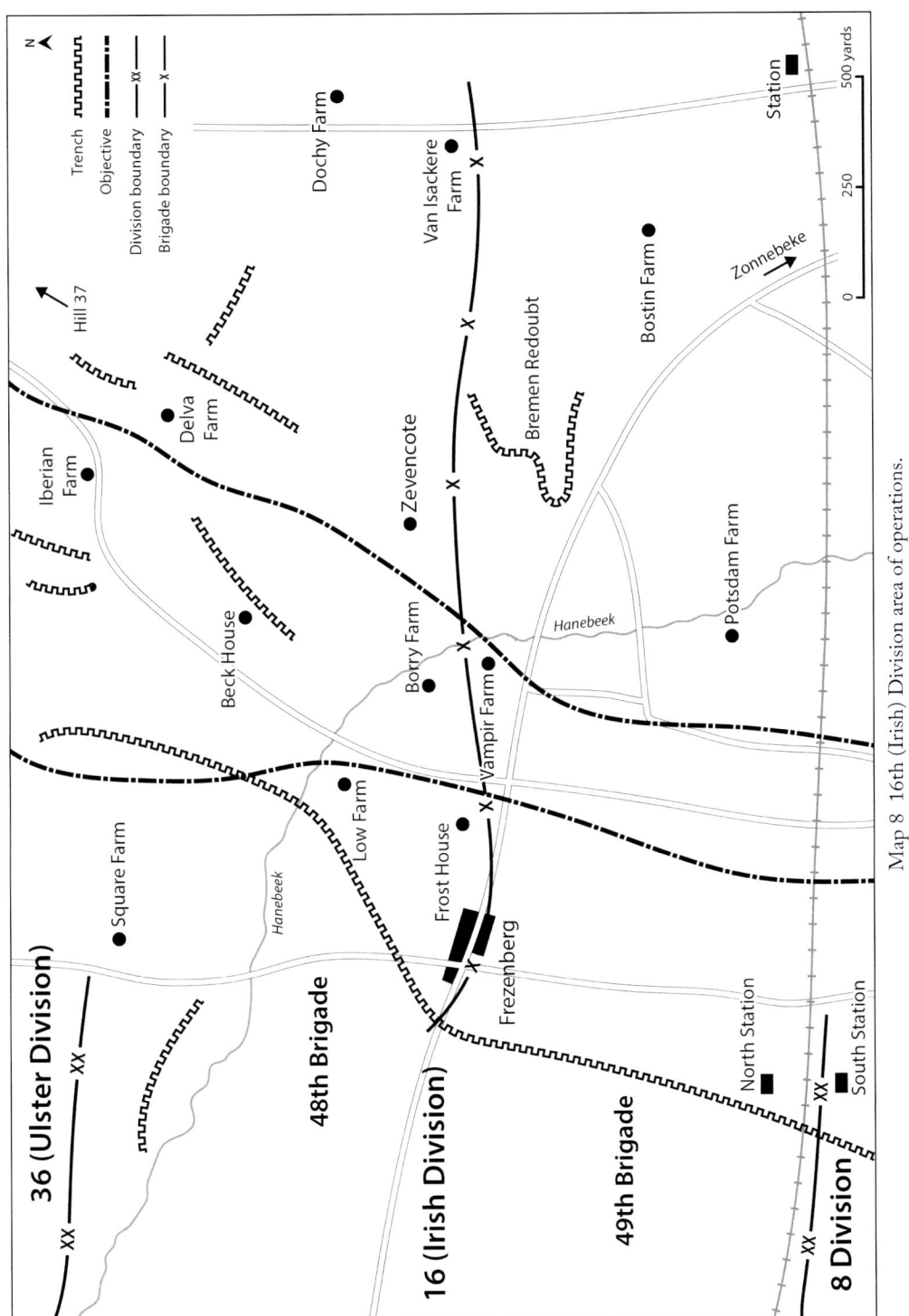

as the red line. This objective was to be reached following an advance and a pause for 20 minutes at the green line.[1]

For both divisions, reaching the red dotted line would have meant an advance of 2,500 yards or just less than a mile and a half to what was known as the Gheluvelt–Langemarck line. On a battlefield which was firm under foot and against resolute defenders, this would have been a considerable undertaking. With the ground conditions and the German defensive system, it was an unachievable target. Worse news was to follow however. Paragraph 7 of the operation order states:

> 3rd Brigade Tank Corps will allot tanks to support the attack as follows:
> 1 Section 'C' Battn. to 16th Division.
> 1 Section 'F' Battn. to 36th Division.[2]
> These tanks cannot be guaranteed owing to the uncertain weather conditions, but should be available if there is no more rain before the operation.[3]

Given that the Tank Corps had been warning that the conditions were totally unsuitable for tanks since before the opening of the offensive, this paragraph was wildly optimistic. As it transpired, the opinions of the Tank Corps Officers should have been given more credence. Brigadier General Baker-Carr of the Tank Corps recalled:

> On the 16th of August, I made a desperate effort to send a dozen or more tanks to assist in an attack near St Julien, but in spite of the most determined and gallant efforts of the crews, not a single tank managed even to reach our own front line.[4]

An important asset in neutralising defensive strongpoints was therefore, not available to the attacking battalions.

The 48th Infantry Brigade Operational Order was issued on 14 August and reiterated much of what is contained in the Corps Operations Order, focusing on specific deployments relevant to that Brigade. The attacking battalions were confirmed as 7th Royal Irish Rifles on the right and 9th Royal Dublin Fusiliers on the left. The 2nd Royal Dublin Fusiliers were in support, bolstered by a company from 8th Royal Dublin Fusiliers, the remainder of whom were in reserve.

The success of the Irish divisions depended greatly on II Corps' assault on the southern side of the railway line. If this attack was not successful, the Germans would be able to target the Irish with enfilade fire. On the other side of the railway line from 7th Royal Irish Rifles, the 2nd Middlesex Regiment and 2nd West Yorkshire Regiment of 23rd Infantry Brigade were tasked with the advance.

As previously mentioned, 7th Royal Irish Rifles did not reach their assembly positions until 2:30 a.m. 16 August, having been shelled heavily on the way forward and sustaining several

---

1 The initial oepration order referred to the objectives as the Blue line and ultimately the Green line, however, these were changed for an unknown reason in an amendment to the operations order on 9 August.
2 Each section numbered 12 MK IV tanks.
3 TNA WO 95/969/2: Appendix 152 XIX Corps Operation Order No. 79.
4 Baker-Carr, *From Chauffeur to Brigadier*, p.202.

casualties in the vicinity of the Menin Gate. Once in position, they were again shelled heavily around 4:00 a.m. 45 minutes before Zero hour. The objective for the battalion was the position where the Hanebeek was bridged by the Ypres-Roulers railway line. This entailed an advance with the railway embankment on their right. Whilst this embankment provided some cover from German enfilade fire from the II Corps area, the embankment itself was home to several German machine gun posts and there was one major reinforced defensive structure known as 'Potsdam Farm' just before the objective. Potsdam Farm was a group of pillboxes built into, and straddling the Ypres-Roulers railway which covered the approach to Zonnebeke and the Passchendaele Ridge. They were named Potsdam after a farm between the railway and the Ypres-Zonnebeke road. The Germans named the group *Lindenhof* after the same farm.[5] To the left of Potsdam as the 7th Rifles advanced were other reinforced structures known as Mitchell's Farm (*Kaffeegut*) Vampir (*Strohgut*) Borry Farm (*Quergut*) and Beck House (*Kaminhof*). All the named features were garrisoned by multiple machine guns.

As if the horrendous ground conditions were not enough to contend with, the attacking troops were laden with equipment to enable them to support themselves as the advance unfolded. In addition to his rifle and bayonet, each soldier carried the following:

> 120 rounds small arms ammunition. In his pack, towel and soap, oil tin, holdall, one iron ration and one day's preserved ration. Two water bottles, one with cold tea, ground sheet, one rifle grenade, two flares, three sandbags, wire cutters, entrenching tool and box respirator. Bombers carried 8 grenades instead of the small arms ammunition.[6]

The advance commenced at 4:45 a.m. from what was known as the Black Line, coinciding with a massive artillery bombardment on German positions. The 7th Royal Irish Rifles attacked with three companies in line and one in support. Immediately the British barrage commenced, the Germans retaliated with a heavy artillery bombardment on the Black Line and machine-guns opened up on the advancing troops from Potsdam, Borry Farm and from machine gun posts on the embankment.

The 7th Royal Irish Rifles struggled to keep up with the creeping barrage as they fought their way towards the Green Line and eventually it moved ahead of them, the troops enduring the galling spectacle of the enemy machine guns continuing to fire from the strongpoints as the barrage passed over them.

Of the three companies in the advance, the centre and left companies were held up by sustained machine gun fire with all of their officers being hit. The company on the right were able to advance and cleared some machine gun posts along the embankment, sending back 30 prisoners. The battalion war diarist continued:

> This company then moved along the Railway and across the Hannebeeke. Some of them were seen to follow the barrage to the Red Dotted line, a few of the centre and support

---

5   Peter Oldham, *Pill Boxes on the Western Front: A Guide to the Design, Construction and Use of Concrete Pill Boxes 1914–1918* (Barnsley: Pen & Sword Military, 2011), p.135.
6   Thurlow. *The Pill-Boxes of Flanders* p.20.

104 A Bad Day I Fear

Companies appeared to have followed them through. With the exception of these few the whole line came to a standstill.[7]

The Green Line was reached at 5:16 a.m. Just short of Potsdam Farm and opposite Mitchell's Farm, a small party under the command of Lieutenant William Kingston, a 26 years old single man from Durrus, County Cork, came across another fortified bunker. Lieutenant Kingston led his men in trying to work his way around the bunker from the embankment side and was shot dead in the act of firing his revolver at the machine gunner through the firing aperture. Commissioned in May 1915, William Kingston had been living in Belfast at the outbreak of war and had served with the Young Citizen Volunteers before moving to Dublin. He was promoted Lieutenant in September 1916.[8] His commanding officer, Lieutenant Colonel Francis DSO, later wrote:

> Although wounded, Lt. Kingston pressed on to where an enemy machine-gun was in action and attacked the enemy with bombs and his revolver. While doing so the gun was turned on him and he was killed instantly. His gallant attempt to save his men was one of the finest examples of self-sacrificing heroism I have ever known.[9]

Shortly after Lieutenant Kingston was killed, the remnants of his platoon were decimated by shellfire. The 2nd Royal Dublin Fusiliers sent forward A Company under the command of Captain Black MC and along with what remained of the right company of 7th Royal Irish Rifles, they managed to consolidate a position close to the railway embankment short of Potsdam.

The 2nd Middlesex Regiment, on the other side of the railway line were advancing in conjunction with 7th Royal Irish Rifles. At 5:45 a.m. they reported that no British troops could be seen in the vicinity of Potsdam. At 6:32

Lieutenant William Kingston. (Great War Ulster Newspaper Archive)

---

7 TNA WO 95/1975/2: 7th Royal Irish Rifles War Diary.
8 TNA WO 339/3815: Lieutenant William Kingston service record. Kingston had been mentioned in despatches.
9 *The Northern Whig*, 6 September 1917.

a.m. it was reported that the left company [closest to the railway embankment] had been held up and no further advance was possible.[10]

As was the norm at that time, once attacking troops went forward, the commanding officer had great difficulty receiving accurate information on which to base further decisions. Lieutenant Colonel Francis of 7th Royal Irish Rifles sent out four orderlies and an officer to ascertain when the Green line had been reached. Nothing was ever heard from them again. The officer was 19 years old Second Lieutenant Adam Cyril Darley Hill from Deramore Drive off the Malone Road, Belfast. Posted as 'Missing' his death was presumed by the War Office and his father informed by letter in September 1918.[11] He is however, believed to be buried at Tyne Cot Cemetery, Special Memorial 79. His father arranged for the inscription, 'Missing' to be placed on the headstone.

Unbelievably, a small party of men had managed to circumvent Potsdam by moving between it and the embankment. It is believed that they may have reached the objective of the red dotted line however, they came under sustained machine gun fire from pill-boxes between Vampir and Potsdam Farm and from beyond that near Mitchell's Farm, and nothing more was heard from them.

Captain Cowley of the attached company from 8th Battalion Royal Dublin Fusiliers met with Lieutenant Colonel Francis at his Headquarters and received orders to go forward to the Green Line, clarify what the situation was, and report back. The 8th battalion Royal Dublin Fusiliers war diary records the disposition of this company:

> Captain Cowley took in B&D Coys (less 7 Platoon still attached to the Bde Carrying Company) with 2Lts Peasey, Warren, Marlow, Green, Mallon and Father Doyle as a composite Company.[12]

Captain Cowley split his resources, sending two officers, Second Lieutenant's Green and Marlow and 40 men to support the 7th Royal Irish Rifles, whilst he took the remainder to support 9th Royal Dublin Fusiliers.

The party supporting 7th Royal Irish Rifles reached just short of Potsdam where the two officers were wounded. On hearing this, Father Doyle went forward to offer assistance. As he was doing so, all three were killed by shellfire.

Father Willie Doyle SJ MC was a revered figure amongst Irish troops, renowned for ignoring danger to carry spiritual assistance to those in need. Respect for him transcended religion and political views and he was as respected by the men of the Ulster Division as he was by the men of his own Division. A soldier from the Ulster Division wrote of Father Doyle after the battle:

> Father Doyle was a good deal among us. We couldn't possibly agree with his religious opinions, but we simply worshipped him for other things. He didn't know the meaning of fear, and he didn't know what bigotry was. He was as ready to risk his life to take a drop of water to a wounded Ulsterman as to assist men of his own faith and regiment. If he risked his life looking after Ulster Protestant soldiers once, he did it a hundred times in his last few days.

10 TNA WO 95/1713/1: 2nd Middlesex Regiment War Diary.
11 TNA WO 339/61839: Second Lieutenant Adam Cyril Darley Hill service record.
12 TNA WO 95/1974/3: 8th Royal Dublin Fusiliers War Diary.

The Ulstermen felt his loss more keenly than anybody and none were readier to show their marks of respect to the dead hero priest than were our Ulster Presbyterians. Father Doyle was a true Christian in every sense of the word, and a credit to any religious faith.[13]

One of the men from his own battalion, Private Patrick Marren 18788, from Sligo forwarded a poem in Father Doyle's memory to his local newspaper an excerpt of which follows:

He is gone from amongst us, may his soul rest above,
The pride of our regiment whom every man loved,
His life's work is o'er he has finished his toil,
So may God rest the soul of our brave Father Doyle[14]

None of the three killed have a known grave and all are commemorated on the Tyne Cot Memorial. All evidence indicates that Father Doyle and Second Lieutenants Marlow and Green met their deaths on 16 August however, many records, including those of the Commonwealth War Graves Commission indicate that their deaths occurred on 17 August. This is likely due to reports of deaths not being consolidated until the action was over.[15]

Second Lieutenant Charles Dwyer Marlow was 22 years old and from Oldcastle, County Meath, where both of his parents were Schoolteachers. He had enlisted in the 28th London Regiment (Artist's Rifles) in April 1915 and had served in France from August 1915. He was commissioned in September 1916, being posted to 8th Royal Dublin Fusiliers, and had been slightly wounded on 7 August 1917, remaining on duty. He is also commemorated in St Bride's Church of Ireland, Oldcastle.[16]

Second Lieutenant Arthur Vivian Green was 21 years old and from Holland Park, Knock, Belfast. Educated at the Royal Belfast Academical Institution in the city, he was employed as an Exchange Clerk with the Bank of Ireland, Londonderry. He was appointed to the Inns of Court Officer Training Corps in January 1916 and was commissioned as Second Lieutenant in the Royal Dublin Fusiliers in December 1916.[17] His elder brother, Second Lieutenant Percy Harold Green, 9th Royal Inniskilling Fusiliers, was killed in action during the German Spring Offensive, March 1918.

At 8:45 a.m. the Forward Artillery Observer (FOO) of 16th Division Artillery reported that an enemy counterattack was developing. This was the first documented report and was corroborated by a report from 2nd Middlesex Regiment at 9:50 a.m. In accordance with the German Scheme F, the counterattack was carried out by the reserve battalions of *Bavarian Infantrie Regiment Nr.21* supported by the *Eingreif* Division, 12th Reserve Division, which required more time to move forward from its base near Passchendaele. At 10:15 a.m. General Watts ordered

---

13   Tom Johnstone, *Orange Green and Khaki. The Story of the Irish Regiments in the Great War 1914-1918* (Dublin: Gill & McMillan, 1992), pp. 290-1
14   Full text of the poem was published in *The Sligo Champion*, 2 September 1917.
15   For a comprehensive account of Father Doyle's life and death, see the excellent Carol Hope, *Worshipper and Worshipped. Across the Divide: An Irish Padre of the Great War. Fr. Willie Doyle, Chaplain to the Forces, 1915-1917* (Brighton: Reveille Press, 2013).
16   TNA WO 339/72149: Second Lieutenant Charles Dwyer Marlow service record.
17   TNA WO 339/67470: Second Lieutenant Arthur Vivian Green service record.

the commanders of 16th and 36th divisions to commence a barrage in front of the Black Line and the commander Royal Artillery to commence a barrage of German strongpoints across the front and including Potsdam, Vampir and Borry Farm.[18] Whilst this barrage was intended to discourage the German counterattack, it also spelt the death knell for those Irish troops in the open between the Black Line and the line of German bunkers.

A small party of 7th Royal Irish Rifles and 2nd Royal Dublin Fusiliers maintained a position on the railway line until late afternoon and actually made contact with troops from 2nd Middlesex Regiment before being forced to withdraw to the Black Line under cover of darkness.

The Brigade after action report indicates that 7th Battalion Royal Irish Rifles went into the battle with a strength of 21 officers and 423 other ranks and sustained casualties of 17 officers and 269 other ranks, a casualty rate of 64 per cent.[19] Of those casualties, the Commonwealth War Graves Commission database records 85 fatalities.

Amongst the 85 killed that day was Private Nathaniel Dunlop aged 20 from Cullybackey, County Antrim. A signaller with the battalion, Nathaniel was a carpenter prior to enlisting and was an active member of the United Free Church, Cullybackey, where his name appears on the Roll of Honour. His commanding officer wrote to the family stating:

> He was held in the highest esteem by the officers, NCOs and men of his company.[20]

Nathaniel's Mother received a Dependant's Pension of five shillings a week for the loss of her son.

Another who fell that day was Corporal Michael Joseph Flood aged 18 from Slane, County Meath. He had been with the battalion on the Western Front since December 1915 when he was aged 16. In his Will, he left all his possessions to his married sister, Josephine.

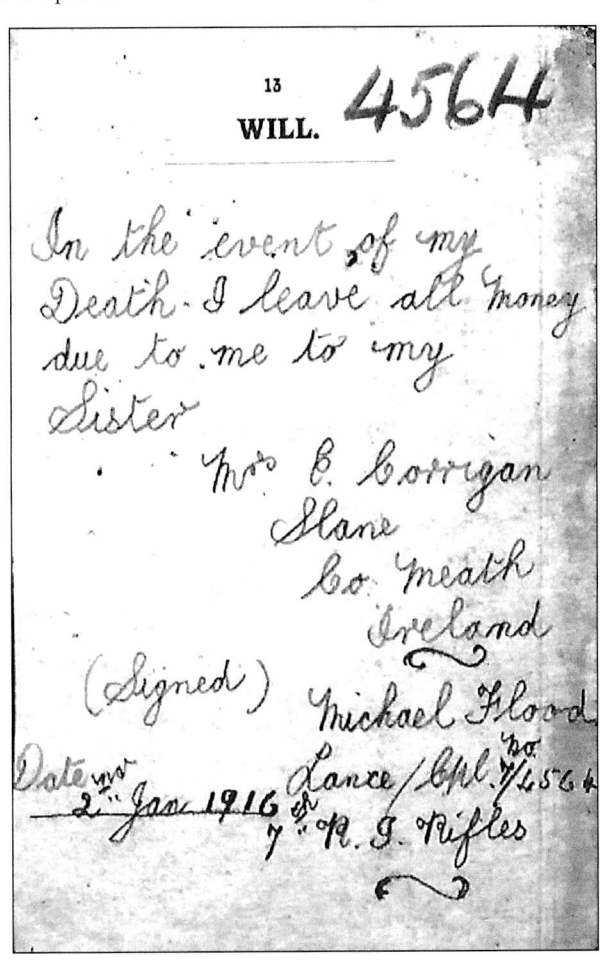

Private Michael Flood. (Will. National Archives Ireland)

18 TNA WO 95/960/1: XIX Corps War Diary.
19 TNA WO 95/1974/3: 8th Royal Dublin Fusiliers War Diary.
20 *The Ballymena Observer*, 7 September 1917.

Neither man has a known grave and both are commemorated on the Tyne Cot Memorial to the Missing.

Attacking to the left of 7th Royal Irish Rifles were 9th Royal Dublin Fusiliers. They left the assembly positions simultaneously with 7th Royal Irish Rifles, having been heavily shelled by the Germans just prior to Zero hour, and had gone only a few yards when they came under sustained machine-gun fire from Vampir and from the Bremen Redoubt, a fortified trench system behind Vampir. Second Lieutenant Robert Francis Hickey attached to B company sent back a message by runner timed at 5:40 a.m. which unfortunately due to the chaos existing, was only received at 7:30 a.m. The message outlined that the attackers were held up around 100 yards short of the strongpoint and that most of the party were dead or wounded. On receipt of this message, the commanding officer sent out Second Lieutenant Richard Arthur Walcott Martin with two men and the original runner to ascertain the situation. The two soldiers were killed soon after leaving the HQ however, it is believed that Second Lieutenant Martin reached the attacking party and on his return, was shot dead by a sniper within 20 yards of the HQ. Whatever message he carried was verbal as none were recovered from his body.

Twenty-seven years old Second Lieutenant Martin was from Monkstown, County Dublin, and was employed as a cable clerk prior to obtaining his commission in 1916. He is commemorated on the Tyne Cot Memorial to the Missing as is Second Lieutenant Hickey. It is believed that Second Lieutenant Hickey had succumbed to his wounds late on 16 August.

As his son was posted as 'wounded and missing' his father Robert Hickey, like many others tried to do what he could to find out further information. This included a newspaper appeal which was replied to by an Edward Harkin in January 1919. This was 22492 Private Edward Harkin from Maryborough, Queen's County, who had been discharged as no longer fit for military service in October 1918. He stated:

> I wish to tell you that on the morning of August 15th [sic] 1917, we went over the top and Mr Hickey got hit with a sniper's bullet in the back which came out his breast, he was running from behind a tree to a shell hole when he got hit, so I crept out and pulled him in, dressed his wound and did all I could for him. The firing was so bad that I lay there with him until night, so I went back to see if I could get stretcher bearers, but they were all killed or wounded. The Germans put up a heavy barrage then and I did not get out until the following evening, there were only 25 left of the battalion and no-one could get up to any of the wounded as the Germans were over where we were stopped in the morning, so I think any one was wounded never got a chance. Mr Hickey was very weak when I left him. I don't think he would have lasted much longer as he drank all the water we had between us, and had no chance of getting more. I cannot give you any more information as to what befell him afterwards.[21]

Following the death of Second Lieutenant Martin, it was at this stage that Captain Cowley and his party of forty-five moved forward to ascertain the situation. He later described what occurred:

---

21 TNA WO 339/69891: Second Lieutenant Robert Francis Hickey service record.

> Upon reaching a point about 200 yards in front of BLACK LINE, we came under heavy rifle and machine-gun fire apparently from three points, (a) BORRY FARM, (b) Line VAMPIR FARM – POTSDAM, (c) High ground to south of railway. This caused us many casualties including an officer. We took cover in shell holes and advanced by rushes. On gaining ground I saw in front and opposite VAMPIR FARM what appeared to be a firing line in shell holes and gullies. By glasses, I could see the 9th and 2nd battalion's 'flashes' on the shoulders of some. The next rush brought us nearer and I could see that they were nearly all dead or wounded being particulary thick along D.25.b [a point midway between the Black line and Vampir]. The ground near us was dotted with numerous dead. The frontal and enfilade fire against us had by this time caused some 22 casualties out of the 45 in the B half of the composite company … We joined up to two officers and 10 men of C Coy 2nd RDF whom we found in shell holes.[22]

The party of the 2nd Royal Dublin Fusiliers were commanded by Captain Arthur Evanson Glanville. In a written account he recalls meeting with Captain Cowley's party:

> Aug 16, attack at dawn. Given away by Sgt Phillips.[23] Boche puts up terrible barrage before zero as we are moving into position. Burrowes hit in eye.[24] I was in rear of Coy and finding Coy halted went up to front to see what was happening. Burrowes gone, Coy lost. However, I take command and with help of Wolfe who was acquainted with orders, I move Company into position.[25] A & B Coys in front wave completely wiped out. I got order from Bn. to reinforce in full daylight over shellholes full of water, under hellish fire, and to collect as many of Coy as possible and give the signal to advance but one after the other is shot down. I was nearly buried by shellfire but remained untouched. We reach front wave – mostly dead about 50 yds from Boche front line of pill boxes. There is one other officer – Major [sic] of the 8/9 RDFus. Completely exhausted, I place myself and about 10 men who have survived in his hands. We remain all day and night and next day in shell holes. It is death to move – to raise oneself an inch out of the mud. We dare not expect reinforcements so Wolfe goes back to see if he can get any orders for us. Fortunately he is able to send a runner to us with word to retire at night and better still with a bottle of rum. Strengthened by the rum, we straggle back to the old line. The attack has failed everywhere. We march or rather drag ourselves back to Ypres heedless of shellfire – wishing we were dead but thankful to be alive all the same. At Ypres we get a lorry back to our bivouacs a remnant of 30% – too fed up at the pals we have lost for nothing to appreciate our good fortune at being alive. I was awarded Divisional Parchment Certificate for work in the Ypres sector in August 1917. It was my first actual conflict with the Boche and I had no desire for another.[26]

---

22 TNA WO 95/1974/3: 8th Royal Dublin Fusiliers War Diary.
23 The reference to Sgt Phillips appears in a number of accounts and publications and refers to a Sgt Phillips of an unnamed Welsh Regiment who had deserted to the Germans with plans of the attack. Despite my own research and that of others, this story cannot be proven and may be apocryphal.
24 Lieutenant Alfred Edward Burrowes was from Cork and had previously served at Salonika, where he had been Mentioned in Despatches. On 16 August he was struck by a shell fragment in the right eye, necessitating its removal. TNA WO 339/44285: Lieutenant Alfred Burrowes service record.
25 Lieutenant William Cooper Wolfe.
26 IWM: Doc 21037 Captain Arthur Evanson Glanville papers.

Captain Cowley expanded on the experience of the composite party as the day wore on:

> Opposite us were a line of square apparently intact concrete dugouts extending with intervals from D.26.a.2.0 to VAMPIR.[27] I could see none but wounded and dead to my north and none of our men at all to the south. The enemy had a machine gun in front of us at D.26.a.21, in addition to those on our flanks at BORRY FARM.[28] Their snipers and machine-guns were active firing at us from three sides and from dugout loopholes. We succeeeded in keeping our end up especially with the Lewis Guns, but the latter I had to stop as we were running through too much S.A.A. and I expected a counter attack. In the afternoon we got in several wounded of the attack. I concluded that with half my men casualties and machine-guns on both flanks, I could not take these dugouts, so started to consolidate the shell holes I was in. In the afternoon we got in several wounded of the RIR, including an officer from in front of D.26.a.31.[29] These said that they were survivors of a support company who had moved across to the left to support 9th RDF.[30]

Captain Cowley and his composite party remained in this position overnight and in the early hours of the morning saw the German troops opposite him relieved. They were most likely troops of *Infanterie Regiment Nr.84* of 3rd Reserve Division. This Division was relieved from the line on 18 August being replaced by 54th Division. The German 3rd Reserve Division was known to the Germans to have poor morale and was not regarded as a top class fighting unit.[31] Captain Cowley remained in the same position until dusk on 17 August when he marched his men back to the Black Line.

The 9th Battalion Royal Dublin Fusiliers went into the battle with a strength of 17 officers and 353 other ranks. Of these, 15 officers and 229 other ranks became casualties, a 66 per cent casualty rate.[32]

One of those killed was Private Reginald Isaac Jeffares 26218, a 26 years old married man. Reginald had grown up in County Wexford and had been married a year before his death. From available information, it appears that Reginald fell about 100 yards forward of the Black Line. His remains were exhumed from the battlefield in 1924 and identified by his identity disc. He was subsequently buried at Railway Dugouts Burial Ground (Transport Farm) Plot VI.S.22. His widow Margaret, resident with her family at Dalkey, County Dublin, arranged for the inscription, 'Not lost, but in thy care till by and by we meet' to be placed on his headstone. Reginald is commemorated on the war memorial at St Mary's Church of Ireland, New Ross, County Wexford. Two of his sisters Ruby and Violet, also appear on the Roll of Honour, having served as Nurses in the Great War.

---

27 The full map reference is 28.D.26.a.2.0 and refers to a point halfway between Potsdam and Vampir.
28 Map reference is 28.D.26.a.21. This refers to a point 100 yards behind Vampir.
29 Map reference is 28.D.26.a.31. This refers to a point beyond Vampir and just in front of the Bremen Redoubt.
30 TNA WO 95/1974/3: 9th Bn. Royal Dublin Fusiliers War Diary.
31 Intelligence Section of the General Staff, American Expeditionary Forces, *Histories of Two Hundred and Fifty-One Divisions of the German Army Which Participated in the War 1914-1918* <http://www.gwpda.org/1918p/USintel_germanarmy14-18.pdf> (accessed 24 January 2023).
32 The Commonwealth War Graves Commission data base records 85 men from the battalion died during this action.

Another 26 years old to fall that day was Captain James Owen Williams Shine. He was the third and last remaining son of Colonel James Shine, Royal Army Medical Corps and Mrs Shine of Abbeyside, Dungarvan, County Waterford, to fall in the war. His younger brother Second Lieutenant John Denys Shine, 2nd Battalion Royal Irish Regiment was killed in action on 25 August 1914, aged 19. His youngest brother, Second Lieutenant Hugh Patrick Shine, 1st Battalion Royal Irish Fusiliers, was killed in action on 25 May 1915 aged 18, near Ypres.[33]

Captain James Shine was commissioned from the Royal Military College, Sandhurst in 1909 and had been wounded at the Battle of the Somme on 1 July 1916. He has no known grave and is commemorated on the Tyne Cot Memorial and along with his brothers on the Waterford War Memorial, Dungarvan, County Waterford.[34]

Captain James Owen William Shine. (Open source)

The 2nd Battalion Royal Dublin Fusiliers were the support to the two attacking battalions, with two companies, A and B, detailed to follow behind the 7th Battalion Royal Irish Rifles and the 9th Battalion Royal Dublin Fusiliers as 'moppers up'. As they awaited Zero Hour, they were subjected a heavy German bombardment which caused many casualties. B Company, under the command of Captain Byrne, moved up behind 9th Royal Dublin Fusiliers with instructions to 'mop up' Vampir and the trenches in its vicinity. Unfortunately, they were annihilated before reaching their objective which was believed to be garrisoned by five machine guns. The actions of A Company, under the command of Captain Black MC have already been mentioned in connection with 7th Royal Irish Rifles. C Company also moved up in support but could make no progress either, being pinned down with sustained machine-gun fire short of a trench emplacement known as, 'Bit Work' which was short of Vampir Farm. The remnants remained there until ordered back to the Black Line on the evening of 17 August.

33 Tom Burnell, *The Waterford War Dead* (Dublin: History Press Ireland, 2010), pp.258-9.
34 Members of the Shine family still reside in the family home at Abbeyside, Dungarvan, County Waterford.

The 2nd Royal Dublin Fusiliers attacked with 14 officers and 293 other ranks. Of these, 7 officers and 115 other ranks became casualties, a casualty rate of just over 40 per cent. Of this number, 39 men were killed in the advance.[35]

One of those killed was 20 years old Private James Meehan 9138. From Waterford Street, Dublin, James had been married in 1914 and was the father of a two year old daughter, Margaret. He had been with the battalion since July 1915 and had been wounded in December of that year. With no known grave, James is commemorated on the Tyne Cot Memorial. In November 1917, he was posthumously awarded the Military Medal for gallantry in the field.

Second Lieutenant George Stride Falkiner aged 19, was the second son of Henry and Euphemia Falkiner of Terenure, County Dublin. He was educated at St Stephen's Green School and St Blundell's, Tiverton, Devon, before being admitted to the Royal Military College, Sandhurst in 1916, being commissioned in October of that year.[36] He had joined the battalion in December 1916 and had been wounded in a trench raid in May 1917. Like James Meehan, he is commemorated on the Tyne Cot Memorial. In a double family tragedy, his elder brother, 22 years old Second Lieutenant Frederick Ewen Baldwin Falkiner was killed five days later on 21 August. Frederick had enlisted in 7th Battalion Royal Dublin Fusiliers in 1914 and had been a Sergeant attached to the machine gun section when the battalion landed at Suvla Bay, Gallipoli, in August 1915. Commissioned in December 1915, he was posted to 15th Royal Irish Rifles in the 36th (Ulster) Division. He was awarded the Military Cross for gallantry at Messines, the citation stating:

> For conspicuous gallantry and devotion to duty. At a critical moment when the whole line was held up by machine guns firing from a very strong concrete emplacement, he detailed a Lewis gun to engage the enemy in front whilst he, with a Sergeant, worked round to the rear and charged the gunners. A fierce hand to hand fight ensued. As the Sergeant had already been severely wounded on the way, the officer was left single-handed; nevertheless with the greatest pluck and gallantry he killed two of the enemy and captured the gun and about 30 prisoners.[37]

Frederick transferred to the Royal Flying Corps in July 1917, being posted to 57 Squadron on 15 August. On 21 August he was Observer in a DH4 aircraft which took off at 5:30 a.m. on a reconnaisance flight. The pilot was Lieutenant Cecil Barry, aged 20 from Kanturk, County Cork, who had transferred to the Royal Flying Corps from the Royal Irish Regiment. The aircraft was shot down by 20 years old Leutnant Ernst Udet of *Jasta 37*, with both pilot and observer being killed.[38] Both pilot and observer were buried by the Germans however, in 1923 they were exhumed and buried at Tyne Cot Cemetery, Plot 1.AA.20. Both George and Frederick Falkiner are commemorated on the War Memorial at Dublin Unitarian Church, St Stephen's Green, Dublin.

---

35 CWGC data base.
36 George was initailly deemed unfit following a medical examination, but was successful on appeal. See TNA WO 339/78218: Second Lieutenant George Stride Falkiner service record.
37 *The London Gazette*, 17 September 1917.
38 Henshaw, *The Sky their Battlefield* p.88. Leutnant Ernst Udet later became a German ace with 62 victories.

The 48th Brigade Machine Gun Company suffered severely from the German counter barrage. Two guns moved forward at 5:40 a.m. to support the infantry and target Potsdam Farm, but both were destroyed by shell fire before coming into position. Both machine guns attached to 7th Royal Irish Rifles were able to engage the enemy for a short time before being put out of action. The two machine guns attached to 9th Royal Dublin Fusiliers were destroyed before they could be brought into operation. Five officers and 36 other ranks from the Machine Gun Company became casualties, a casualty rate of 35 per cent.

The 48th Brigade Trench Mortar Battery had two mortars attached to each of the attacking battalions however, all of them were put out of action due to German shelling before Zero hour. One of the officers of the TMB to fall was 35 years old Second Lieutenant Andrew Wynne Storrar, from Dublin Street, Carlow, the son of a Major in the Army Veterinary Corps. Andrew Storrar had been a Dentist prior to obtaining a commission in 1916. His servant, Private Baker, later wrote to his mother describing the circumstances of his death:

> Mr S at HQ on Thursday morning Aug 16 just before daybreak. We went over the top, there were no trenches, only shell holes, we arrived near the Bremen Redoubt. The 2nd Dubs passed the Redoubt on the right, the 9th Dubs on the left, and while Mr Storrar was deciding which way to go he was unfortunately killed by a sniper or machine gun bullet as he was kneeling down. The bullet passed through his helmet into his head, not one word was uttered. We made the wounded as comfortable as possible, and by that time it was too light for us to make a move, so we were compelled to stay until 9.30 in the evening. When dark, I took all Mr S' belongings off him and before we got back the Germans opened a very heavy barrage. When we arrived back, I reported his death to the CO … All the boys were sorry to lose Mr S. He was always very cool, always in front and very brave, doing his duty until the last.[39]

Second Lieutenant Storrar was initially buried on the battlefield close to Vampir Farm. His remains were later recovered, identified and reinterred at Potijze Chateau Grounds Cemetery, Plot II.E.18.

Unusually, Second Lieutenant Storrar's Will written in April 1917 is contained within his service record. Thoughtfully written, it contains the following:

> In the event of my death in action, I bequeath to my dear old housekeeper, Maria Whelan, Burrin Street, Carlow, Ireland, the sum of Fifty Pounds (£50) as a slight token of my regard for her and in remembrance of her unfailing kindness and unswerving devotion to me during 9 years of service.[40]

An article in *The Carlow Sentinel* of 25 August indicated that Andrew Storrar had visited friends in Carlow a few weeks prior to his death. Second Lieutenant Storrar is commemorated on the Carlow Memorial Arch at Leighlinbridge Memorial Garden, County Carlow.

---

39 TNA WO 339/61283: Second Lieutenant Andrew Wynne Storrar service record.
40 TNA WO 339/61283: Maria Whelan appears on the 1911 Census at Dublin Street, Carlow with Andrew Storrar.

Second Lieutenant Storrar Headstone Potijze Chateau Grounds Cemetery. (Authors Collection)

The 49th Infantry Brigade attacked on the left of 48th Infantry Brigade. Their attack was led by 8th Royal Inniskilling Fusiliers on the right and their sister battalion, 7th Royal Inniskilling Fusiliers on the left. The 7/8th Royal Irish Fusiliers were in support and 2nd Royal Irish Regiment were in reserve. Their objectives on the green line and the dotted red line respectively meant an advance of a similar distance to 48th Brigade. The divisional boundary was on the left of 7th Inniskillings with 9th Royal Irish Fusiliers of the 36th Division's 108th Brigade the next battalion in line.

Misfortune was to strike 49th Infantry Brigade even before Zero, when the Brigadier and his HQ Staff were overcome by gas in the HQ dugout, having to be removed to hospital. The commanding officer of 7/8th Royal Irish Fusiliers, Lieutenant Colonel Kenneth Charles Weldon DSO took over as Acting Brigadier.

In the path towards the final objective of the 8th Royal Inniskilling Fusiliers was the heavily fortified strongpoint of Borry Farm (*Quergut*), which was garrisoned by a company of Germans and at least three machine guns. To the left of Borry Farm and just in front of it as the 8th Inniskillings advanced was another fortified farmhouse, Low Farm (*Ostermorgengut*).

Against such formidable defences, the depleted 8th battalion was always going to experience great difficulty, and so it transpired. The attack was to be carried out in waves of two lines with 20 yards between each line, and 100 yards to the next wave.

First Company of *Infanterie Regiment Nr.19* under the command of Oberleutnant Weiseman were based at Low Farm. At dawn on 16 August, they observed the 8th Inniskillings advance towards them and opened fire at a distance of 70 metres. Despite one of their machine guns being put out of action by shellfire, the regimental history observed:

> Despite this unfortunate glitch, the frontal offensive was broken. The enemy collapsed and could not return fire.[41]

At the same time, the defenders of Low Farm observed an attack developing against Borry Farm:

> Around the same time as the dawn attack, two English waves could be identified south east of *Ostermorgengut*, immediately in front of the right flank of the flank division (54th Infantry Division) A third wave came in a row to the right, in the left open flank, and panned left to *Ostermorgengut*. There, the left flank group, and the flank machine guns on *Ostermorgengut-Est* fire on both waves. They suffer bloody losses. The sections which had penetrated the furthest form shooting nests immediately in front of the flank division (54th Infantry Division). At 6:15 a.m. the front and left flank are secure.[42]

Repeated attacks were made against Low Farm throughout the day but despite this the defenders managed to hold out despite suffering many casualties:

---

41 Oberleutnant Hans Jager, *Das K.B.19 Infanterie-Regiment Konig Viktor Emanuel III. Von Italien* (Munchen: Schick, 1930) p.387.
42 From this passage it is believed that Borry Farm was held by men of 54th Division, most likely *Infanterie Regiment Nr.84*.

Before long the machine gun crew of *Ostermorgengut-Est* are killed or incapacitated. The gun commander, Lance Corporal Schefthaler of the 1st Machine Gun Company defended valiantly. Although wounded in two places, he manned the machine gun, shooting with his left hand, with the right aiming. He fired almost the entire munition store (5000 rounds) at the enemy and was responsible for heavy enemy losses. Only after suffering a neck injury and losing his right eye to a splinter, did he abandon the gun at 7:00 a.m. Amidst this state of emergency, Unteroffizier [Corporal] Kellermann of the 1st Company, without further ado or further prompting order, took up the abandoned machine gun and, with the assistance of Unteroffizier Giffert, opened fire on the enemy, who then withdrew.[43]

The failure to take Low Farm and beyond it Borry Farm, caused great difficulty, not only for 8th Inniskillings who were pinned down and unable to advance. But also for 7th Inniskillings to their left who were subject to enfilade fire from both locations.

The reserve battalion in the brigade, 7/8th Royal Irish Fusiliers had identified specific tasks for each of their companies. C company, under the command of Second Lieutenant Charles Lennox Henry aged 22 from Lisburn, Co. Antrim, were tasked optimistically with 'mopping up at Borry Farm' once it had been captured by 8th Inniskillings. The company went forward to assist in the attack and were decimated with Second Lieutenant Henry being killed.

To their left, D company 7/8th Royal Irish Fusiliers under the command of Captain Edward Eaton Sargint MC had dealt with their own objective at Beck House, the battalion war diary recording:

> At 5.50 am OC D Coy reported that Borry Farm had not yet been taken and that sniping and MG fire from this farm was holding up the whole right attack. Captain Sargint proposed to try and work round the flank, but this attempt failed.[44]

The remnants of the 8th Inniskillings remained pinned down and it was impossible for them to move forward. The British Artillery barrage ordered on the Green Line at 10:00 a.m. by XIX Corps, must have added to the toll of dead and injured. Later in the day, they were withdrawn to the Black line and were relieved at 1:00 a.m. 17 August by 6th Connaught Rangers. On 16 August, 8th Inniskillings sustained 336 casualties including 114 men killed.

The strength of the defence at Borry Farm proved that it was a pivotal part of the German defences and it remained so as Thurlow recorded:

> On 22 August, the 15th Division again attacked, Borry Farm being included amongst the objectives allocated to 13th Battalion Royal Scots and 11th Battalion Argyll and Sutherland Highlanders, but so heavy was the enemy MG fire that hardly any of the men of the leading companies survived. On the same evening a desperate effort was made by the 6th Camerons to take both Borry and Beck Farms, but without success. On 20 September, 9th (Scottish) Division was assigned the task of capturing this portion of the German defensive system and finally Borry Farm and the concrete works to the south of it were taken by the 4th Regiment, South African Brigade.[45]

---

43 Jager, *Das K.B.19 Infanterie-Regiment Konig Viktor Emanuel III. Von Italien*, p.389.
44 TNA WO 95/1978/3: 7/8th Royal Irish Fusiliers War Diary.
45 Thurlow, *The Pill-Boxes of Flanders*, p.27.

Amongst those to fall on 16 August was 19 years old Second Lieutenant Jack Carrothers who had written home with such enthusiasm after the Battle of Messines. Initially reported as wounded in a Telegram from the War Office, when no further information was forthcoming, the family began their own investigations to establish what had happened to him. An enquiry through the Red Cross resulted in the interview of a Private WH Ferns 40347, 8th Inniskillings, who stated that he saw Second Lieutenant Carrothers being carried wounded on a stretcher to a captured German pillbox. This informant indicated that the pillbox was later hit by shells and the wounded killed.

The fact that Jack was wounded was corroborated by a number of other sources including his Batman, Private RH Osborne 43845, who was himself wounded and was being treated in hospital at Ebrington Barracks, Londonderry. His statement was summarised as follows:

> Informant saw him on a stretcher and helped carry him down. He spoke to informant and said he was wounded in the leg about the knee and said 'It was a nice little Blighty wound' and said that he was glad that he (the informant) was alright. He had only that one wound. Informant helped stretcher bearers who were already carrying him to just behind the front trench and left him outside Square Farm 10 o'clock night of 16th waiting to be dressed. It was Brigade HQ and there was heavy shelling round there at the time.[46]

A fellow officer, Second Lieutenant Arthur Hodder Robbins made strenuous efforts to find out details as he highlighted in a letter to the family on 6 September 1917:

> As far as I can tell he was wounded through the knee, it was a glorious 'Blighty' early in the day. Then after dark he was carried to an advanced medical post by two men, one of whom I know well and is a good and reliable man and he told me that he was handed over to the Doctor. I have also seen him and he saw and dressed your brother and sent him back further still. The doctor was the last to see him and there was a strong rumour around when we came out that a 'Skin' officer and two bearers had been hit on their way down. I refused to believe this or more that it was your brother's party for he was my best pal. I loved him dearly. At daybreak, I sent an Orderly to the Advanced Dressing Station to find if I could find anything about him but was unsuccessful. Later, I saw the Padre who knows your brother very well and he had not seen him pass down. The next day I sent to the next station down the line where everyone passed and particulars of all cases are taken, again without success…I'm very much afraid that we shall never see him again and you've no idea how much I miss him.[47]

Jack's death was confirmed by the War Office in a letter to his parents in February 1918. He has no known grave and is commemorated on the Tyne Cot Memorial to the Missing.

Private Charles Seaman 28143 was a member of Second Lieutenant Carrother's company. Also aged 19 and from Florencecourt, County Fermanagh, he had enlisted in December 1915

---

46 TNA WO 339/67178: Second Lieutenant John Carrothers service record.
47 PRONI: D1973/12. Arthur Hodder Robbins remained with the Inniskillings being promoted to the rank of Captain. He was killed in action on the first day of the German Spring Offensive, 21 March 1918.

and had been posted to 8th Inniskillings in March 1917. In a letter to his mother on the eve of the battle Seaman wrote:

> Just a few lines hoping to find you all well as it leaves me. You need not worry about me as there is times we cannot write. I got your letter yesterday and I was very glad to get it … I think there is no fear of me getting a pass for the next six months but I suppose the war will be over before then. No more to say at present.[48]

Charles Seaman was also killed on 16 August and is also commemorated on the Tyne Cot Memorial.

One officer of the battalion who had a fortunate escape, was Second Lieutenant John Lanigan Charlesworth. Injured in the attack on Borry Farm, he was taken prisoner. He recounted the circumstances to an Army Board following his repatriation in November 1918:

> At Zero we advanced under a heavy fire and were held up by a pillbox known as BORRY FARM on our maps. There was a sunken road before this place which I tried to cross. A sniper shot me through the left shoulder at a range of about 20 yards. After I had lain in the open for some time, it now being too light to crawl back unobserved and useless to crawl forward, two Germans came to the door of the pillbox and motioned to me to come in. I went.[49]

The 7th Royal Inniskilling Fusiliers were to the left of their sister battalion. To the left of 7th Inniskillings was the divisional boundary with 36th Division and the 9th Royal Irish Fusiliers were the battalion to the left of 7th Inniskillings. B & D Companies of the Support battalion, 7/8th Royal Irish Fusiliers also supported the 7th Inniskillings attack. The difficulties of getting all the companies briefed and into position was highlighted in the battalion war diary:

> 15 August. Moved at 10.30 pm to assembly positions in preparation for attack. It should be understood that no intercourse had been possible between Battn HQ and its two front companies, C and A from dawn in the morning until 8.30 pm at night. C Coy stood fast. A Coy relieved by a Coy of 7/8 Royal Irish Fusiliers and moved in behind C Coy. D & B coy's moved up from the rear and took up position on the northern side of the Hannebeeke continuing the line of C & A coys, linking up with the Coys of 9th Royal Irish Fusiliers of 36th (Ulster) Division, the line taken up by them being strictly in the 36th Div area, but special leave was given for the battn to use this so to simplify its advance, there being streams which might have impeded its advance on its objectives otherwise. It was not until D & B Coys had passed Bn HQ's that Zero Hour – 4:45 a.m. was received … Everything was ready by 2:30 a.m. all last orders including Zero time having to be given verbally to the OC's C & A Coys owing to their being in position when it was impossible to show a light.[50]

---

48 The Inniskillings Museum, *The Fermanagh War Memorial Book of Honour 1914-1921* (Enniskillen: Inniskillings Museum, 2014), p.468.
49 TNA WO 339/63982: Second Lieutenant John Lanigan Charlesworth service record.
50 TNA WO 95/1977/2: 7th Royal Inniskilling Fusiliers War Diary.

On the 7th battalion front, the main strongpoints to be captured were, Beck House (*Kaminhof*) Delva Farm, and Iberian (*Marienhütte*). Beck House was given as an objective to D Company 7/8th Royal Irish Fusiliers commanded by Captain Edward Eaton Sargint MC.

In common with the other Irish battalions, 7th Inniskillings were severely understrength – 20 officers and 372 other ranks however, the war diary records that they were ready for the challenge:

> Every man knew the objective and had had the objectives etc thoroughly ground into him whilst every NCO, L/Cpls included and every signaller and runner had visited the Corps model and had the position and lay of the ground over which they were to attack explained to them.[51]

When the attack commenced accompanied by the artillery barrage at 4:45 a.m. the German artillery replied immediately however, the attacking companies had vacated the front line by that stage.

There is a remarkable account of the battalion's actions from Captain Victor Henry Parr MC contained within, *The Book of the 7th (S) Battalion Royal Inniskilling Fusiliers* by Garret Alexander Cooper Walker MC. Extracts from this account have been woven into those from the battalion war diary, German Regimental histories, and personal accounts, to piece together the actions of the battalion on 16 August.

> At Zero hour I was in the front line trench at D.19.c.50.40 [this is a position midway between Beck House and Iberian Farm and about 100 metres short of Beck House] and behind me was the battalion Headquarters party under the command of Captain Hester.[52] From this party I detailed two runners to remain with me throughout the attack. My idea at this time was to leave Captain Hester in command of the advance party (signallers, snipers, runners, etc) so that I should be free to leave them at a moment's notice in case I should be required elsewhere. At zero hour we advanced about 100 yards to the left of A Company's third wave so as to be clear of our own trench. We made straight on for Delva Farm. As we passed Beck House, I noticed that it had already been captured by our men and some prisoners were taken.[53]

From the account of Captain Parr, it seems that Beck House fell very easily to Captain Sargint of the 7/8th Royal Irish Fusiliers and his men. The account of the defenders of *Kaminhof* as the Germans named Beck House, tells a story of a desperate struggle:

> Meanwhile, the masses of Englishmen under our fire gradually reach *Kaminhof* [Beck House]. Assault aircraft support their advance. Yet *Kaminhof* is held, even as the fire

---

51 TNA WO 95/1977/2: 7th Royal Inniskilling Fusiliers War Diary.
52 From Earl's Court, London, Captain Edgar Hazel Hester was killed on 16 August. His body was recovered from the battlefield beyond Delva Farm in 1921 and identified by personal effects. He is buried at Bedford House Cemetery (Enclosure No. 4 XIV.F.31).
53 Garret Alexander Cooper Walker, *The Book of the 7th (S) battalion Royal Inniskilling Fusiliers* (Dublin: Privately published, 1920), p.117.

raining down from all sides thins out the ranks of defending troops. Platoon Commander, Unteroffizier Zipfel is fatally wounded and died on 22 August. If the junction to their left is maintained, the company commander's position is not hopeless. This considered, he gives orders to hold the position. The English identify the weak defence area, however, and ready themselves to penetrate the area between *Kaminhof* and the left flank of the 2nd platoon of the 4th company. Yet, they do not anticipate the bravery of 2nd platoon commander, Vizfeldwebel [Staff Sergeant of the Reserves] Bickel and his three detachment commanders, Uffz. Georg Maher, Gefreiter [Lance Corporal] Konrad Hofmann and Uffz. Witzleben. They and their 17 men receive the oncoming Englishmen with hand grenades and sniper fire, meaning the enemy, suffering heavy losses, must take cover 10m in front of the 2nd platoon and engage in a bitter firefight, bringing a machine gun into position. Uffz. Maher is severely wounded (Died 3rd September) Gefr. Hofmann dies. Vzfw. Bickel rises, not wanting to give way, and motions to the left, signaling for help from the 1st company. Hit in the head, he sinks to the ground. The Englishmen now storm past the platoon's flank, Uffz. Witzleben, (who was later awarded an honorary cross for his actions on the 16 August) finds his way to *Kaminhof*. At the same time, the Englishmen form a frontal assault against the rest of the 2nd platoon. The remaining six to seven men position themselves by their dead and wounded comrades and allow the assault troops to rush over them. They then gather themselves, running to the join the 1st company.

Meanwhile, *Kaminhof* is still held. As the left flank is penetrated, Leutnant Kötter sends a group to approach the front at a right angle, so that the now consolidated 4th company was fighting against three fronts at the same time. But it is no longer possible to prevent the enemy from advancing on both penetrated flanks. The English assault troops surround the 4th Company from the rear, cutting them off. Lt. Kötter then gives orders for the evacuation of *Kaminhof*, retreating over the Hanebeeke flowing behind the company.[54]

Having successfully captured Beck House, Captain Sargint left some of his men there as a garrison and, having seen the danger posed by Borry Farm to his right, headed for it, intending to try and outflank it to assist 8th Inniskillings, but was unable to do so.

Captain Parr continues:

> We continued on our way and crossed the Zonnebeke at a point midway between Pommern Castle (*Gartenhof*) and Beck House. There was no difficulty in crossing the stream, but a line of wire entanglements on the right bank, which had escaped out artillery bombardment caused us some difficulty. On arrival at the southern end of Iberian strongpoint I noticed that there was considerable rifle fire going on and in the next few minutes my signalling Serjeant was hit by a bullet. I ordered the snipers who were with me to advance to the eastern end of the strongpoint and take up a position until I joined them. As far as I could see there did not appear to be any of our troops in Iberia, though it was then 6:30 a.m. Shortly after this we noticed a German looking out of one of the dug-outs. I arranged that all dugouts in the vicinity be thoroughly searched. In one we found 20 Germans and two machine-guns. At first they hesitated to come out, but on being threatened with a revolver they came out

---

54 Jager, *Das K.B.19 Infanterie-Regiment Konig Viktor Emanuel III. Von Italien* p.385.

unarmed. This particular pill-box was a concrete machine-gun emplacement facing in the direction of Frezenberg. In all we searched about three dug-outs and got forty prisoners and three machine-guns. At the time I could not spare any of my men as escort, so I ordered the prisoners to report to Square Farm, which I understand now they did. As a precaution I took the breech blocks from the machine guns and threw them into a shell hole. The clearing of these dugouts had caused some delay to our advance, so we proceeded straight away in the direction of Delva Farm. When I came to Delva, I noticed that B company were extended in shell craters in front of the farm. Captain D. H. Morton had been wounded during the attack and was lying in a shell hole close by. This officer explained the situation to me.[55]

In an unfortunate coincidence, 16 August was Captain David Hamill Morton's 24th birthday. Born at Newtownstewart, County Tyrone, he was the son of a Presbyterian Minister. In the German counterattack that developed later in the morning, Captain Morton was captured and received treatment from the Germans at a Field Hospital at Bielefeld, Germany. A prisoner for the remainder of the war, he was repatriated to the United Kingdom on 3 December 1918. He related how he was captured in an account for an Army Board:

On 16th August 1917, I commanded B Company 7th Royal Inniskillings in an attack on the enemy's positions near Hill 37, West NW of Zonnebeke. My company was in support of the leading company, D Company. On reaching my objective, a line running N & S 50 yards east of Delva Farm, we commenced to consolidate our position, but were greatly hindered by crossfire from enemy machine-guns and snipers. About 10 minutes after arriving at my objective, I was wounded in the left side about one and half inches from the hip joint by a bullet from a machine-gun or sniper, rendering me unable to stand.[56] I immediately sent orders to my senior Platoon commander to take command of the company, but this officer was killed before doing so. The enemy then laid down a heavy machine-gun barrage, crossfiring from both flanks and as I was lying in a deep shell hole, I was unable to observe his attack. About four hours later I was discovered by the Germans and removed to Delva Farm and from there to a German Dressing Station together with a wounded Private from my own Company.[57]

Following his conversation with Captain Morton, Captain Parr continued to try and ascertain the situation as he described:

My first idea was to locate D Company and I sent a runner to find their whereabouts. In a short time, Captain H.W. Ruddock came back personally to report to me. He then told me that he had reached a line 150 yards in front of Delva Farm, that his casualties were slight up to this, but that he was under intense machine-gun fire, and not in touch with troops on either flank.[58]

---

55 Walker, *The Book of the 7th (S) Battalion Royal Inniskilling Fusiliers* p.118.
56 Captain Morton was also wounded in the forehead later that day.
57 TNA WO 339/20231 Captain DH Morton service record.
58 Garret Alexander Cooper Walker, *The Book of the 7th (S) Battalion Royal Inniskilling Fusiliers* (Dublin: Privately published, 1920) p.118.

At that stage, Captain Ruddock's D Company were the farthest forward of any of the Division's troops however, the fact that he had no support on either side spelt danger.

Herbert William Ruddock was a 29 years old married man who had been born in Dublin. At the outbreak of war, he was employed as an Engineer and was resident in Vancouver, British Columbia. He returned to the United Kingdom and was commissioned Second Lieutenant in April 1915. He had been with the battalion in France since February 1916, participating in the actions at Guillemont and Ginchy on the Somme, and at Messines. Due to the casualties suffered by the battalion in the first two weeks of August, he had been promoted Acting Captain on 13 August. Taken prisoner on 16 August and interned in Switzerland, he described his view of the attack of 16 August:

> Whilst in command of D company 7th R. Innis Fus. I received orders to attack the enemy on the morning of 16th August, my objective being roughly 1200 yards away. In the line of advance there were several enemy strongpoints. The principle one being DELVA FARM, about 800 yards from POMMERN CASTLE. The latter an old German strongpoint was our jumping off position. This was used for a similar purpose by a company of the 9th Royal Irish Fus. (36th Division) who were attacking on my left. C Company 7th R. Innis. Fus being on my right. The 1st wave of my company advanced for five or six hundred yards and appeared to suffer heavy casualties from rifle and MG fire. In DELVA FARM on the right, they encountered thick barbed wire. I moved up the 2nd wave as there appeared to be only about a dozen men left. I observed the enemy clearing out of the position. We worked round to the right and eventually captured the farm. We inflicted heavy casualties on the enemy as he retired. The advance was continued for about 200 yards further. It was then held up owing to intense MG fire particularly from the right. I sent several runners to get in touch with C company, but they did not return. By this time I only had about 15 men left and had great difficulty in digging in owing to sniping and MG fire. We were then reduced to 10 men, four men being hit while working. After a short while, I went back to advanced Bn. HQ at DELVA FARM and saw Captain VH Parr MC (2nd in command for tactical purposes) I explained my position and received orders to hang on at all costs. From what I could ascertain, C company had been held up 300 yards behind my position. I then went forward and formed a defensive flank on the right with a Lewis Gun. The enemy shortly after counter attacked in force and worked round my right flank. I received a bullet wound in the ear, and whilst L/Cpl P. Flood (Stretcher Bearer) was attending to my wound the enemy rushed us from a position 50 yards off and took both of us prisoner. From what I could see the few men I had left fell back as soon as I was hit.[59]

As he considered the situation Captain Parr became aware of rumours that the troops to his left – those of 36th (Ulster) Division were retiring however, he believed this to be wounded troops making for the rear. Using his field glasses, he observed Hill 35 to his left and it confirmed his suspicions as he saw men retiring from in front of the hill.

---

59   TNA WO 339/40301: Acting Captain Herbert William Ruddock service record.

This observation is crucial to the assessment of what actually happened on 16 August. Captain Parr mentions no time that he made this observation however, the XIX Corps summary of 16 August contains the following:

> 6:49 a.m. Reported by 36th Div. Artillery. Message from Liaison officer with 12th Royal Irish Rifles timed 6:40 a.m. says, 13th Royal Irish Rifles retiring. (13th RIR are the left battalion of right brigade)[60]

At this point it is not clear whether the troops were retiring due to fire from German strongpoints or from the German counterattack. The history of *Bavarian Infanterie Regiment Nr.21* gives a clue as to timing:

> At 8 am, a runner brought a division order sent from the brigade to the regiment: 'Enemy incursion on both sides of the Ypres-Roeselare railway up to the Hannebeeke. The 21st Inf. Reg. is to push the enemy back and recapture our front line.'[61]

This puts the timing at around 7:00 a.m. British time and given that *Infanterie Regiment Nr.21* were to the rear of *Infanterie Regiment Nr.19*, it would have taken them some time to move forward to commence the counterattack.

Captain Parr immediately realised the danger as his men were unsupported either to the right or left. He established defensive flanks and sent a message outlining the position to Brigade HQ at Square Farm. He continued:

> At 8.30 am I got word that we are being counter-attacked so I went out in front to ascertain if this were true. I saw the enemy were advancing towards D company who were 'firing rapid' and appeared to have the situation well in hand. Another message came when I was there from B Company in which I was informed that Lieutenant Woods had been killed.[62] I went across to where he had been and on my arrival I saw the Germans advancing from a northerly direction with apparently Hill 35 and Delva Farm as their objectives. When I first saw them they were advancing in two lines at about five paces interval, their right flank was almost on Hill 35 which appeared to be undefended and they were then only 400 yards away from where we stood. I shouted to the men who were near me to open fire, but my voice did not carry very far.[63]

In an attempt to form a defensive line, Captain Parr established a defensive flank from Delva Farm to Iberia, to counter the threat from Hill 35 however, such was the casualty rate that he found it difficult to gather sufficient numbers to do so:

---

60   TNA WO 95/960/3: XIX Corps War Diary.
61   Reber, *Das K.B. 21. Infanterie Regiment*, p.209.
62   Lieutenant Norman Hill Woods MC was 24 years old and from Holywood, Co. Down. Pre war he was an Insurance Clerk with the London & Lancashire Fire Assurance Company, Donegall Square West, Belfast. He is commemorated on the Tyne Cot Memorial.
63   Walker, *The Book of the 7th (S) Battalion Royal Inniskilling Fusiliers* p.119.

> Within the next fifteen minutes, I succeeded in collecting various parties of stragglers, in all amounting to about 40 men and I endeavoured with these to reform a line. Unfortunately, the casualties had been so heavy that it was difficult to find any NCO's to put in charge of the men. When I reached Ibernia [sic] I could find no organised body of Royal Irish Fusiliers, but with the assistance of Captain Sargint, we succeeded in restoring the situation for a while. The enemy's barrage fire was very intense at this time and severe casualties were sustained. It was then that Captain Sargint, my runner and myself were all hit.[64]

Captain Edward Eaton Sargint MC was aged 22. He had been born at Tipperary in July 1895, the son of a Bank Clerk. He had enlisted in the 21st (Service) Battalion Royal Fusiliers (4th Public Schools) in October 1914 and had been commissioned in May 1915. He was promoted Acting Captain in June 1917 and had been recommended for a bar to his Military Cross on 11 August for, 'excellent work and gallantry in remaining with his company when wounded when all his Coy HQ was wounded or killed.' Captain Sargint has no known grave and is commemorated on the Tyne Cot Memorial and on the Roll of Honour at Abbey School, Dublin.[65]

For the men of *Bavarian Infanterie Regiment Nr.21*, moving forward to the attack was difficult in itself:

> The remaining companies of both battalions had meanwhile gone beyond the *Wilhelm-Stellung* [Wilhelm Position] the 8th Company taking up the position of the 6th. Traversing the sodden shelled fields, running through the artillery fire zone and crossing the corroding barbed wire, which forced the troops to advance in columns as well as the view of the now visible Tommys, the emerging machine gun fire and the wall of smoke and fumes hanging over *Marienhütte* (Iberian) had the combined effect of seriously mixing the units. They were now tasked with driving the Englishmen from the concrete placements; the majority of these now equipped with machine guns. This task had a dispersive effect, with the battle now proceeding in the form of separate assaults against each of these footholds. The commanders nonetheless succeeded in keeping together the core of their men, attacking the British with such vigour that they also pulled the other companies' troops forward with them.[66]

As the counterattack developed, the Acting Brigadier of 49th Infantry Brigade, Lieutenant Colonel Weldon needed to make decisions rapidly:

> The fact that no progress had been made by the 8th Inniskillings rendered the position at Delva untenable with the result that the whole line fell back to Iberia, the existence of only one officer can be established. The 7/8th Royal Irish Fusiliers Coy holding Iberia had no officers and only 22 OR and these were carried back with the 7th Inniskillings … The left flank at Iberia had been seriously threatened and uncovered by the retirement to Iberia and Delva and also by the Germans advancing to attack 48th Bde on my right. I decided that

---

64 Walker, *The Book of the 7th (S) Battalion Royal Inniskilling Fusiliers* p.119.
65 TNA WO 339/3785: Acting Captain Edward Eaton Sargint MC service record.
66 Reber, *Das K.B. 21. Infanterie Regiment*, p.213.

I must send the 2 RIRegt to hold the original front line. I anxiously awaited the arrival of 6th Connaught Rangers who it was reported to me had left their bivouac at 9:45 a.m.[67]

The 2nd Royal Irish Regiment utilised three companies to hold the Black line throughout the day to facilitate the withdrawal of the remnants of 7th Inniskillings and 7/8th Royal Irish Fusiliers to join them.

By 11:10 a.m. 49th Infantry Brigade was back at the Black Line as the war diary of 7th Inniskillings recorded:

> The situation is serious, apparently we took our objectives Hill 37 and Delva Farm, but the 9th RIF of 36th Div gave way before a counter attack and left the Battn with both flanks in the air, the 8th Inniskillings having been held up apparently by Borry Farm. The remains of the Bde now hold our original front line including Beck House but are very disorganized. I fear we could not hold this line without reinforcements. Casualties very heavy.[68]

At this stage, the chaos and confusion of the battle caused communications to go awry, with the lack of accurate information reaching Brigade Headquarters causing erroneous orders to be issued, which caused great consternation within 7th Inniskillings:

> 1.30 pm First message received from Bde. Did not answer any of the previous messages but stated that Borry Farm had to be taken at all costs… The 8th Inniskillings will make up their strength up to 300 strong calling on CO's 7 Innis Fus, 7/8 RIF and 2 RIRegt for men. With these men 8 Innis. will take Borry Farm, garrison it and push forward as far as the river joining up with the Dublins on the right west of Bremen Redoubt, the left to be east of Borry Farm. Touch with garrison of Beck House to be maintained. This attack must be carried out at all costs to support 2 Dublins at order of the Divisional Commander. CO 8 Inniskillings will notify Brigade of the hour he is ready to attack. The RA are firing on Borry Farm and will be switched off as soon as the hour for attack is notified. The message giving the hour must be sent by two different runners. If the power buzzer is working the message will be sent by this means also. Artillery support is being arranged for the hour notified.[69]

The Headquarters of 7th Inniskillings were bewildered by this order and unusually expressed their consternation in the war diary:

> This was not a practical order and simply proved that the Bde Hq's had not the slightest conception of the situation.[70]

Following a reply to Brigade which clarified the situation, this order to attack was cancelled.

---

67 IWM: Doc. 7190 Lieutenant Colonel Kenneth Charles Weldon Papers.
68 TNA WO 95/1977/2: 7th Battalion Royal Inniskilling Fusiliers War Diary.
69 TNA WO 95/1977/2: 7th Battalion Royal Inniskilling Fusiliers War Diary.
70 TNA WO 95/1977/2: 7th battalion Royal Inniskilling Fusiliers War Diary.

The confusion which existed is illustrated by the fact that following the German counterattack, Beck House was held by neither side as Lieutenant Colonel Weldon recorded in a report following the action:

> Enquiries have since been made and it is almost certain that on vacating Beck House at 9 am on 16th, it was held by neither side up until the Connaught Rangers took over the front line at 3.15 am 17th.[71]

This information was corroborated by 7th Inniskillings:

> Meanwhile the situation at Beck House was indefinite. Neither side held it but both had a few troops facing it about 150 yards apart with this place in the middle.[72]

What remained of 49th Infantry Brigade held the Black Line until relieved by 6th Connaught Rangers and were then withdrawn to the Vlamertinghe area.

The casualties within the Brigade were horrendous. The 7th Inniskillings attacked on the morning of 16 August with 14 officers and 372 other ranks. When relieved, the roll call showed a strength of 7 officers and 114 other ranks. Of the 265 casualties, 78 were killed. Of those killed with the battalion, at least one had an unusual background for an Inniskilling. Private Rupert Marcellious Wilson 29029, was 19 years old when he was killed. He had been born in 1898 in New Hampshire, USA, and was resident there until the outbreak of war. He travelled to the United Kingdom and enlisted in the Inniskillings at North Shields, County Durham. With no known grave, he is commemorated on the Tyne Cot Memorial and on a family memorial at Forest City Cemetery, South Portland, Maine, USA.

Also aged 19 was Captain Cornwall Nathaniel Brownlow Walker. The only son of Cornwall and Adaline Walker, he was from Fitzroy Avenue, Belfast, and had been educated at Coleraine Academical Institution. A Second Lieutenant, he had been at the front since July 1916 and had been authorised to wear Captain's insignia only on 13 August. Initially reported as wounded and missing, his death was confirmed in February 1918. He was recommended for the Military Cross for his actions on 16 August however, the battalion war diary somewhat harshly states that the recommendation was 'Thrown out by the BG commanding 49th Inf Bde, this officer being missing.'[73]

With no known grave, Captain Walker is commemorated on the Tyne Cot Memorial to the Missing.

A year older than Captain Walker was Private Alfred Henry Marsh 41174, from Cheriton, Folkestone, Kent. Alfred had been a reinforcement for 7th Inniskillings due to problems recruiting sufficient numbers and was attached to C company. He had previously served as Private 21671 with the East Surrey Regiment. Seriously wounded and captured, he died at a German military hospital at Hamburg on 30 August 1917. He is buried at Hamburg Cemetery.

Captain Victor Henry Parr MC who provided the in-depth account of the battalion's actions, survived the battle. Aged 29 and the son of a Farmer from Athboy, County Meath, he had been

---

71 IWM: Doc. 7190 Lieutenant Colonel Kenneth Charles Weldon papers.
72 TNA WO 95/1977/2: 7th battalion Royal Inniskilling Fusiliers War Diary.
73 TNA WO 95/1977/2: 7th Battalion Royal Inniskilling Fusiliers War Diary.

a student at Trinity College, Dublin before the war. He had been awarded the Military Cross for gallantry at Guillemont in September 1916. For his part in the Battle of Langemarck he was awarded the Distinguished Service Order, the citation stating:

> For conspicuous gallantry and devotion to duty when in command on an advanced battalion headquarters. On his way there he mopped up three machine guns and 50 prisoners. On the battalion being forced back, through both its flanks being exposed, he was responsible for its orderly retreat. Practically all the officers were killed, wounded and missing and the casualties by this time were about 60 per cent. He himself was wounded, but by his resolute action the advance of the enemy was delayed and the troops in the rear given time to take up covering positions.[74]

Promoted to Major, Victor Hall was captured during the German Spring Offensive, March 1918. When repatriated, he returned to Athboy, residing there until his death in 1966.

Such were the casualties of both 7th and 8th Inniskillings that a decision was made to amalgamate them on 23 August 1917. A Special Order was issued by Lieutenant Colonel Herbert Nugent Young DSO, commanding officer 7th Inniskillings:

> Officers and Other Ranks of the old 7th and 8th battalions of the Royal Inniskilling Fusiliers are from this date amalgamated as one battalion. As such they must continue to accrue fresh honours for their parent Regiment. Both battalions have records of which any battalion in the British Army would be proud to possess. Let it now be the aim of all to win a name for the combined battalions which will if possible even surpass the record of either.[75]

As support battalion, 7/8th Royal Irish Fusiliers were in the thick of the action from the outset as has already been noted from the actions of Captain Sargint. As the day progressed they became intermingled with both 7th and 8th Inniskillings and were steadily reduced in numbers as casualties mounted and by the end of the day had sustained 229 casualties including 51 killed.

Second Lieutenant George Coombes DCM MM, was one of those killed with the battalion. From Haslemere, Surrey, he had enlisted in the Cavalry in 1902. A champion boxer, by the outbreak of war he was married with two sons and embarked for France on 15 August 1914 with the 9th Lancers (Queens Royal) with the service number 4894. He was wounded on 1 September 1914 and was gassed on 27 April 1916. By that time, he had been awarded the Distinguished Conduct Medal, the citation stating:

> For conspicuous gallantry, when in charge of a working party behind the bombers after the explosion of a mine, he displayed the greatest courage and resource, and volunteered for and carried every dangerous and difficult task during 48 hours under very heavy fire.[76]

---

74 Jim Condon, *Officers of the Royal Inniskilling Fusiliers in World War 1* (Droitwich Spa: Privately published, 1993), p.254.
75 Walker, *The Book of the 7th (S) Battalion Royal Inniskilling Fusiliers* p.121. Lieutenant Colonel Young was awarded a bar to his DSO in October 1918 and was killed in action on 25 October whilst commanding 11th Battalion Sherwood Foresters (Notts and Derby Regiment). He is buried at Pommereuil British Cemetery (Plot E.7).
76 *Ancestry* <www.ancestry.co.uk>

In March 1916, he was transferred to 7th Royal Inniskilling Fusiliers, service number 29224 in the rank of Company Serjeant Major and was awarded the Military Medal for gallantry in the field. He was appointed to a permanent commission in the 7/8th battalion Royal Irish Fusiliers on 14 February 1917.

Attached to C Company, Second Lieutenant Coombes was killed in the advance on 16 August as his company supported 8th Inniskillings. Initially reported as wounded and missing accounts were sought after the battle from men from his platoon as to his fate. Unfortunately these did not provide much clarity beyond confirming that he was dead. Private Murray 22898 reported:

> I was alongside of him at Ypres-Menin Road when he was blown to pieces by a shell. I was just behind his back. This was about 200 yards from the B line in No Man's Land. It was daylight. We had to retire. He was a good officer and belonged to my company and platoon.[77]

Another soldier, Private Bray 13464, gave a conflicting account:

> On the 16th August 1917 I was beside 2nd Lt. G Coombes when he was killed by a bullet in the head. I saw him lying dead. We were at Ypres at the time.[78]

In October 1919, Second Lieutenant Coombes' remains were uncovered from the battlefield and identified by his identity disc. He fell just beyond Beck House close to the banks of the Hanebeek river. He was reburied in Dochy Farm New British Cemetery Plot II.B.2.[79]

The attrition rate amongst platoon commanders was high. Another who fell was 26 years old Second Lieutenant Arthur Conway Young. Born at Kobe, Japan, where his father was the editor of an English language newspaper. Arthur Young had initially enlisted in the Inns of Court Officer Training Corps and was commissioned in October 1915. Initially reported as 'wounded and missing' enquiries were made on his father's behalf through the Red Cross as to his fate. A Corporal in his company, Thomas Robilliard, taken prisoner and interned in Switzerland, was interviewed and claimed that he had been killed on the morning of 16 August.[80] Some confusion then arose as to the whereabouts of the remains of Second Lieutenant Young. A letter to his father from the War Office in November 1917 stated that he had been, 'Killed in action or died of wounds on or shortly after 16 August 1917.' His burial being reported by 5th Battalion Oxfordshire and Buckinghamshire Light Infantry on 8 November. In response to a request for further details, his father received another letter from the War Office in May 1918 stating that:

> Second Lieutenant Young is buried 150 yards east of Bory Farm [sic]. The grave has been registered in this office and has been marked with a durable wooden cross with an inscription bearing full particulars.[81]

---

77 TNA WO 339/95118 :Second Lieutenant George Coombes DCM MM service record.
78 TNA WO 339/95118 :Second Lieutenant George Coombes DCM MM service record.
79 Enquiries have been undertaken with the CWGC to have Coombes' decorations included on his headstone.
80 Corporal Thomas Robilliard 21892 was a native of Guernsey, Channel Islands.
81 TNA WO 95/339/45248: Second Lieutenant Arthur Conway Young service record.

Second Lieutenant George Coombes DCM MM gravesite. (Author)

This grave however, was lost. In September 1919, the remains of Second Lieutenant Young were recovered during battlefield clearance and identified through personal effects. The Commonwealth War Graves Commission documents indicate that the remains were recovered from in front of Somme Farm – to the west, not the east of Borry Farm. He is now buried at Tyne Cot Cemetery, Plot IVG.2. His parents who were committed pacifists arranged for the inscription, 'Sacrificed to the fallacy that war can end war' to be placed on his headstone.

The 2nd Royal Irish Regiment were the reserve battalion of the brigade and were moved up rapidly into the front line once the advance commenced. A party from C Company assisted in the initial capture of Beck House and many of these men became casualties. Thereafter, the battalion consolidated on the Black line enduring artillery and machine gun fire for most of the day until relieved by the Connaught Rangers in the early hours of 17 August. In the attack, the battalion lost 17 men killed.

A comment in the war diary of 7/8th Royal Irish Fusiliers pays tribute to the tenacity and endurance of Stretcher Bearers adding the remark that, 'Enemy snipers apparently respected them whilst working'.[82]

One man carrying out such duties was Lance Corporal Frederick George Room 8614, 2nd Royal Irish Regiment.[83] In the course of the battle, Lance Corporal Room was in charge of a party of Stretcher Bearers and performed this arduous duty under the most trying of circumstances without regard to his own safety. For his actions that day he was awarded the only Victoria Cross awarded to anyone in either Irish Division, despite there being many cases which could have been deemed suitable. The citation states:

> For most conspicuous bravery when in charge of his company Stretcher Bearers. During the day the company had many casualties, principally from enemy machine guns and snipers. The company was holding a line of shell holes and short trenches. L/Cpl Room worked continuously under intense fire, dressing the wounded and helping evacuate them. Throughout this period with complete disregard for his own life, he showed unremitting devotion to his duties. By his courage and fearlessness he was the means of saving many of his comrades lives.[84]

The citation was published in *The London Gazette* of 17 October 1917 and Lance Corporal Room was presented with the medal by King George V at a medal ceremony at Durdham Downs in his native city of Bristol on 8 November 1917.

Frederick George Room was born in Bristol on 31 May 1895, the third son of William James and Bertha Eaton Room, nee Rees. At the time of the birth, William Room was a grain porter. By 1911, Frederick, then aged 16, was employed as a motor engine fitter at the Western Engineering Company, Bristol. He was also a member of 1st Bristol Cadet Battalion, Church Lad's Brigade in the St George's area of Bristol. Frederick enlisted soon after the outbreak of war on 29 August 1914 at Colston Hall, Bristol. He initially joined Southern Command Cavalry Depot at Bristol before being posted to 10th Reserve Cavalry Regiment at The Curragh, County Kildare.

82　TNA WO 95/1978/3: 7/8th battalion Royal Irish Fusiliers War Diary.
83　Some accounts refer to him as Acting Lance Corporal. His military records show that he was promoted Lance Corporal on 11 August 1917 and to Corporal on 30 August 1918.
84　*The London Gazette*, 17 October 1917.

Second Lieutenant Arthur Conway Young gravesite. (Author)

Following training with the Cavalry he was posted to the Royal Irish Regiment and he embarked for France joining 2nd Royal Irish Regiment on 26 July 1915.

He was wounded in the hand on the opening day of the Battle of the Somme, 1 July 1916 and spent three weeks at No 11 Stationary Hospital, Rouen, rejoining the battalion after treatment. An Acting Lance Corporal, he was promoted to paid Lance Corporal on 11 August 1917. The award of the Victoria Cross was gazetted on 17 October 1917, whilst Frederick was at home on leave. Following the award, he remained with the battalion being promoted Corporal on 30 August 1918. He contracted influenza during the Spanish Flu pandemic in October 1918 and recovered despite being hospitalised. As he had enlisted for the duration of the war, he was demobilised, being transferred to Class Z Army Reserve on 5 March 1919.

Lance Corporal Frederick George Room VC. (Open source)

At a medical board in January 1919 prior to his discharge, he was assessed as having disordered action of the heart which was aggravated by nervousness, due to being in close proximity to a bomb which exploded having been dropped by a German aeroplane in October 1918. He was assessed as being under 20 per cent disabled and was awarded a weekly pension of 6 shillings. Following discharge from the military, he obtained employment as a lathe machine operator with Brecknell, Munro and Rogers Engineers in Bristol.

On 2 August 1919, he married Ellen Elizabeth Sargent at Bath, Somerset. A modest and very shy man, he shunned the limelight and intensely disliked the publicity which the award brought to him. He remained in poor health throughout the 1920's and died aged 36 on 19 January 1932 at Ham Green Sanatorium, Bristol, after a long illness. He was buried at Greenbank Cemetery, Bristol, in a ceremony attended by the Royal British Legion and the Church Lads Brigade, of which he had been an active member. Frederick and Ellen had no children and Ellen never remarried. She was interred alongside Frederick when she died in 1966.[85]

---

85   Thanks are due to Clive Burlton for additional biographical material in relation to Frederick Room VC.

Lance Corporal Frederick George Room VC Wedding. (David & Jennifer Kingscott)

Further down the medical evacuation chain, the officers and men of 112 Field Ambulance at the Mill, Vlamertinghe, were working flat out:

> 16 Aug Heavy fighting. Cases began to come in about 7:30 a.m. Rush greatest at midday. Practically no cases previously dressed at ADS. First train away at 1:00 p.m. 10 trucks with 14 men in each on palliases. Became very dissatisfied with rate of registration owing to crush in the narrow room. Opened fresh channels giving three passages for 16th, 36th and other troops, this greatly hastened registration. Second train at 3:00 p.m. with 140 cases. Third train at 5:00 p.m. 150 cases. At 6:00 p.m. dismissed Dressing room staff and brought in reduced staff. Was quite clear at 8:00 p.m. and from that only had very rare lorry loads to deal with. Passed through – Officers W 28 OR W 1305 S 54 of those, 16th Div made up 575.[86]

The fact that it was mentioned that few cases were being dressed at the Advanced Dressing Station is indicative of the pressure that these locations were under from continual German shellfire. It was likely thought that moving wounded down the casualty evacuation chain was of greater importance than risking lives by prolonging their stay for treatment in a dangerous environment. The celebrated war correspondent Philip Gibbs subsequently wrote in a best-selling postwar book:

> There was an old mill-house near Vlamertinghe, beyond Goldfish Chateau which was made into a CCS and scores of times when I passed it, I saw it crowded with the walking wounded who had trudged down the fighting line taking 11 hours, 14 hours sometimes to get as far. They were no longer 'cheerful' like the gay lads who came lightly wounded out of the earlier battles, glad of life, excited by their luck. They were silent, shivering, stricken men, boys in age, but old and weary in the knowledge of war. The slime of the battlefields had engulfed them. Their clothes were plastered to their bodies. Their faces and hands were coated with that whitish clay. Their steel hats and rifles were caked with it. Their eyes, brooding, were strangely alive in those corpse like figures of mud, who huddled round charcoal stoves, or sat motionless on wooden forms waiting for ambulances. Yet they were stark in spirit still. 'Only the mud beat us' they said. Man after man said that. 'We should have gone much farther except for the mud.'[87]

Exhausted and catastrophically depleted, by mid afternoon on 16 August, the 16th Division was back at its start position with the exception of a few parties holding on grimly in shell holes in front of resolutely defended pill boxes and bunkers.

An order was subsequently forwarded to XIX Corps by Fifth Army HQ at 2:08 p.m. ordering both divisions to carry out a further advance and establish a line which included the capture of Borry Farm and points across 36th Division's sector.[88] This was not a practical order and showed an ignorance of the situation on the ground due to the depleted strength of 16th Division and as we shall see, 36th Division. The commanding officers of both divisions told Lieutenant

---

86 TNA WO 95/1967/2: 112th Field Ambulance War Diary.
87 Philip Gibbs, *Realities of War* (London: William Heinemann, 1920), p.393.
88 TNA WO 95/960/3: XIX Corps War Diary, Appendix 272.

General Watts at XIX HQ that they were unable to undertake this attack, with General Watts informing Fifth Army accordingly at 8:00 p.m. Comment is made in many of the war diaries of the attacking brigades and battalions as to the reasons for failure. These will be analysed further along with observations from 36th Division units in a following chapter.

7

Thursday, 16 August 1917 36th (Ulster) Division

As with 16th Division, 36th Division attacked with two Infantry brigades in line. The 108th was on the right, the attacking battalions being 9th Royal Irish Fusiliers on the right and 13th Royal Irish Rifles on the left. Their support battalion was 12th Royal Irish Rifles. The 11th Royal Irish Rifles were in reserve.

The final objective for 36th Division was a line from a point just beyond Gallipoli Copse on the Zonnebeke-Langemarck road, to Aviatik Farm. At its farthest, this represented an advance of 2,200 yards or one and a quarter miles. The advance for the 108th Brigade was shortly less than that, at a mile.

The 9th Royal Irish Fusiliers had a number of substantial strongpoints to negotiate to reach their objectives. Hill 35 was so named as it was 35 metres above sea level. Visited by the author in November 2021, it is a gradual rise which would be insignificant, save for the fact that in the low-lying shell-shattered ground, it provided observation and was more importantly, drier ground.

Beyond Hill 35 and at the same height, was a strongpoint known as Gallipoli. This remains a farm of the same name today and at that time was heavily fortified. In front of this strongpoint were numerous belts of barbed wire which were to be dealt with by the Artillery prior to the advance. The Green Line which was the first stage of the advance ran between Hill 35 and Gallipoli.

The method of attack is described in the divisional history of 36th Division:

> Each Brigade was to attack with two battalions in the front line, one in support about 1000 yards in rear and one in reserve in the old British front and support lines. Each battalion was to attack on a two company front in four waves. The second and fourth waves were to be only half the strength of the first and third owing to companies having been reduced for the time being to three platoons. The objective of the leading companies was the line Gallipoli-Schuler Farm, the old Green line of the first offensive, still so-called. On this line the rear companies were to pass through to the final objective, the original leading companies following in close support. The supporting battalions were then to move up and

Hill 35 from Black Line. (Author)

Gallipoli Farm from Hill 35. (Author)

take over the Green Line. A Company from each of the supporting battalions was allotted to the leading two battalions on each brigade as 'moppers up'.[1]

To the right of 9th Royal Irish Fusiliers was the divisional boundary and attacking alongside them were 7th Royal Inniskilling Fusiliers of 16th Division. For the Irish divisions, this was the most vulnerable and problematic area. No matter how much training, familiarisation, and camaraderie existed between the two divisions, they were still separate entities with different methods of operating and these differences were liable to be exacerbated when under severe pressure in the heat of battle.

The start position for both the Fusiliers and the Inniskillings was Pommern Castle, a network of trenches just beyond the Steenbeek. The preparations for the attack did not escape the notice of the Germans who noted on 15 August:

> At late dusk, the 4th Company commander, Leutnant Kötter, observes cigarettes lighting up across no man's land. He identifies strong enemy deployments at *Gartenhof* (Pommern Castle) and *Pfingstmorgengut* (Bank Farm). He sends a detailed report to the battalion and requests destruction fire. At 9:45 p.m. he assists the request with rocket flares. He notifies the 1st, 2nd and 3rd companies. The destruction fire is insufficient and lacklustre. There are few artillery spotters on the frontline. The observations are soon confirmed: at 10:10 p.m. the 1st Company commander, Oberleutnant Weisemann reports that the enemy is readying itself.[2]

The Artillery support for 36th Division was impressive as Falls recorded:

> It was provided by 36th and 61st divisional Artilleries and the 108th and 150th Army Field Artillery Brigades. For the creeping barrage there were 14, 18 pounder batteries giving about one gun to around 20 yards. There were four 18 pounder batteries for distant barrage to search hidden ground and deal with strongpoints beyond the creeping barrage while the six 4.5 howitzer batteries fired 100 yards ahead of the latter, resting on all known strongpoints and MG emplacements. The pace of the barrage was 100 yards in five minutes with a pause of 35 minutes in front of the Green Line. There were three gas shell bombardments prior to the attack, the last being on the night of 15th. For these there was allocated 100 rounds per 18 pounder and 50 rounds per howitzer.[3]

In normal circumstances 100 yards in five minutes seems relatively pedestrian and was predicated on the Artillery bombardment having destroyed all the barbed wire defences and having neutralised the garrisons of the strongpoints. However, the state of the ground had not been factored into the equation which was bound to slow the attackers and had in fact ruled out the support of tanks.

When the attack commenced, the right of the Fusiliers was in touch with the left flank of their sister battalion, 7/8th, of 16th Division and 7th Inniskillings. The 9th battalion attacked

1　Falls, *The History of the 36th (Ulster) Division*, p.114.
2　Jager, *Das K.B.19 Infanterie-Regiment Konig Viktor Emanuel III. Von Italien*, p.376
3　Falls, *The History of the 36th (Ulster) Division*, p.115.

Thursday, 16 August 1917 36th (Ulster) Division 139

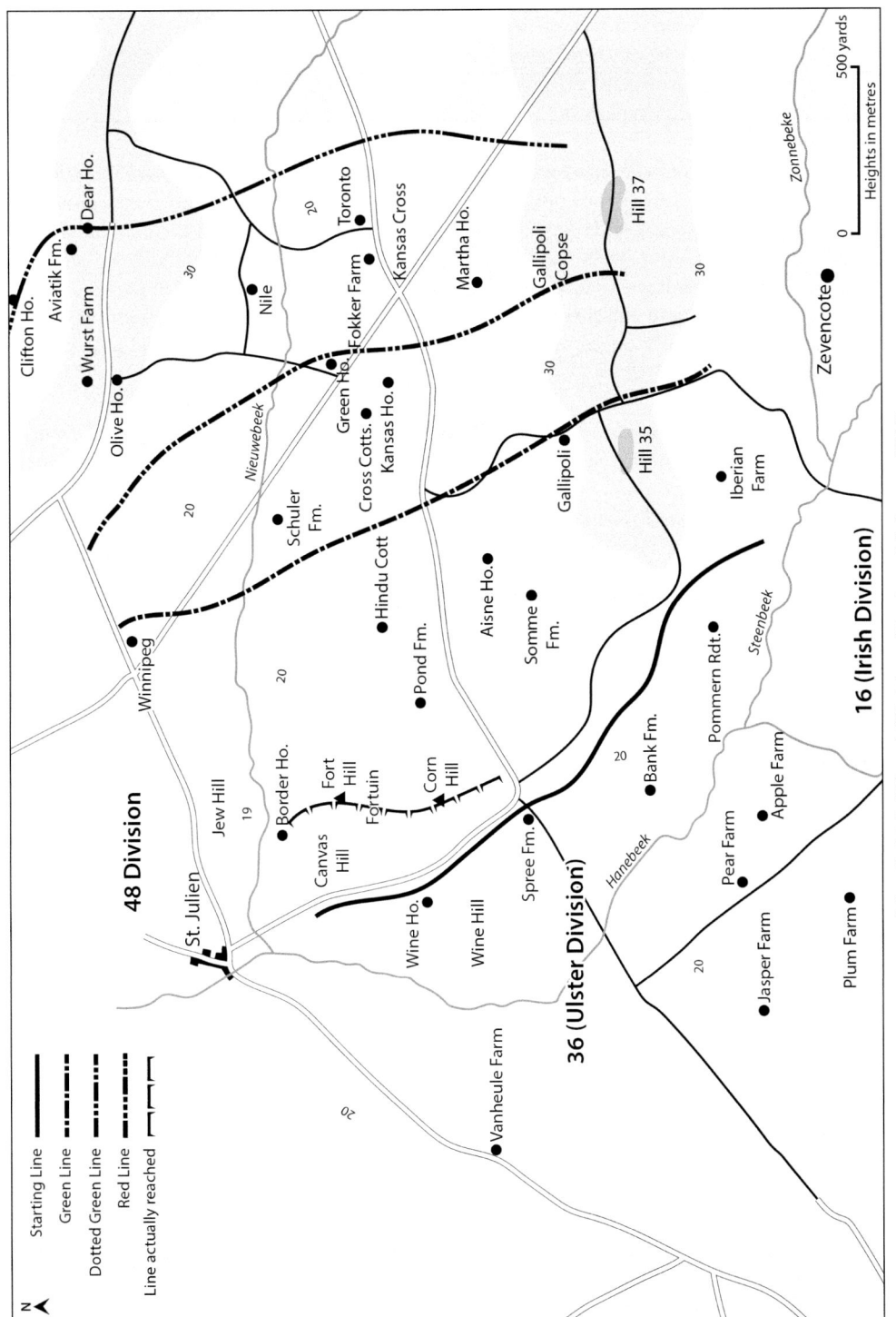

Map 9 36th (Ulster) Division objectives, 16 August 1917.

with A and B companies in front supported by C and D companies. Each company was formed in waves, with each wave in two lines, giving the battalion an attacking force of eight lines. The distance between each line was 10 yards and between waves 100 yards. The battalion war diarist recorded how the advance developed:

> At Zero, waves advanced from assembly positions. The normal position was roughly kept by right attacking and support companies till front wave reached a hastily entrenched position south of strongpoint on Hill 35 where enemy opened fire on us and each Company merged its two waves into one on account of casualties. Before this trench and strongpoint were taken, both companies had merged into one wave. A & C Coys on right had heavy casualties almost at zero and merged into one wave before they had advanced more than 200 yards. Strong opposition was met on Hill 35 which held up the advance for 20 minutes in which time 7/8 RIF had got ahead of us as had the barrage.[4]

It was at this stage that the plan began to disintegrate. As the two divisions were forced to overcome different strongpoints with dissimilar strengths and problems, it was a given that the advance was going to become disjointed. It was immediately obvious to the attackers that the Artillery bombardment had failed to deal with the reinforced concrete pillboxes and bunkers and as a consequence, the creeping barrage raced ahead of the attackers with fatal effects. The war diarist continued:

> When Hill 35 was taken, one Platoon was detached to consolidate it and the remainder pushed on until centre had reached double row of wire S and E of Gallipoli which was only cut in one or two places. This held up the advance. Heavy MG and Rifle fire was brought to bear on us from dugouts in Gallipoli and long range MG fire from the direction of Aisne House, Martha House and Hill 37.[5]

The results of the artillery bombardment on the barbed wire defences at Gallipoli had actually assisted the Germans, as the partial destruction had left gaps which attracted the attacking troops as a means of advancing. The German defenders however, had trained machine guns on these gaps which resulted in carnage.

According to the battalion war diaries of the supporting battalions, the 11th and 12th Royal Irish Rifles, the advance stalled and men began to retire around 6:30 a.m.[6] The 108th Brigade Machine Gun Company war diarist records that the advance appeared to have stalled before 6:00 a.m.

> Zero + 15, W Battery 4 guns placed a standing barrage which lasted until Zero + 70. At that time the guns ceased fire and should have advanced to Gallipoli but on account of the situation, this was not possible.[7]

---

4   TNA WO 95/2505/2: 9th Royal Irish Fusiliers War Diary.
5   TNA WO 95/2505/2: 9th Royal Irish Fusiliers War Diary.
6   TNA WO 95/2505/2: 12th Royal Irish Rifles War Diary and WO 95/2506/1: 11th Royal Irish Rifles War Diary.
7   TNA WO 95/2506/5: 108th Brigade Machine Gun Company War Diary.

In command of C Company, in the second wave of the 9th Royal Irish Fusiliers attack was Lieutenant David Hamilton Wright, aged 28 and from Fahan, County Donegal. He had been an Accountant with the Londonderry and Lough Swilly Railway before enlisting in the Royal Inniskilling Fusiliers. He received a temporary commission in April 1915 and had been with the battalion since December 1916. He was captured during the attack and was imprisoned as a Prisoner of War at Limburg, Karlsruhe and Holzminden before being repatriated in December 1918. In an account of his capture for an Army Board he outlined what happened on 16 August:

> I was in command of the extreme right Coy of our Division and was on the point of organising an attack on an enemy concrete strongpoint from which several guns were in action when I observed that the left flank which apparently also met strong opposition had retired. I endeavoured to get in touch with the officers in charge (by runner) to hold onto the ground gained, as retirement then meant further heavy losses without result. I then withdrew the small force at my disposal a few hundred yards and occuped a more favourable position. The 16th Division on my right had also a few isolated posts in the area. The enemy by this time had launched a heavy counterattack which notwithstanding our vigorous resistance, overran us and we were completely cut off. I put up a defence for a further two hours in the hope that the ground would again be retaken, but was overpowered in an organised bombing attack on our position when the ammunition had run out.[8]

Lieutenant Wright realised the danger of having no support on his left flank and withdrew as he states 'to a more favourable position'. This would have straightened the battalion's line, but made the position of 7th Inniskillings and 7/8th Royal Irish Fusiliers of 16th Division more vulnerable to attack.

If the timings and the above account are correct, the withdrawal started well before the German counterattack developed and was triggered by the failure to overcome the Gallipoli defences.

With many of the leading company's officers killed and wounded, the commanding officer of 9th Royal Irish Fusiliers, Lieutenant Colonel James Stafford Somerville, went forward with a party to Hill 35 to rally his troops and was mortally wounded.[9]

Under heavy machine gun fire, the remnants of the battalion could not advance further and when the German counter attack began they were pushed back to the Black Line by the rapid advance of *Infanterie-Regiment Nr.21*, the reserve battalion of 5th Bavarian Division:

> On the right flank, the 9th Company suffered almost no losses as they crossed the MG fire strewn areas beyond the *Wilhelm-Stellung*. As they rushed forward, they saw the British flooding back and pursued them with rapid fire. The actions of the machine gun platoon under Leutnant König deserve particular merit. Despite the difficult ground conditions and obstacles, the Unteroffizier Hölzel and Gefreiter Walter's guns kept pace with the company, and despite fire coming from the right, they took perfect aim pursuing the fleeing

---

8   TNA WO 339/32232: Lieutenant David Hamilton Wright service record.
9   Lieutenant Colonel Somerville had been CO since March 1917. Commissioned into the Royal Inniskilling Fusiliers in 1890, he had commanded 1st battalion at Gallipoli until wounded there in May 1915. He is buried at Brandhoek New Military Cemetery, No.3. Grave II.F.17.

English. Both men were wounded, Unteroffizier Hölzel took up command of the platoon. The company rushed forward again. Some stubborn English gunners defending from shell craters were taken out with hand grenades. Those who raised their hands in time were taken prisoner. Several Lewis guns fell into our hands.[10]

An impotent observer was Acting Captain Edwin Albert Godson MC of the battalion, who was attached to 108th Infantry Brigade:

16 August, 'Der Tag' again. Hopes ran high. Zero was at 4:45 a.m. too dark to see. First messages were not too hopeful. As soon as it seemed light enough I went out to near Jasper Farm for observation. Saw many men moving on Hill 35 but could not make much of the situation, but at 6:45 a.m. I saw flares lighted on the right near Gallipoli Copse and reported by runner to Bde HQ. Came back afterwards and said that I did not think that the show seemed to be going too well. Went out again about 8:30 a.m. and sometime afterwards saw many of our men coming back and then Germans in the battery position on Hill 35. Things looked bad so I moved up to the front line near Bank Farm. There I found chaos. Battalions all mixed up and back. I went along the line trying to cheer up the men and telling any officers I met that the Black line must be held, there must be no question of going back from there.[11]

The fact that Captain Godson saw flares near Gallipoli Copse is of interest as this is the only indication I have come across that any party of either Irish Division had reached that far. Certainly, no-one came back from there and the fact that this location is beside the heavily fortified Hill 37 which was pinning men from both divisions down may suggest that this was an isolated small party who were later cut off and either killed or captured.

In his excellent, *Blacker's Boys*, Nick Metcalfe records that the battalion went into action on 16 August with a strength of 23 officers and 640 other ranks. They sustained 442 casualties including 139 killed in action – the highest number of fatalities of any battalion in the Ulster Division and indicative of the strength of the German defences and the impenetrable nature of the barbed wire defences around Gallipoli.[12] This equates to a casualty rate of 66 per cent.

The amount of casualties and the condition of the battlefield made the recovery of the wounded a trial. The battalion stretcher bearers worked to exhaustion to recover men whose only chance of survival was to be taken to the rear. The dangers in this work were obvious and one stretcher bearer who was killed was Private Edmund Gray 14201. Aged 27 and from Mullaghglass near Bessbrook, County Armagh, Edmund was a Hackle Maker in the Linen trade. He was also a member of Bessbrook company, Ulster Volunteer Force, and had signed the Ulster Covenant at Bessbrook Orange Hall. He had enlisted in September 1916 and was a stretcher bearer attached to A Company. Private Gray has no known grave and is commemorated on the Tyne Cot Memorial. He is also commemorated on the Roll of Honour at Bessbrook Presbyterian Church.

10 Reber, *Das K.B. 21. Infanterie Regiment*, p.214.
11 IWM: Doc. 10995. Captain Edwin Albert Godson MC Papers.
12 Nick Metcalfe, *Blacker's Boys: 9th (Service) Battalion, Princess Victoria's (Royal Irish Fusiliers) (County Armagh) & 9th (North Irish Horse) Battalion, Princess Victoria's (Royal Irish Fusiliers) 1914-1919*. (Woodstock: Writer's World, 2012), p.143

Another stretcher bearer who fell was 20 years old Private William Proctor 23071, from Albert Place, Armagh. A factory worker, he had enlisted in November 1915. Posted as Missing, William's remains were recovered by 728 Labour (Exhumation) Company in February 1920. The remains were found just in front of Gallipoli and it is likely that William was one of those cut down at the impenetrable barbed wire defences. His remains were interred at Tyne Cot Cemetery, Plot XXV.F.4. Following the battle, his sister received a letter from the battalion Chaplain Reverend Samuel Mayes, who wrote:

> I deeply sympathise with you on the death of your very gallant brother. He was killed while trying to carry in wounded men. I was speaking to him shortly before his death, and although tired and exhausted after a most tiring day, he carried on his work of mercy. You have every right to be proud of the deeds of your gallant brother. May God help you in your time of trial.[13]

Private Edmund Gray. (Christine Tyrell)

Of the 23 officers of the battalion who took part in the attack, 20 became casualties, including six who were killed. One of the six, 21 years old Lieutenant William Graham Boyd also fell at the Gallipoli defences. Born at Ballyjamesduff, County Cavan, where his father was a Presbyterian Minister, William was educated at the Royal Belfast Academical Institution and following the death of his father, was resident at Carrickfergus when he enlisted in the Royal Irish Rifles in April 1915, being commissioned in August of that year and joining the Royal Irish Fusiliers. Initially posted as missing after the battle, enquiries were made as to what had happened to him and statements were taken from witnesses. Serjeant Joshua Pentland 16424 from Tandragee, County Armagh, was Lieutenant Boyd's Platoon Serjeant. He stated:

> That he saw his officer wounded in a shell hole with blood on his head and also appeared to be hit about the stomach. He offered him water, but Lt. Boyd was unable to make any response.[14]

13　Fiona Berry, *Names Carved in Stone* (Armagh: The Mall Presbyterian Church, Armagh, 2016), p.124.
14　TNA WO 339/44470: Lieutenant William Graham Boyd service record. Pentland was captured during the German Spring Offensive of March 1918. He survived the war and subsequently served with the Ulster Special Constabulary.

He further mentioned that Corporal O'Neill was wounded beside the Lieutenant and may be able to give further information.

Corporal Charles Bernard O'Neill 18532, a career soldier from Dublin was subsequently interviewed and reported the following:

> On 16th August 1917 I was in command of No 4 Section, No 5 Platoon, B Company, 9th Royal Irish Fusiliers. Lt. Boyd's Platoon was immediately on my right during the advance. At a strongpoint known as Gallipoli, I regret to state that a shell burst just above our heads and several of us were wounded. I went to where I saw Lt. Boyd laying and found that he was mortally wounded and he died soon after.[15]

Lieutenant Boyd was accepted as having died on 16 August 1917 in February 1918. He has no known grave and is commemorated on the Tyne Cot Memorial to the Missing. His two younger brothers, Thomas and Robert also served with the Regiment.

Two other officers of the battalion who fell are buried alongside each other in Brandhoek New Military Cemetery No 3. Lieutenant James Matthew Stronge, aged 26, was the only son of Sir James Henry Stronge D.L. and Ethel Margaret Stronge of Tynan Abbey, Co. Armagh. James Stronge had married Winifred Alexander, the daughter of Colonel Henry Alexander at Carrickmore, County Tyrone, on 10 July 1917, five weeks before his death. Lieutenant Stronge was the battalion's Transport Officer and by rights should have been far from the action.[16]

Lieutenant William Graham Boyd.
(Great War Ulster Newspaper Archive)

Attached to B Company, Thirty-four years old Second Lieutenant Samuel Levis Trinder was from Innishannon, County Cork. Samuel Trinder had been living in South Africa where he had served in the Natal Light Horse in German South West Africa following the outbreak of war. He returned to the United Kingdom to obtain a commission and joined 9th Battalion Royal Irish Fusiliers in October 1916. Shot in the head and back, Second Lieutenant Trinder died of

---

15 TNA WO 339/44470: Lieutenant William Graham Boyd service record. Corporal O'Neill was himself wounded during the attack. Following convalescence, he rejoined the Battalion and was wounded again in September 1918. He served with the Royal Irish Fusiliers until 1922.
16 TNA WO 339/14288: Lieutenant James Matthew Stronge service record.

Lieutenant James Matthew Stronge Headstone. (Author)

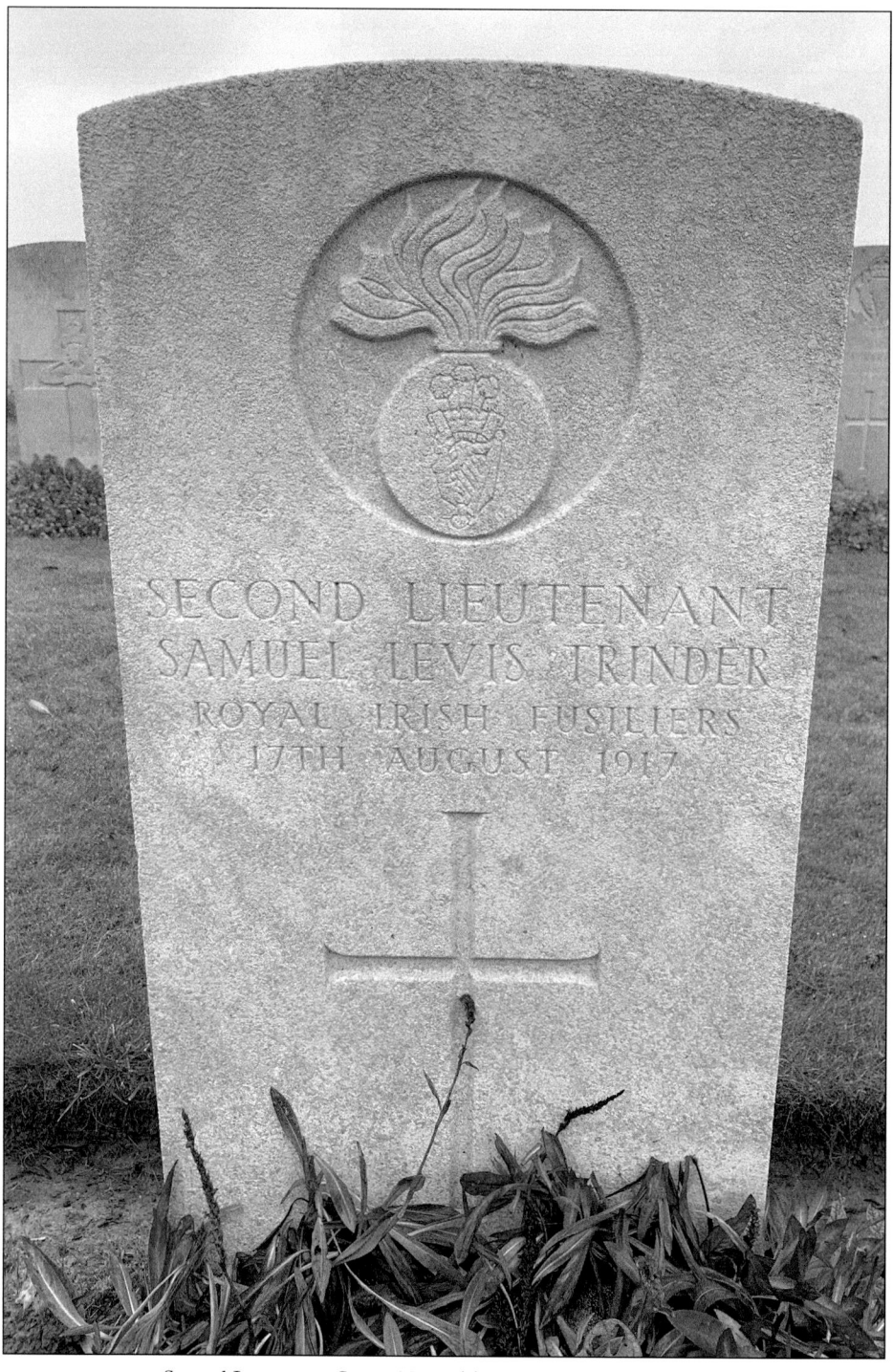

Second Lieutenant Samuel Levis Trinder Headstone. (Author)

wounds at No 44 Casualty Clearing Station, Brandhoek, on 17 August. He is commemorated on the Great War Memorial at St Fin Barre's Cathedral, Cork.[17]

Another officer who died of wounds and is buried in the same cemetery was 19 years old Captain Thomas Graham Shillington who had been commanding A Company. From Portadown, Thomas Shillington had received his commission when only 17. He was wounded in the left thigh and right calf in the advance at the Somme on 1 July 1916 and recovered to rejoin the battalion in December 1916. In the advance on the morning of 16 August, he was shot in the throat and died at No 3 Australian Casualty Clearing Station, Brandhoek, on 18 August. In addition to his burial location, Captain Shillington is commemorated on Portadown War Memorial and on the war memorial at Castle Park School, Dalkey, County Dublin, which he had attended.[18]

Captain Thomas Graham Shillington. (Great War Ulster Newspaper Archive)

Attacking alongside the 9th Royal Irish Fusiliers were 13th Royal Irish Rifles. Attacking in the same formation as 9th Royal Irish Fusiliers with the leading two companies in waves, they initially made good progress and kept up with the creeping barrage until they reached the strongpoint known as Somme, *Wiesengut* to the Germans. A company found themselves being pushed too far to the right due to uncut wire and B company on the left came under heavy attack from Somme where the German defenders of 12th company *Infanterie Regiment Nr.19* put up initial stout resistance:

> The 2nd platoon at *Wiesengut* took position in the trench in front of the bunker and engaged in infantry and machine gun fire. With this, the enemy attack initially came to a halt. Increasing numbers of support troops forced the enemy back against the flank. As the 11th company then retreated and *Wiesengut* came under attack from the left-rear, an evacuation was put in effect. A machine gun in this position was left immobilised.[19]

From the German account, it is obvious that Somme was abandoned by them. It was recaptured in the afternoon. The account of the 13th Royal Irish Rifles indicates that the platoon detailed to consolidate the position, led by Second Lieutenant Trevor Armstrong Phenix failed to do so.[20] However, evidence indicates that Second Lieutenant Armstrong may have been harshly

17 Metcalfe, *Blacker's Boys*, p.143.
18 TNA WO 339/17419: Captain Thomas Graham Shillington service record.
19 Jager, *Das K.B.19 Infanterie-Regiment Konig Viktor Emanuel III. Von Italien*, p.379.
20 TNA: WO 95/2506/3 13th battalion Royal Irish Rifles War Diary.

judged. Aged 18 and from Sydenham, East Belfast, it would appear that his platoon did hold Somme whilst those who had advanced beyond it were halted by an artillery barrage as the Regimental history of *Infanterie Regiment Nr.19* recorded:

> A large section of the enemy sought to get into position again roughly 200 m away. As the company commander knew that our barrage fire lay there, he requested this with signal cartridges. This was effective and rigorous, the English could hold up no longer, all fled; only at *Wiesengut* could 50 enemy troops remain, marooned. Midday proceeded quietly in this position. Gradually, 18 men presented themselves to the company commander 12th company. The company commander now determined to take the concrete dugout *Wiesengut* with these 18 men alone. Four men remained as a support detachment in the company commander's dugout, while the rest advanced toward *Wiesengut* with cries of Hurrah! at 1:45 p.m. which the English men had vacated in their retreat.[21]

The battalion's companies on the left, B & C, suffered heavily from the German bombardment losing two officers, 20 other ranks and a Lewis gun just before Zero and as they advanced, they lost a further two officers and five NCO's within 100 yards.

The advance faltered and halted and in reality did not reach much beyond the fortified bunkers of Somme. The attackers faced withering machine gun fire from Gallipoli to their front right, Aisne House, directly in front beyond Somme, and from Pond Farm and Hindu Cottage to their left. There was simply no way forward as the creeping barrage had long left them behind.

The machine gun support to the battalion from 108th Brigade Machine Gun Company could not assist in making a breakthrough as the war diary recorded:

> The two Guns under Lt. Bles attached to 13 RIR moved forward with the rear wave of the attacking infantry and in the early stages, one gun and the team were destroyed by shell fire. Lt. Bles and four men carried on with the remaining gun but shortly afterwards the four men became casualties and Lt Bles was left on Gallipoli with the gun. He got the gun into action and accounted for a number of the enemy but after being in this isolated position for seven hours he saw the enemy preparing to rush him, so retired after dismantling the gun. He reached the Black Line safely after crawling the whole way.[22]

This account shows the extent to which the 13th Rifles' A Company had been forced to the right, being mixed with 9th Royal Irish Fusiliers at Gallipoli. The officer named was Second Lieutenant Jean-Marie Delacours-Bles, Machine Gun Corps. For his actions in assisting the advance, he was awarded the Military Cross, the citation appearing in *The London Gazette* on 18 October 1917:

> For conspicuous gallantry and devotion to duty when in charge of two guns in an attack. After all his men had become casualties he brought one of his guns into action and engaged a party of the enemy. He remained with his gun until he saw the enemy preparing to rush his position and then he crawled back to our line.[23]

21 Jager, *Das K.B.19 Infanterie-Regiment Konig Viktor Emanuel III. Von Italien*, p.379
22 TNA WO 95/2506/5: 108th Brigade Machine Gun Company War Diary.
23 *London Gazette*, 18 October 1917.

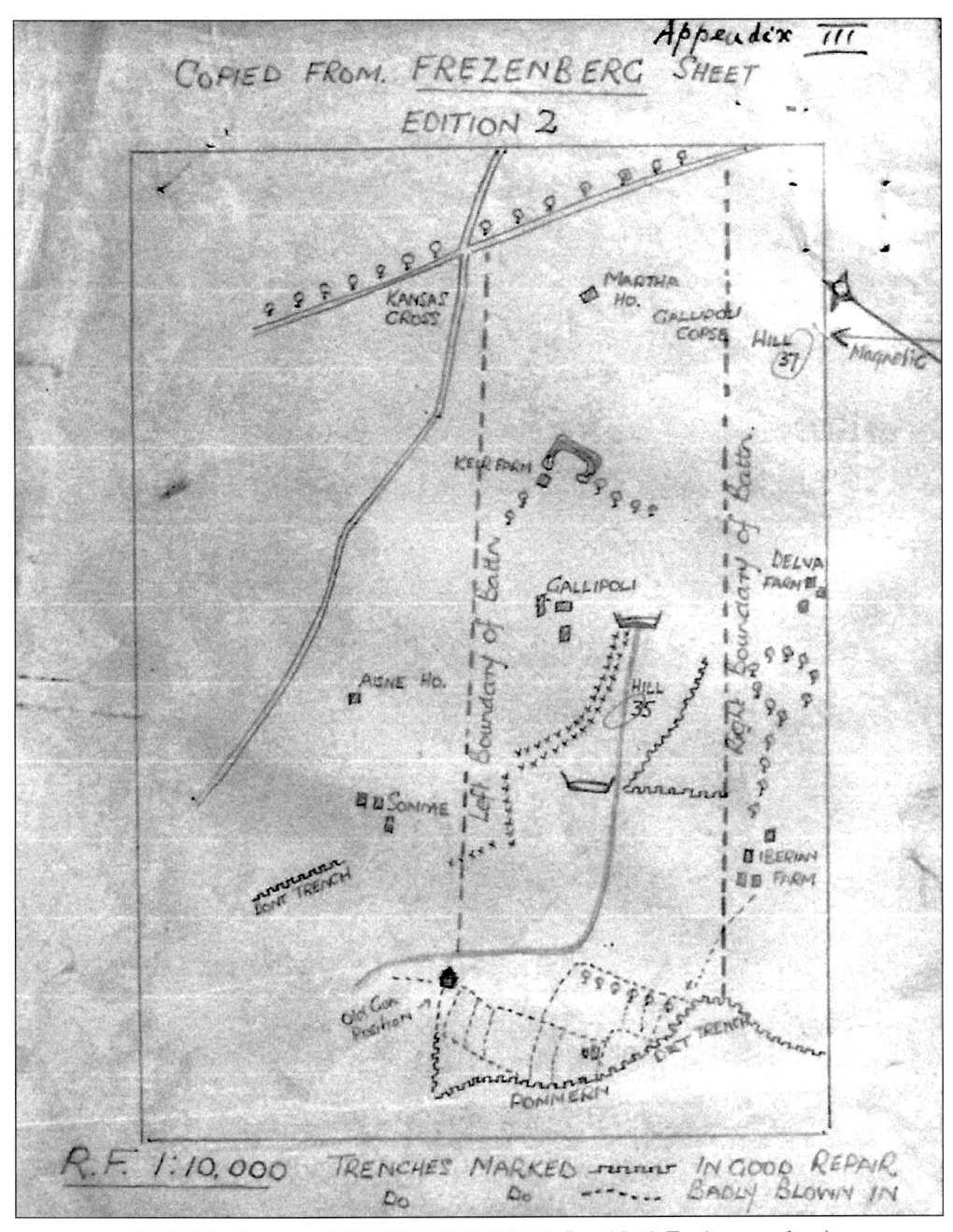

108th Brigade sector. (TNA: WO 95/2505/2 9th Royal Irish Fusiliers war diary)

150　A Bad Day I Fear

Unable to go forward and with many officers and NCO's killed, the battalion began to retire. The battalion war diary states the following:

> Retirement started on the left about Zero plus one hour and on the right, Zero plus 2 hours.[24]

This puts the retirement beginning before 6:00 a.m. and corroborates the view of Lieutenant Wright of 9th Royal Irish Fusiliers who was to the right of the 13th Rifles. In common with the commanding officer of 9th Royal Irish Fusiliers, Lieutenant Colonel Robert David Perceval-Maxwell of 13th Royal Irish Rifles gathered a party from Headquarters and led an advance to regain the initiative. In doing so, he was shot through the left thigh by a machine-gun and five other officers were wounded. Any hopes of making a further advance were lost. During this abortive advance, the 13th Battalion Royal Irish Rifles sustained 305 casualties including 92 killed.[25]

Thirty-two years old Private Paul Lynch from Holborn Street, Sligo, was one of those killed. In 1919 in a battlefield clearance, his remains were discovered just beyond Somme, one of a number of sets of remains found in that area and indicative of the withering machine gun fire which must have cut the Riflemen down. Private Lynch was identified by his identity disc and was interred in Tyne Cot Cemetery, Plot V.H.5. His headstone bears the cryptic inscription, 'ever remembered by A.R.K.'[26] Paul Lynch had enlisted in the Sligo Royal Garrison Artillery as a Boy aged 14, in 1897. He remained with this Militia unit until October 1899 when he enlisted in the Regular Army, joining the Connaught Rangers, regimental number 6751. He served in South Africa being awarded the Queen's South Africa Medal with clasps for Cape Colony and Orange Free State. Following this campaign he was discharged as medically unfit. The 1911 Census of Ireland shows him as resident with his widowed mother, Bridget, at Holborn Street, Sligo. At that time he was employed as a general labourer. At the outbreak of war he enlisted in the East Lancashire Regiment, regimental number 11413 and embarked for the Western Front in January 1915. He later transferred to 13th Royal Irish Rifles with the regimental number 40240.[27]

Of the officers who fell, Second Lieutenant Joseph Laverty was a 30 years old former school principal from Derriaghy, County Antrim. Principal of Castlerobin National School, he had obtained his commission in 1916 and after a short time with the Heavy Branch Machine Gun Corps (the forerunners of the Tank Corps) he was posted to 13th Royal Irish Rifles where he was attached to 108th Trench Mortar Battery. He has no known grave and is commemorated on the Tyne Cot Memorial.

Twenty-seven years old Captain John Nugent Cahill is also commemorated on the Tyne Cot Memorial and on the Kilkenny Great War Memorial. From a military family, he was born at Ballyconra, County Kilkenny, and had been commissioned into the Royal Irish Regiment

24　TNA WO 95/2506/3: 13th Royal Irish Rifles War Diary.
25　Lieutenant Colonel Perceval-Maxwell was from Finnebrogue House, Downpatrick, County Down. He had been prominent in raising 13th Battalion and had been wounded on 1 July 1916.
26　This has been identified as Mrs A R Kerr, Thornhill, Sligo.
27　Private Lynch is commemorated at the soon to be dedicated Sligo Great War Memorial Garden.

Somme Farm from Pond Farm. (Author)

prior to being attached to the 13th Royal Irish Rifles. The following obituary appeared in the *Waterford News*:

> Captain J N Cahill, Royal Irish Regiment (Attached Royal Irish Rifles) was killed in action on 16th August. He was the eldest son of Colonel J N Cahill, Ballyconra, County Kilkenny. Captain Cahill's Colonel writes of him,' He was hit leading his company like the gallant soldier he was. We were all so fond of him and I always considered him as good a company commander as there was…He had trained and led one of the best companies going. We buried him that night at dark and I will get a proper cross put up as soon as possible.' Johnnie Cahill was a great favourite with everyone who knew him. A good all round sportsman, he was a fine rider across the country and was well known with the Kilkenny Hounds and other packs in the South of Ireland.[28]

Captain Cahill's Widow Mary later wrote to War Office enquiring about some of her husband's personal effects with a degree of touching naivety:

---

28 Tom Burnell and the Kilkenny Great War Memorial Committee, *The Kilkenny War Dead* (Kilkenny: Tom Burnell, 2014), p.37.

I have already received two packages by mail and one small registered package by post from Messrs. Cox & Co. quite safely. Very many thanks. But unfortunately there are some of his things missing which I value very, very much. I would be so glad if you could get them for me, perhaps his servant would be able to get them. They are a silver cigarette case with the initials 'JNC' on front, he always carried it with him, and a large silver watch, also a brown canvas holdall (round) with name on. I do not care so much if you cannot find these other things, but I should like more than anything, to get back the silver cigarette case as it is a souvenir. I am sorry for troubling you.[29]

The War Office diplomatically replied:

Owing to the abnormal conditions adhering to active service, delay in the recovery and transmission of such effects is frequently unavoidable, but if any further articles of the late officer's property are at any time forthcoming, they will at once be forwarded to you.[30]

Also killed whilst attached to the battalion was Captain Horace Dorset Eccles, Royal Army Medical Corps. Aged 47, Captain Eccles had been born at Croydon, Surrey. His father was an assistant librarian at the British Library. Horace qualified as a Doctor and emigrated to New Zealand before the turn of the century, practicing at Manganui on the country's North Island. He volunteered for service with the 8th New Zealand Contingent in the Boer War, serving as Surgeon Captain. On return from South Africa, he remained in the Auckland Mounted Rifle Volunteers, rising to the rank of Lieutenant Colonel. At the outbreak of the Great War he attempted to obtain a commission in the New Zealand Expeditionary Force, but was informed that only junior officers were required. Undaunted, he applied for, and was granted leave for the duration of the war. He travelled to England in 1915, and obtained a commission in the Royal Army Medical Corps. Posted to 108th Field Ambulance, he was attached to 13th Royal Irish Rifles as Medical Officer for the attack. Posted as Missing, Captain Eccles' remains were uncovered during battlefield clearance in January 1920. It is a mark of the man that the remains were not found near battalion HQ, but far to the left of the 13th Rifles position, between Pond Farm and Border House. It is possible that he may have gone to the aid of an injured officer of either 13th or 14th Royal Irish Rifles, as the as yet unidentified remains of a Second Lieutenant of the Royal Irish Rifles were uncovered at the same time and from the same location.[31] Captain Eccles now rests at New Irish Farm Cemetery, Plot XVI.C.20. On his headstone is the inscription, 'He gave up all for England, RIP'.

As the support battalion for 108th Brigade, 12th Battalion Royal Irish Rifles had three companies, A, C & D in line behind 13th Royal Irish Rifles and 9th Royal Irish Fusiliers. B Company were to act as 'moppers up'. Battalion Headquarters was at Uhlan Farm, some distance behind the Black Line. The battalion was 460 strong, less than half active service

---

29　TNA WO 339/69114: Captain John Nugent Cahill service record.
30　TNA WO 339/69114: Captain Cahill's younger brother, Acting Captain Patrick Leopold Cahill, was killed in action with the Royal Munster Fusiliers on 21 March 1918.
31　Research indicates that there are five second Lieutenants from these battalions who, to date, remain unidentified.

strength. As the assault commenced, the three support companies moved into the trenches vacated by the attacking battalions. The battalion war diarist recorded:

> No information could be obtained until 6:30 a.m. when it was reported that the infantry were retiring on our left. At 6:45 a.m. Major Connor reported that our left flank appeared to be in the air and our troops had retired to a line behind Somme Farm.[32]

A concerted German counterattack was reported by the battalion at 9:00 a.m. by this time the three supporting companies had become intermingled with the attacking battalions and by 9:30 a.m. were back at the Black Line. One of those retiring was Rifleman Robert McGookin 6548, aged 20 from Larne, County Antrim, and he recorded his experience:

> We had been given the order to retire and were doing so in companies, that is, one company kept up a rapid fire while the other company retired a hundred yards or so, then they kept up a rapid fire to cover the retirement of the company who had done the same for them. When we were ordered to retire, one of the German guns was placed in the open and had already knocked a lot of our lot out. Our Captain snatched a rifle from his servant and shot the gunner, and another man moving forward to take his place received the same medicine from the rifle in the hands of Captain Luce. He shot seven men who went to fire the gun and after that they didn't send any more forward to make a target for the Captain.[33]

The Captain mentioned was Arthur Aston Luce aged 34, who had been born at Gloucester. For his actions on 16 August, he was awarded the Military Cross, the citation reading:

> For conspicuous gallantry and devotion to duty when in command of his company. In spite of very heavy casulaties he held on when the troops on his flanks had retired and the attacking enemy were 300 yards behind his right flank. He killed three of the enemy with his own hand.[34]

Both the 1911 Census and the register from his marriage in 1918, remarkably show that Captain Luce was a Clerk in Holy Orders.

When the Black Line was reached, the conditions were grim as Rifleman McGookin recalled:

> Eventually we completed the retirement to the old German front line from where we had started, but at a part where the trenches were waist deep in water. The trench I was in contained four dead bodies, floating backwards and forwards in the water and men were running over the top of them, it was a ghastly sight.[35]

32　TNA WO 95/2506/2: 12th Royal Irish Rifles War Diary.
33　Catherine Minford et al, *It Wasn't All Sunshine: An Ordinary Man's Account of the First World War* (Larne: Larne Borough Council, 2012), p.90.
34　*The London Gazette* 7 March 1918. Captain Luce was discharged with the Silver War Badge in January 1919 and resided in Dublin until his death aged 95 in 1977.
35　Catherine Minford, et al, *It Wasn't All Sunshine*, p.90.

Here consolidation took place and the battalion assisted in holding this line until relieved at 2:30 a.m. on 17 August.

For their part, the men of *Infantrie Regiment Nr.21* were pleased at how their counterattack had progressed:

> A bit further to the left, a concrete house is being cleared out. The Tommys are being led out, one after the other, and are immediately assigned as stretcher-bearers. They are not ham-handed and set about their work willingly. We inform the battalion commander of where we met the I. and II. battalions. A status report from the III. battalion is written for the regiment. It is urgent. An English officer was found crouching in a marshy hollow. His round, watery blue eyes and his freshly shaved face gave away his astonishment at how quickly everything had happened. We take him with us. He is a little tubby and tries his hardest to keep up with us. We are in a hurry, however, and cannot wait. Tired out, but nowhere near as dripping with sweat as our gentleman companion now was, we came upon the Headquarters. A few minutes later, the brigade was able to communicate news of the successful counterattack. Gripped by victorious joy, the Regiment savoured the feeling of triumph over the English infantry as they had done following the Fresnoy assault. Our loot amounted to some three officers and 157 prisoners of the 36th Division. Several German machine guns had been recovered. As far as prisoner statements can be believed, it is apparent that the Englishmen had not gone into the attack with very high hopes. Already during the advance, the Englishmen had shouted to severely wounded German soldiers that they should stay calm since a German counterattack would soon be on its way.[36]

The 12th Royal Irish Rifles involvement in the advance cost them 171 casualties, 26 of whom were killed.

One of those killed was 27 years old Rifleman William John Watson 19298 from Ballymena, County Antrim. William was employed at the Braidwater Spinning Mill, Ballymena, prior to enlisting and had signed the Ulster Covenant opposing Home Rule for Ireland at the Protestant Hall, Ballymena, on 28 September 1912. William embarked for France on 5 October 1915 and was wounded in the right arm at the Battle of the Somme in 1916. Before returning to active service, he spent a period with 18th (Reserve) Battalion Royal Irish Rifles at Clandeboye Camp, County Down. Whilst there, he completed his Will in favour of his father, Robert. In common with many of his comrades, William has no known grave and is commemorated on the Tyne Cot Memorial to the Missing and also on the Ballymena War Memorial.

Another commemorated on the Tyne Cot Memorial is Second Lieutenant James Alexander Patterson Bill. Aged 21, he had been born at Edinburgh, but was resident at University Street, Belfast, and a student when he enlisted in the Royal Army Medical Corps in December 1915. He remained with the RAMC until August 1916 when he transferred to the Royal Irish Rifles and received his commission in January 1917. Initially reported as wounded and missing, enquiries were made to establish his fate which resulted in the following report:

---

36   Reber, *Das K.B. 21. Infanterie Regiment,* p.217.

This officer was last seen about D.19.b.10.90. He was lying on the ground apparently wounded in the groin or lower abdomen. Rfm. Matthews went out to dress him but was killed in the act of doing so, and it is supposed that the same bullet also hit Mr Bill.[37] The men had by this time started coming back and Mr Bill was left behind apparently severely wounded.[38]

Rifleman William John Watson. (Will. National Archives Ireland)

The report, made by Second Lieutenant Stokes of the battalion is open to speculation as to its accuracy however, it would appear that no further enquiries were made and the status of Second Lieutenant Bill was changed to 'missing believed killed' on 22 August. From the location given above, it would appear that Second Lieutenant Bill was wounded between Somme and Hill 35 and had been following the attack of 9th Royal Irish Fusiliers.

A wounded officer who was more fortunate was Second Lieutenant William Abraham Hayden. Aged 27 and from Ashley Avenue, Belfast, pre-war he had been an assistant in a wholesale drapery business. He was initially posted as 'missing believed killed', most likely on receipt of the following report from Second Lieutenant Montgomery:

> I was with 2nd Lt. Hayden when he was wounded. We were on the crest of Hill 35 at the time. He was struck in three places by machine-gun bullets, the jaw, neck and left side of the back. I bandaged his wounds and had to go forward leaving him in a shell hole. I did not see him again. He was conscious at the time, but compained of intense pain in his back.[39]

Remarkably, Second Lieutenant Hayden survived. Recovered from the battlefield by the Germans, his injuries were treated and it was found that he was shot in the left lung. Following treatment, he was detained as a Prisoner of War at Limburg and Furstenburg.

---

37 The only fatality attached to the battalion named Matthews is Rfm. Thomas Matthews 203 and he is recorded by the CWGC as having been killed on 15 August.
38 TNA WO 339/83449: Second Lieutenant James Alexander Patterson Bill service record.
39 TNA WO 339/83449: Second Lieutenant James Alexander Patterson Bill service record.

Repatriated following the Armistice, he emigrated to the United States in 1921, residing in San Francisco and gaining employment as a Wholesale Dry Goods Salesman. He married, became a naturalised United States citizen, and died at San Francisco in 1950.

The reserve battalion of 108th Brigade, was 11th Royal Irish Rifles. At Zero hour they moved forward in the rear of 12th Royal Irish Rifles. They had only three companies with which to advance, A, B, and D, as C company had ceased to exist due to gas casualties sustained whilst holding the line in the days leading up to the advance.

The battalion war diary recorded the experience of the three companies following 12th Royal Irish Rifles:

> 4:45 a.m, Barrage fire opened and A and D Companies advanced from assembly positions. B Coy followed D. 6:40 a.m. Attack reported held up on our front. Battalions retiring on Black Line. 7:35 a.m. Bn Hq ordered to proceed to Black Line to reorganise front line.[40]

The commanding officer, Lieutenant Colonel Philip Laurence Kington Blair-Oliphant DSO faced a daunting task, especially as the war diary further recorded:

> 8:55 a.m. Troops seen retiring in large numbers over Hill 35. Retirement of Bn's on flanks noticed.
> 9:10 a.m. Adjutant proceeded to Uhlan Farm to inform 108th Bde of situation which was reported as follows: Troops falling back on Black Line and some not halting at that line.[41]

Fortunately, Lieutenant Colonel Blair-Oliphant was able to bring some stability to the situation and the Black Line was consolidated utilising the remnants of the attacking battalions.

On 16 August, the battalion had 18 men killed. One who has a known resting place is 17 years old Rifleman James McKinney 3742. Born in 1900, James spent his early years at Ballymena Workhouse and by aged 11, was boarding with the Hollinger family at Ahoghill, County Antrim. He enlisted in the Royal Irish Rifles at Randalstown and joined 11th Royal Irish Rifles in France on 8 December 1915. James was killed in the advance on 16 August and his remains were recovered in September 1919. Recovered from his remains were a knife and a letter which enabled him to be positively identified. Interestingly, his remains were recovered to the left and beyond Somme, near Aisne house, indicating how spread out the attackers had become. Rifleman McKinney is buried at Tyne Cot Cemetery, Plot VII.B.1. He left the balance of his pay and allowances to the Hollinger family who had cared for him.

Buried at Ypres Reservoir Cemetery is 21 years old Second Lieutenant Joseph Hamilton Millar Andrews. From Templemore Park, Londonderry, he had been a hardware assistant when he enlisted in the Royal Irish Rifles in May 1915 being posted to 17th (Reserve) battalion. Andrews was commissioned the following October. Initially reported as 'missing believed

---

40 TNA WO 95/2506/1: 11th Royal Irish Rifles War Diary.
41 TNA: WO 95/2506/1: 11th Royal Irish Rifles War Diary.

Rifleman James McKinney gravesite. (Author)

158   A Bad Day I Fear

killed', enquiries were made to establish his fate. A report was received from a Rifleman Horner 2235, D company 11th Royal Irish Rifles who had also been wounded:

> Lt Andrews was killed at the dressing station, he had been shot through both arms. He was taking shelter in a shell hole when he was hit, but I did not see him get hit. I saw him fetched away by stretcher bearers about half an hour afterwards. There was machine gun fire all around us and we had to keep low and could not get near one another. The dressing station had cellars, some of the cases were left outside as there was not room inside till the ambulances fetched them away. Lt. Andrews was outside when the shell fell.[42]

In September 1921, Second Lieutenant Andrew's remains were recovered from the battlefield and identified by his identity disc. The location of the recovery casts doubt on the above account as the remains were recovered between Somme and Hill 35, far in advance of any Dressing Station locations. He is buried at Ypres Reservoir Cemetery, Plot X1.B.21. and is commemorated on the War Memorial at the Diamond, Londonderry.

On the left of the 36th Divisonal Front were 109th Infantry Brigade. They assembled for the attack with 14th Royal Irish Rifles on the right and 11th Royal Inniskilling Fusiliers on the left. A company of 9th Royal Inniskilling Fusiliers were detailed as 'moppers up' behind the attacking battalions, with the remainder of 9th Inniskillings further to the rear as support. The 10th Royal Inniskilling Fusiliers were in reserve, further to the rear.

The headquarters of 14th Royal Irish Rifles were at Spree Farm which was located at a junction on the Wieltje-St Julien road. The 14th Rifles were well within range of the German strongpoint at Somme however, directly in front of them was a complex of bunkers and pillboxes centred on Pond Farm which was a major German headquarters facility housing a large medical bunker.

The author met the current owner of Pond Farm, Mr Stijn Butaye, in November 2021.[43] He confirmed that the hospital bunker (now buried) was in excess of 40 metres long. To give some idea of the task facing the 14th Rifles, he also confirmed that between Spree Farm and Schuler Farm were 38 concrete pillboxes and bunkers. Some were small, giving cover to two men and others were larger shielding a team of men armed with one or more machine guns. He also stated that the ground between his farm and Spree farm was marshy and prone to flooding even in normal circumstances.

One bunker remains in the farmyard (known as *Haeseler*) and is testament to construction techniques of 106 years ago.

Beyond Pond Farm was Hindu Cottage, which was another strongpoint, garrisoned by machine guns.

Situated at a junction, Spree Farm was a natural target for the German artillery. As it had been constructed by the Germans, its location was known exactly and it was heavily shelled on the night of 15/16 August. The battalion war diary recorded the preparations for the advance:

---

42   TNA WO 339/45662: Second Lieutenant Joseph Hamilton Millar Andrews service record.
43   Mr Butaye is a Great War enthusiast and has an excellent museum on his farm containing many items recovered from his land. It is well worth a visit. See *Pondfarm* <www.depondfarm.be>

Haeseler Bunker at Pond Farm. (Author)

We were relieved about 1:00 a.m. by the 9th Inniskillings and moved to our forward HQ Post in Capricorn Trench. No casualties on the way up but things very hot. Arrived in trench to find it blocked with everybody. HQ took shelter in a slit trench behind the parados, things not so bad later so made our way to the dugout. Company Officers reported for final instructions and left about 3:00 a.m. to get their men into position.[44]

The German counter bombardment increased in intensity around 4:00 a.m. and before Zero, a direct hit on a dugout at Spree Farm had horrendous consequences:

> 4 am heavy bombardment on our line, one direct hit on our dugout, killed six and wounded many. Dugout full of wounded, can only bandage a few of them as we have no more dressings. Their suffering is terrible and we cannot move.[45]

It is believed that most of the casualties were from the 109th Brigade Trench Mortar Battery which drew men from each of the battalions in the Brigade. They were to play a vital role in the advance as the 109th Brigade war diary outlined:

---

44 TNA WO 95/2511/2: 14th Royal Irish Rifles War Diary.
45 TNA WO 95/2511/2: 14th Royal Irish Rifles War Diary.

Two Stokes Mortars will be employed in the advance, the remainder of the 109th T.M. Battery's efforts will be devoted to supplying these mortars with ammunition. The two Mortars will follow immediately in rear of the support battalion and will take up position in both Assaulting Battalion Sectors on the Dotted Green Line. The role of these Mortars is mainly defensive, but OC Detachments will look out for any opportunity of assisting any part of the line held up by a Strongpoint, and the positions selected in the Dotted Green Line should be such that the barrage could be put down in front of the Dotted Red Line, in case our line of advanced posts on the red line is penetrated by the enemy.[46]

Corporal Jim Donaghy of 10th Inniskillings had luckily been on leave for the battle and discovered the fate of his friends on his return:

> When I got back I found that nearly all my friends in the Trench Mortar Battery had been killed when one of the captured German dugouts they were in exploded. Over half the battery were killed including most of the officers.[47]

One of the officers referred to by Corporal Donaghy was Second Lieutenant Alexander Henry McCullagh. Aged 20, he had been born at Tullow, County Carlow, where his father was a School Principal. In December 1915, the family was resident at Upper Ballinderry, Lurgan, County Armagh, when Alexander enlisted in the Royal Irish Fusiliers, being posted to 10th (Reserve) battalion. He applied for a commission in April 1916 and following training with an Officer Cadet battalion at The Curragh, received a commission in the Inniskillings in January 1917. He was one of a draft of eight officers who joined the 11th Inniskillings on 7 August, nine days before his death, and was attached to the Trench Mortar Battery. Alexander's family received a

Second Lieutenant Alexander McCullagh. (Great War Ulster Newspaper Archive)

---

46 TNA WO 95/2509/1: 109th Brigade War Diary.
47 Gardiner Mitchell, *Three Cheers for the Derry's* (Londonderry: YES publications, 1991), p.141.

Second Lieutenant Alexander McCullagh gravesite. (Author)

telegram indicating that he was wounded and missing on 21 August 1917. On 4 October 1917, they received a further telegram stating that he had been killed on 16 August. It was not until October 1919 that Second Lieutenant McCullagh's remains were recovered in the vicinity of Spree Farm. He was identified from a cheque found in his possession.[48] He now rests at New Irish Farm Cemetery, Plot VII.D.9.

Also attached to the Trench Mortar Battery was Private William Brown, aged 20 from Brookeborough, Co Fermanagh. William had enlisted in the Royal Inniskilling Fusiliers in November 1915 and had been posted to 11th battalion. He had arrived in France in early 1916. At the Battle of the Somme, William was a stretcher bearer and was mentioned in the battalion war diary for his exemplary work. He had been posted to the Trench Mortar Battery early in 1917. News of his death came in a letter to his mother, Charlotte, from the Presbyterian Chaplain to 10th Inniskillings, Reverend James Gilbert Paton:[49]

> I am sorry to have to tell you of the death of your son 27583 Pte W J Brown of 109 TMB on 16/8/17. He was in the big battle of that date when he was killed. He will probably be reported missing believed killed, but it would be cruel to ask you to hope as the dugout in which he was sitting was either smashed by a shell or blown up by a mine. I am Chaplain to the 10th R. In. Fus. but the TMB was under my care and so I knew them all well. Your boy was a good boy and a brave soldier and had won the respect and esteem of his officers and men who all desire to extend to you their heartfelt sympathy. I pray that God will comfort and sustain you in your hour of sorrow.[50]

Private Brown has no known grave and is commemorated on The Tyne Cot Memorial and also on the Brookeborough War Memorial.[51]

Following the explosion which so decimated the Trench Mortar Battery, Reverend Paton was obviously a busy man. The mother of 25 years old Private Harry McIlroy 23187, also of

Private William Brown. (Peter Johnston)

---

48 TNA WO 339/67935: Second Lieutenant Alexander Henry McCullagh service record.
49 Reverend James Gilbert Paton was born in Scotland in 1883. By the Armistice he was the holder of the Military Cross and two bars. Paton died at Belfast in 1936.
50 Original correspondence held by Brown family and used with their permission.
51 Also commemorated on that memorial is William's uncle, Sergeant William John Brown 730, 1st Battalion Royal Inniskilling Fusiliers who died of Enteric Fever (Typhoid) at Ladysmith, South Africa on 21 April 1900 whilst on active service during the Second Anglo-Boer War.

11th Inniskillings, received exactly the same letter. From Cullybackey, County Antrim, Harry McIlroy had worked in the Maine Linen works at Cullybackey prior to enlisting and was also a member of the Orange Order and Ulster Volunteer Force. He had been wounded in March 1916 and again on 29 June 1916 when he was shot in the leg. He is also commemorated on the Tyne Cot Memorial to the Missing.

It is also believed that the Regimental Serjeant Major of 14th Royal Irish Rifles, Frederick Jacquest, may have been seriously wounded in this incident. Aged 35 and from Bromley, Kent, Frederick Jacquest had served with the Grenadier Guards from the late 1890's, before transferring to the Royal Irish Rifles in 1914. He died of his wounds on 17 August and is buried at Lijssenthoek Military Cemetery, Plot XVII.H.1.

The advance of the 14th Rifles mirrored that of many of the other battalions, an orderly advance until they met withering machine gun fire from reinforced concrete bunkers and pill boxes. The battalion war diary gave a very downbeat assessment:

> 5:45 a.m. Sergeant McIlveen just arrived with a message from Lt. Ledlie, D Company, that he was held up by MG Fire from Pond Farm and wanted support up. Support cannot be found. They have melted into the blue somewhere but certainly not out in front. Reports from the wounded that many of our brave officers have gone down, some killed, some wounded, and that the men are holding on.[52]

This diary entry was further elaborated on by Falls in the postwar divisional history:

> On the right, 14th Rifles had to cross ground far worse than even the ordinary, completely under water in fact. In their passage they came under withering machine-gun fire from Pond Farm. Lieutenant Ledlie made a fine attempt to capture this place surrounding it on three sides with the few men remaining to him when he reached it and killing any Germans who showed themselves. With his numbers so greatly depleted, he waited for support before making an attempt to rush it, sending back two messages, but no support came, the men could not face the machine gun fire. They had already suffered greatly from the Artillery barrage which the leading waves had avoided. At 8.00 am seeing that his position was hopeless, he withdrew his men 150 yards covering his retirement with Lewis Gun fire.[53]

James Crawford St John Ledlie, had been promoted to Acting Captain on 20 July. Born at Cork in 1885, he was a member of a family prominent in the Drapery business, Robertson Ledlie Ferguson, who owned department stores in many of the major cities in Ireland.[54] He was commissioned into the Special Reserve of the Royal Dublin Fusiliers on July 1915 and was posted to the 14th Royal Irish Rifles in July 1916.

For his actions on 16 August, Acting Captain Ledlie was awarded the Military Cross, the citation stating:

---

52 TNA WO 95/2511/2: 14th Royal Irish Rifles War Diary.
53 Falls, *The History of the 36th (Ulster) Division*, p.117.
54 This included the Bank Buildings in Belfast where James worked before the war.

RSM Frederick Jacquest gravesite. (Author)

For conspicuous gallantry and devotion to duty. He led his company in the attack in the most gallant manner and held his ground with a handful of men when others were forced back. He collected scattered men and established a party in a strongpoint which held up the enemy's advance. By his example and leadership he encouraged his exhausted men and held his post until relieved.[55]

Acting Captain Ledlie dug in at a feature known as Corn Hill in front of the Black Line and received much needed supplies and a few reinforcements to enable him to maintain his position.

The position at Corn Hill was the farthest forward that 14th Royal Irish Rifles were able to consolidate and that was only 120 yards in front of the Black Line. The battalion war diary gave a gloomy assessment of the day's fighting:

General report from 8 am – During the whole day, the Boche never ceased his bombardment on our line. We had to shift our HQ as we could not live in it. News came dribbling in that we were having heavy casualties and wanted reinforcing, but reinforcements could not be found. Towards afternoon we found the 11th Inniskillings holding an advanced post at Corn Hill which we visited and found that Lt Ledlie was digging himself in first in front of this place and wanted help – we sent him all we could and stores. We then took up our position in the forward line as it was the only safe place. Received instructions that 8th RIR are to relieve us at night – everyone delighted as we are done up. About 9 pm, Lt Reddy sent up an SOS as the Boche were coming to the attack. Our artillery opened after a considerable pause and both sides started to it. We stood to in our trench and were prepared for it, but we must have broken up his assembly as he did not come on. It was a weary wait in the line as we did not know what was coming next, All arrangements made to hand over to the 8th Rifles and as many wounded as we could find cleared before dark. This was the worst part of the whole business as we had no advanced Aid Posts left, shell fire having demolished most of them. The wounded had to be carried long distances and several medical officers were knocked out. Many plucky things have been done today and men risked their lives over and over again to bring in wounded. The whole thing has been a miserable failure for reasons which are obvious to us all. Our men did all that was asked of them, but the peculiar attitude of the enemy and his methods were not appreciated by the powers that be. Our Divisional and Brigade staff did everything that was humanly possible as we know from past experience how well they look ahead and the splendid system they work on. Even for all our losses and failure our confidence is not shaken in our Division and the aim and object of us all is to bring back to our men the splendid fighting spirit which we have always had. We went into this battle knowing that things were not right, and that spirit is fatal, but all round us the signs were very clear and we could not blame either officer or men. They did their best and from our point of view could have done no more. We went into action with 19 officers and 480 men. Our casualties were 10 officers and 222 men.[56]

---

55 *The Edinburgh Gazette*, 11 March 1918.
56 TNA WO 95/2511/2: 14th Royal Irish Rifles War Diary.

The Commonwealth War Graves Commission records that 103 men from the battalion were killed on 16 August or, as with RSM Jacquest, died of wounds the following day. This is a casualty rate of just over 46 per cent, not the highest of the attacking battalions however, the fatality rate of just over 20 percent of those who went into battle puts them on a par with 9th Royal Irish Fusiliers who had a similar percentage killed.

Of the 103 who died, only 24 have a known grave and the fate of 19 years old Rifleman Robert John Brooks 47053, is indicative of that of many of the fallen of 14th battalion. From Princes Risborough, Buckinghamshire, Robert was the eldest son of Frederick and Ada Brooks. He had enlisted in the Rifle Brigade, regimental number S/28948, and had transferred to 14th Royal Irish Rifles as part of a large draft in February 1917. Initially posted as missing, his mother applied for and was granted a Dependant's Pension of five shillings per week in November 1918. In a battlefield clearance, his remains were found in January 1920. The map reference of the discovery of his remains shows that he fell directly in front of Pond Farm. He now rests at New Irish Farm Cemetery, Plot XIX.A.19 and is also commemorated at Princes Risborough, where the Market House and clock are dedicated as the town war memorial.

One of the majority from the battalion who fell and who are commemorated on the Tyne Cot Memorial to the Missing, was 26 years old Second Lieutenant Samuel Hugh Walker from Belfast. Born near Donaghcloney, County Down, his father, also named Samuel, was a cambric weaver, a specialist in the Linen industry. By the outbreak of war, the family was resident at Dee Street, East Belfast, and Samuel was a Methodist Minister having served at Pettigo, which sits on what is now the border between County Fermanagh and County Donegal. Samuel resigned from the Ministry and enlisted in the 16th Royal Irish Rifles (Pioneers) as a private soldier in January 1915. He embarked for France with them in October 1915 and by March 1916 had attained the rank of Serjeant. He obtained a commission in September 1916 and was posted to 14th Royal Irish Rifles.

No 3 Company of 9th Royal Inniskilling Fusiliers followed the initial advance of 14th Royal Irish Rifles. They acquitted themselves well however, were also forced to retire as the war diary records:

> No 3 Coy, at 12:20 on the morning of the 16th moved out from Liverpool Trench to support the 14th RIR. They came under heavy shell fire whilst going along the Wieltje–Gravenstafel Road. When reaching the Black Line, the Company took up the position behind the right Coy of the 14th RIR and moving out to the attack in support of the attack in support of the Bn. The Coy had just got clear of the Black Line, when the enemy SOS went up and a heavy enemy barrage came down. The Company advanced in perfect order maintaining a distance of 50 yards between the attacking waves of 14th RIR and penetrated the enemy defence system about 700 yards. At this juncture, red and green lights were sent up from enemy strong points in front, and a heavy machine gun barrage coming from these strong points and being heavily enfiladed, the Coy had to take cover in shell holes. From this position it could be seen that the troops on our right were retiring. Some minutes later the attacking waves of 14th Royal Irish Rifles were compelled to retire against a heavy counterattack launched by the enemy who were gradually working round the right flank of the Company. The Company had to retire to Capricorn Trench on the Black Line, passing through very heavy machine gun fire. During the retirement the Company became slightly disorganised but were formed up on the Black Line and advanced again about 250 yards

and occupied a strongpoint opposite Pond Farm and held on until relieved by a Coy of 10th Inniskillings.[57]

The strongpoint described was most likely around that consolidated by 14th Royal Irish Rifles at Corn Hill as there was no cover from the right from any other units for a position closer to Pond Farm.

The 11th Inniskillings were positioned on the far left of the divisional front. To their left were 1/5th Gloucestershire Regiment of 145th Brigade, 48th (South Midland) Division. Disaster was to strike the Inniskillings before the advance even began. At around 12:30 a.m. the commanding officer, Lieutenant Colonel Audley Charles Pratt DSO, was exiting the battalion headquarters at the Wieltje dugouts with other officers when a shell landed beside them, mortally wounding Lieutenant Colonel Pratt. He died 15 minutes later and command of the battalion passed to Major John Espenett Knott DSO.[58] In a letter to his wife following the battle, Major General Nugent described what transpired:

> Audley Pratt was killed just as he came out of the dugout where he had been to see his Brigadier. The one shell fell about 10 paces from him and a big piece went through him. He would have known nothing about it, poor old Audley.[59]

Lieutenant Colonel Pratt had been born on 13 May 1874 in County Cavan, and had been commissioned into the Royal Scots Regiment in December 1895, a regiment with whom he served until 1913. Attached to the Reserve of Officers at the outbreak of war, he was recalled to duty and served with 9th Royal Irish Fusiliers, becoming the battalion second in command in November 1914. He became commanding officer of 11th Inniskillings in August 1916 and was awarded the Distinguished Service Order in January 1917. He had been wounded at the Battle of Messines in June 1917.

At the time of his wounding, Lieutenant Colonel Pratt had been standing talking to the commanding officer 9th Inniskillings, Lieutenant Colonel Warren John Richard Peacocke DSO and Bar. Remarkably, he escaped apparently unscathed. Lieutenant Colonel Pratt was initially buried near Wieltje Dugouts however, in a graves consolidation process in July 1919, his remains were exhumed and reinterred at Ypres Reservoir Cemetery, Plot IV.E.23

The 11th Inniskilling's frontage was about four hundred yards. In the leading wave, A company were on the right and D company on the left. B company were behind A, and C behind B. Each of the leading companies had two platoons in line and one in support. The objective of the two leading companies was the Green Line which they were to capture, mop up and hold while the two support companies were to pass through them to the dotted Red Line which they were to capture and consolidate. Companies A and D having consolidated the Green Line, were then to join them. The attack was supported by two machine gun teams from 109th Brigade Machine Gun Company who were to accompany the attacking troops.

---

57 TNA WO 95/2510/3: 9th Royal Inniskilling Fusiliers War Diary
58 Major Knott had been born in Lancashire, and had been a Farmer in County Meath before the war. He initially served as a Trooper with the South Irish Horse before receiving a commission in the Royal Inniskilling Fusiliers in November 1914.
59 Perry (ed.) *Major General Oliver Nugent and the Ulster Division 1915-1918*, p.169.

Lieutenant Colonel Audley Pratt gravesite. (Author)

To the front right of the Inniskillings were the strongpoints of Pond Farm and Hindu Cottage and straight ahead and beyond these was Schuler Farm. To the left and nearly opposite Pond Farm was a formidable complex of bunkers known as Border House (*Prinzenhof*).[60]

In addition to the cover provided by the creeping barrage, the attackers were covered by barrage fire from the remaining guns of 109th Brigade machine gun company. In the circumstances though, this was not as effective as had been hoped, as the war diary recorded:

> At Zero, 12 barrage guns opened at a rate of a belt of 250 rounds per five minutes and eventually slowed to a belt per 10 minutes, a rate of 1765 rounds per hour. The rate of fire was slow as there was not sufficient men to fill the belts. After about 10 minutes a heavy barrage of 5.9 HE was put down by the Germans, this became so heavy at Zero + 15 that it was impossible to continue the fire.[61]

The advance of 11th Inniskillings and their supporting parties resulted in the only ground gained by any of the battalions of either 16th or 36th divisions. The battalion war diarist observed:

> Assembly of the supporting Coys was carried out without serious interference. Heavy shelling was experienced from 1:00 a.m to 2:30 a.m. by the left front Coy.(D). All the battalion HQ Signaller's apparatus, less a Lucas lamp was destroyed by shell fire before zero. Barrage commenced at Zero – 4:45 a.m. and on lifting, Coys at once advanced in good order but were inevitably interfered with by the state of the ground. The right front Coy (A) were met by MG fire from their left front, presumably Caserne and was considerably reduced. An officer and 8 men managed to reach 13.a.30.35 [mid way between Pond farm and Hindu cottage] but were finally held up by heavy MG fire from D.13.a.60.75 [Schuler Farm]. A messenger sent back giving their position was killed and as this party were in the air and unable to move, they retired at night. Some uncut wire was encountered 50 yards N of Corn Hill which caused some delay. The right supporting Coy encountered the same obstacles as the front Coy and by this time were under fire from both Pond Farm and Caserne, Jew Hill and Winnipeg. This Coy was finally held up on a line, C.18.b.37 to C.18.b.64 [Fort Hill/Fortuin/Corn Hill]. Subsequently connection was made with the left and this company assisted in consolidation of Fort Hill which commands all ground to a good all round field of fire. The left front Coy (D) encountered severe opposition from Fort Hill (Caserne) and were held up for some time until they finally stormed it. By this time however, our barrage was 1500 yards away from our troops. While D Coy were thus engaged, the left support Coy endeavoured to push on. Some of their men however became involved in the attack on Caserne and the remainder under the Coy Commander having reached C.18.b.42.53 [Mid way between Pond Farm and Border House] were finally held up by enfilade fire from Pond Farm – 20 strong. The Coy Commander was then killed and a few of the survivors crawled back.[62]

---

60 Mr Stijn Butaye of Pond Farm owns the ground where Border House was situated. One of the many bunkers there measures 60 metres by five metres.
61 TNA WO 95/2511/2: 109th Brigade Machine Gun Company War Diary.
62 TNA WO 95/2510/5: 11th Royal Inniskilling Fusiliers War Diary.

At its farthest, just short of Border House, the greatest extent of ground gained by both divisions was 400 yards.

The modest gains were hard won. In the advance, the battalion had 95 men killed. In common with all of the other battalions who advanced that day, the vast majority of those killed have no known grave. Of the 95, 15 or just over 15 per cent have an identified resting place, with the remainder of the fallen being commemorated on the Tyne Cot Memorial to the Missing.

Further research into the above war diary entry has elicited some further details of the fallen. Mapping of the locations of those whose remains were recovered from the battlefield shows a group of four men, all NCO'S, whose remains were recovered in the vicinity of Hindu Cottage. Of the fifteen whose remains have been recovered, these four are the furthest forward from the Black line and may have been part of the group mentioned in the above diary entry, 'An officer and 8 men managed to reach 13.a.30.35 [mid-way between Pond farm and Hindu cottage] but were finally held up by heavy MG fire from D.13.a.60.75 [Schuler Farm]. The four were:

> Corporal George Machin Twissell aged 36 from Nottingham. George Twissell was married with two children and was employed as a railway clerk pre-war. He had served with the 11th Battalion Sherwood Foresters, regimental number 30418, before transferring to the Inniskillings. His wife had died in 1916 and following George's death, his children were cared for by a Guardian. Following the recovery of his remains, Corporal Twissell was interred at Tyne Cot cemetery, Plot VI.E.12.[63]
>
> Corporal John Dinsmore 14458, was aged 29 and from Shantallow, Londonderry. Born at Carnamoyle, County Donegal, he was married and a father of four. His remains were recovered in October 1918 along with those of Corporal Twissell. In his Will he left all his possessions to his wife, Annie, who was also granted a Dependant's Pension of 30 shillings per week. Corporal Dinsmore is buried at Tyne Cot cemetery, Plot VII.A.4. He is also commemorated on the Roll of Honour at Ballyarnett Presbyterian Church, Londonderry.[64]
>
> Lance Serjeant Robert James Leslie was aged 30 and had been born in Cork where his father was a fish merchant. Prior to the war, he had moved to Dublin and was employed as a brewer's labourer at the Guinness Brewery. At the time of his marriage in May 1915, Robert was already a Corporal in 9th Royal Inniskilling Fusiliers, giving rise to the possibility that he may have been a member of the Loyal Dublin Volunteers, an anti Home Rule organisation, closely affiliated to the Ulster Volunteer Force.[65] Lance Serjeant Leslie's remains were recovered in October 1919 and he was identified from

---

63 Corporal Twissell is also commemorated on the Midland Railway Company Employees War Memorial at Nottingham Railway Station and on the War Memorial at All Souls Church, Radford. His eldest child, Private Arthur Leslie Twissell 44304, 1st Battalion Leicestershire Regiment died aged 18 of Peritonitis at The Curragh Military Hospital on 25 August 1920 and is interred at The Curragh Military Cemetery.

64 Corporal John Dinsmore's name does not appear on the Londonderry War Memorial at the Diamond in the city. A staunch Loyalist, Corporal Dinsmore's youngest son was named Edward Carson Dinsmore.

65 The stated objective of the Loyal Dublin Volunteers was to 'protect the civil and religious liberties of Protestants in Dublin and the south.' A party from the LDV enlisted en masse in the 9th Inniskillings in September 1914 before assignment to C company.

his spoon which bore his service number. He is buried at Tyne Cot Cemetery, Plot VII.A.7. His sacrifice is also commemorated on the war memorial at St Fin Barre's Cathedral, Cork, and on the Guinness Brewery Roll of Honour, Dublin.

Corporal George Speers Clarke 14149 aged 23 was from Ballintra, County Donegal, where his father was a grocer and publican. George had signed the Ulster Covenant opposing Home Rule for Ireland at Ballintra Orange Hall in September 1912 and had enlisted in the Inniskillings at Finner Camp, Ballyshannon, County Donegal. Attached to B company, he had embarked with 11th Inniskillings for the Western Front in October 1915 and had been wounded in March 1916. His remains were recovered in September 1919 and he was identified by his identity disc. He was interred at Tyne Cot Cemetery, Plot VII.C.12.

One whose grave is unknown is Lance Corporal William George Rutledge 28728, also attached to B company. As the advance progressed, B Company followed A on the right of the battalion front. The company commander saw that some men were veering too far to the right, into 14th Battalion Royal Irish Rifles area. Lance Corporal Rutledge ran forward to alert the men and in doing so fell, mortally wounded by machine gun fire.[66] Aged 21 and from Manorhamilton, County Leitrim, where his father was a grocer and farmer, William had joined the battalion in France in early 1916. Five days after his death, on 21 August 1917, he was posthumously awarded the Military Medal for gallantry at the Battle of Messines in June 1917 when he carried wounded men to safety under heavy fire. The medal was presented to his father by Judge Brown at Manorhamilton Quarter Sessions in April 1918. A report was carried in *The Impartial Reporter*, covering the Judge's comments:

> It is a privilege for me to have been invited by the authorities to present to you, Mr Rutledge, this Military Medal gained by your gallant son when he saved wounded men under heavy shell fire in June 1917, and when he attracted the admiration of his whole battalion. Later on 16th August 1917, he lost his life in a hail of machine-gun fire, starting out to save his comrades and nobly doing his duty. So, he doubly won this medal. He showed fortitude, contempt for danger and devotion to duty. What can any man do more? He joined the forces of his country to face the cruellest foe of humanity, and gave his life for his native land. I now present this medal to you, which you will keep as an enduring momento of a devoted and gallant son, who fell when saving the lives of his comrades.[67]

Lance Corporal Rutledge MM is commemorated on the Tyne Cot Memorial to the Missing.

The battalion war diary refers to C company, the support company on the left, as assisting D Company at Fort Hill, but also pushing through them to attempt continue the advance before being halted by enfilade fire at a point between Pond Farm and Border House. At this location the company commander was killed and the few survivors were forced to retire. The company

---

66 William Canning, *Ballyshannon, Belcoo, Bertincourt: The History of the 11th Battalion the Royal Inniskilling Fusiliers (Donegal and Fermanagh Volunteers) in World War One* (Antrim: Canning,1996), p.112.
67 The Inniskillings Museum, *The Fermanagh War Memorial Book of Honour 1914-1921* (Enniskillen: Inniskillings Museum, 2014), p.464.

> HE whom this scroll commemorates was numbered among those who, at the call of King and Country, left all that was dear to them, endured hardness, faced danger, and finally passed out of the sight of men by the path of duty and self-sacrifice, giving up their own lives that others might live in freedom. Let those who come after see to it that his name be not forgotten.
>
> L/Cpl. George Rutledge
> Royal Inniskilling Fusiliers

Memorial scroll for Lance Corporal Rutledge. (Inniskillings Museum) commander was Captain Samuel Fluke. Born at Aughnacloy, County Tyrone, in 1874, Captain Fluke was a vastly experienced soldier. He had enlisted in the Royal Irish Fusiliers in 1893 and whilst serving with the Regiment's 2nd battalion in South Africa in 1901, was promoted in the field to Serjeant by the then General Lord Kitchener, for gallant conduct at Machadodorp. He was also awarded the Distinguished Conduct Medal for the same action.[68] He continued to serve with the Royal Irish Fusiliers until discharged in January 1915 and then enlisted with the Royal Inniskilling Fusiliers and continued in the rank of Company Serjeant Major. He was wounded in April 1916 and later received a commission in that year and was posted to 11th battalion. With no known grave, Captain Fluke is also commemorated on the Tyne Cot Memorial to the Missing. He was posthumously Mentioned in Despatches in December 1917.[69]

The 9th Royal Inniskilling Fusiliers were the support battalion to 11th Inniskillings and 14th Royal Irish Rifles. Their No 1 and 2 company's followed the Inniskilling's advance whilst No 3 company followed 14th Royal Irish Rifles. Their No 4 Company was delegated the task of mopping up and of carrying forward much needed supplies.

No 1 company of 9th Inniskillings advanced behind D Company 11th Inniskillings. The battalion war diary gives detail of the advance:

> The attack commenced at 4:45 a.m. and No 1 Coy moved up in support of 11th Inniskillings in artillery formation. Heavily shelled but no casualties sustained. The Company not being affected by the shellfire opened out into line. The ground which was pitted with shell holes hampered the advance and the rapidity of our own barrage left the Company exposed to heavy machine gun fire which was the means of holding them up. The Company dug in. At this juncture the Coy Commander, Lt ALC Wintle was wounded and very shortly after received a second wound which proved fatal. 2nd Lt Irwin became separated from the Coy and collecting a number of men moved forward and occupied trenches and dugouts near Border House. It was here whilst acting in a gallant manner, the brave officer was killed.[70]

The company commander, Lieutenant Armar Lowry-Corry Wintle was 20 years of age. Born in Peshawar, India, his father was Colonel in the 87th Punjabis and the family home was at Bray, County Wicklow. Educated at the Army School, Maidenhead, and Imperial Service College, Windsor, he received a commission in the Royal Inniskilling Fusiliers and embarked for France with the battalion in October 1915. He received a gunshot wound to the forehead on St Patrick's Day 1916 and following convalescence, rejoined the battalion in April 1917. Wounded twice in the advance, he was treated at No 14 General Hospital, Wimereux, and succumbed to his wounds there on 22 August, being buried at Wimereux Communal Cemetery Plot IV.O.1. He had been acting in the rank of Captain since 20 July 1917. Major General Nugent wrote personally to his mother, stating:

68　Samuel Fluke was also Mentioned in Despatches by Field Marshal Lord Roberts in April 1901.
69　Samuel's son Samuel George Fluke associated with IRA members and was arrested in London during the IRA Bombing campaign of 1939-40. For further details see, Joseph McKenna, *The IRA Bombing Campaign against Britain 1939-1940* (Jefferson: McFarland & Co., 2016), *passim*.
70　TNA WO 95/2510/3: 9th Royal Inniskilling Fusiliers War Diary.

He showed the greatest courage and gallantry and even after he had been wounded once insisted in carrying on, until he fell, mortally wounded. I have recommended him for a Military Cross which he richly deserves.[71]

The award of the Military Cross was gazetted on 11 March 1918.[72] A fellow officer wrote to his father, stating:

I must tell you how proud I am of his conduct before and during the battle. His men were greatly encouraged by his bravery and courage and he has added new laurels to a name well known for it's soldierly deeds, and I can assure that his death is keenly felt by us all. Even when mortally wounded he would not allow the men to carry him in fearing harm should come to them in doing so and remained out until it was dark, as the place was swept by enemy machine gun fire.[73]

The other officer mentioned in the war diary was Second Lieutenant Joseph Frederick (Fred) Irwin MM. Aged 30 and from Limavady, County Londonderry, he had been a draper's assistant at Messrs Irvine & Company, Ferryquay Street, Londonderry, pre-war. Fred Irwin enlisted in the 10th Royal Inniskilling Fusiliers (Derry Volunteers) at their formation in the city in September 1914. He embarked for the Western Front with the battalion in October 1915 and was promoted to the rank of Company Serjeant Major in July 1916. In December of that year he was awarded the Military Medal for gallantry in the field and following attendance at Cadet School, received a commission as a Second Lieutenant in April 1917. Following a battlefield clearance his remains were recovered from behind the Black Line close to Spree Farm, indicating that he may have been seriously wounded and taken back from Border House and succumbed to his wounds behind the front line. He was reinterred in New Irish Farm Cemetery, Plot XV.A.16 and is commemorated on the War Memorial at the Diamond, Londonderry.

No 2 Company of 9th Royal Inniskilling Fusiliers had a more problematic time as the battalion war diarist wrote:

Second Lieutenant Fred Irwin MM. (Ancestry)

---

71 William Canning, *A Wheen of Medals: The History of the 9th (Service) battalion Royal Inniskilling Fusiliers (The Tyrones) in World War One* (Antrim: Canning, 2006), p. 141.
72 *Edinburgh Gazette*, 11 March 1918, p. 954.
73 Canning, *A Wheen of Medals*, p.141.

Second Lieutenant Fred Irwin MM gravesite. (Author)

> No 2 Coy moved out to the attack with No 1 Coy in support of 11th Inniskillings. Owing to the heavy enemy barrage, the Coy lost direction and was obliged to take cover before reaching the Black Line. The Black Line being safely reached the 11th Inniskillings moved out to the attack at Zero. No 2 Coy followed in support but were caught in a heavy Bosche barrage and suffered numerous casualties. Our barrage being too quick, the Coy got mixed up with the attacking waves of 11th Inniskillings. After advancing 200 yards, they came under heavy MG fire from Pond Farm and several strongpoints on their left which held them up. Not being able to advance further on account of the heavy MG barrage. The Company commenced to consolidate on the old trench which ran NNW of Border House. The Coy held this post all day until relieved.[74]

From this account, No 2 Company provided much needed assistance to 11th Inniskilling's A company in securing the ground gained near Border House.

No 4 company of 9th Inniskillings acted as 'mopper's up' and as carrying parties for both attacking battalions of 109th Brigade. They advanced with both 14th Battalion Royal Irish Rifles and 11th Battalion Royal Inniskilling Fusiliers and assisted in the progress made until they too were held up by heavy machine gun fire and were forced to retire and consolidate what gains had been made.

During the advance of 16 August, 9th Inniskillings had 34 men killed. Of those, only six have a known grave with the remainder being commemorated on the Tyne Cot Memorial to the Missing.

The reserve battalion of 109th Infantry Brigade were the 10th Battalion Royal Inniskilling Fusiliers. They spent the eve of the battle in preparation with kit being checked and rations issued, which included chocolate and lemons.[75] A service was also held by the battalion Chaplain, Reverend Paton, and in the evening they moved up to the assembly trenches 800 yards west of Wieltje.

The role of the battalion was to move up and consolidate the Black Line as the other battalions advanced. The battalion war diary recorded the events of the day:

> Zero 4:45 a.m. All companies reported they were on the move. A, B and D Coys to allotted positions in the Black line. C Coy to remain as carrying party. 30 minutes later all reported passing over Old front line. 5:50 a.m. Bde ordered Bn HQ to move forward to Spree Farm which was reached at 6:55 a.m. On arrival, from statements of wounded it was found enemy had held up leading battalion round Pond Farm and the Bde on our right we could see were being driven off Hill 35. This was reported to Bde by runner and orders were received to organize Black line and hold at all costs. This was carried out, most of the men being pushed forward into old trenches in front of Black line which was fortunate as the enemy put down a continuous barrage on dugouts in Black Line during the day. 2nd Lt RB McConnell went forward with his Lewis Gun to help 14 RIR hold and clear point 66 East of Spree Farm and held it all day. Bn relieved during the night by 8 RIR relief being completed by 5:50 a.m.

---

74 TNA WO 95/2510/3 9th Royal Inniskilling Fusiliers War Diary.
75 TNA WO 95/2510/4 10th Royal Inniskilling Fusiliers War Diary.

17 Aug. All ranks behaved with the greatest coolness during a trying time and there were many acts of heroism in attending to wounded, carrying messages etc.[76]

The officer named was Second Lieutenant Robert Brooks McConnell. Aged 21, he had been born at Mountjoy Prison Cottages, Dublin, his father being a master carpenter instructor at Mountjoy Prison. By 1911, the family had moved to Belfast and were resident at Rosewood Street off the Crumlin Road, Robert's father being employed at Crumlin Road Prison. Aged 15, Robert signed the Ulster Covenant opposing Home Rule for Ireland at the City Hall, Belfast, on 28 September 1912. For his actions on 16 August, he was awarded the Military Cross, the citation stating:

> For conspicuous gallantry and devotion to duty. When in command of a Platoon of a reserve battalion, he went forward with his Lewis Gun team to help the leading battalion clear out and man a strongpoint where he remained well in advance all day and most of the following night until relieved, setting a splendid example to his men.[77]

Second Lieutenant McConnell later transferred to the Inniskilling's 1st Battalion and was captured during the German Spring Offensive, March 1918, spending the remainder of the war as a prisoner of war.[78]

In the assault of 16 August, the 10th Inniskillings had 18 men killed, with only five having a known grave. Of those five, the remains of three were recovered close to Spree Farm during battlefield clearance in September 1919, they are:

Private James McClintock 29938, aged 22, was the son of Alexander and Sarah Jane McClintock from Ardagh, St Johnston, Co. Donegal. He is buried at New Irish Farm cemetery grave IV.A.18. Resident in Londonderry at the time he enlisted, his remains were identified by a letter with his address at College Terrace in the city. His parents arranged for the inscription, ' Gave his life for his country and his King. Asleep in Jesus' to be placed on his headstone.

Private William McFawn 15833, aged 23 and from Fountain Place, Londonderry. Attached to B company, he is also buried at New Irish Farm cemetery, grave IV.E.2. Also commemorated on the War Memorial at the Diamond, Londonderry.

Private Alexander Anderson 15285, aged 24, was the only son of Robert and Bella Anderson from Castleroe, near Coleraine. He had been an agricultural labourer prior to enlisting. He is buried at New Irish Farm Cemetery, grave IV.A.10.

One officer was amongst the dead. He was Second Lieutenant Harold Thorne Speares aged 20, from Rathdrum, County Wicklow, where his father was the Clerk of Petty Sessions. Harold had enlisted in the Royal Fusiliers in May 1915 and had embarked for France in October 1915 attached to the 12th (Service) battalion. He was wounded with a gunshot wound to the right leg in April 1916 and whilst convalescing, applied for a commission. He attended Officer Cadet School at Gailes, Ayrshire, and received his commission in September 1916. He has no known

---

76 TNA WO 95/2510/4 10th Royal Inniskilling Fusiliers War Diary.
77 *The London Gazette* 18 October 1917.
78 Robert's younger brother, Samuel, was a Major in 1st Inniskillings and was killed in Burma in April 1942.

grave and like many others, is commemorated on the Tyne Cot Memorial to the Missing and on the County Wicklow War Memorial at Woodenbridge.

A common theme in all of the accounts of the advance from both divisions was the difficulty experienced by the advancing troops in keeping direction as they advanced. This was exacerbated by the atrocious ground conditions and the formidable machine gun fire from the German bunkers and strongpoints. A valuable account which highlights this exists from Second Lieutenant Edward Campion Vaughan of 1/8th Royal Warwickshire Regiment. His battalion, part of 143rd (Warwickshire) Brigade were supporting 145th (South Midland) Brigade a battalion of which, the 1/5th Gloucestershire Regiment, were to the left of 11th Inniskillings.

According to the battalion war diary, after the advance commenced and due to the lack of clarity of the situation, the battalion HQ was moved back and forwards across the Steenbeek three times, eventually positioning itself at Wine House, which was clearly in the 36th Division's area of operations.[79]

Second Lieutenant Vaughan approached the front line from Van Heule Farm and was ordered to take his Platoon and occupy Border House, which was on the boundary between 48th and 36th divisions and was causing great problems through frontal and enfilade fire for 11th Inniskillings and their supporting battalions. He advanced under heavy shellfire which caused many casualties and reached the Steenbeek where he met with what appears to have been a Headquarters party of 14th Royal Irish Rifles, including a Major and a Padre. This indicates that he must have veered far to the right into 36th Division's area. His account continues:

> The Major told me that he was CO of that battalion of Irish Rifles and that they were not advancing any further. He also told me to move my men further away so that we should not be confused. So I took my platoon off to the left and lined the bank, standing in mud up to our knees. We had now entirely lost touch with the rest of the company.[80]

Fortunately for Second Lieutenant Vaughan, he was able to regain contact with his Company and saw the remainder of the battle through uninjured.

The Pioneer battalion of 36th Division, the 16th Royal Irish Rifles had a frustrating day. As the advance began, a party were able to run identifying stakes and markers out towards Hill 35, but this party quickly became involved in a fighting withdrawal along with 9th Royal Irish Fusiliers and 13th Royal Irish Rifles. The remainder of the Pioneers were unable to carry out any meaningful work due to the effective German machine gun fire and as the scale of the withdrawal became apparent, they were ordered back to Ypres. Around 70 men from the battalion performed outstanding duty as stretcher bearers in arduous and exhausting conditions.

The battalion history drew an adverse parallel between the Battle of Langemarck and the Battle of Messines from the Pioneers point of view:

> The battle had not been as meticulously prepared as the Battle of Messines. As far as the pioneers were concerned, they were to operate over ground which they had not seen before, nor had they much time to prepare for the anticipated tasks in the way they had done before

---

79 TNA WO 95/2756/2: 1/8th Royal Warwickshire Regiment War Diary.
80 Vaughan, *Some Desperate Glory*, p.197.

Messines. In addition, because the 36 (Ulster) Division was in reserve and not intended to be committed in the early stages of the battle, the 16th Rifles had been placed initially under the orders of the Chief Engineer XIX Corps. From the Pioneer point of view, this could not have been the ideal way to start a battle.[81]

For similar reasons to those of 16th Rifles, there was little for the Royal Engineer companies attached to 36th Division to do. Both 121st and 122nd Field Companies were largely redundant and spent most of the day standing by unused. The 150th company however were involved in the action. Two Sections, No's 3 and 4 were attached to 109th Brigade. No 4 Section came under severe shell fire as they approached Spree Farm and only four men were left unwounded largely rendering them ineffective. No 3 Section under the command of Second Lieutenant Alan Noel Cam were attached to 11th Inniskillings and made a valiant attempt to assist in securing the advances that they had made:

> No 3 Section under 2nd Lt Cam went forward to 11th Inniskillings at Wieltje dugouts and there waited to go forward… No 3 Section left Wieltje and went forward with Major Knott CO 11th Inniskillings to advanced Bn Hq at Wine House. Lt Cam went forward with the CO and it was decided to consolidate Fort Hill, just south of Border House. Lt Cam came back to get the section and attached infantry out of a shelter trench near Wine Ho. and proceeded to lead them forward near Border House. They ran into MG Fire and Lt Cam was killed around 9:00 a.m. The section tried to get forward but the fire was too heavy and after several attempts was abandoned at 11 am and section returned to Bde HQ at Wieltje.[82]

Second Lieutenant Cam was aged 22 and from Paulerspury, Northamptonshire, where his father was the Church of England Rector. The only son in a family of seven children, he had enlisted as a sapper in the Royal Naval Division Engineers in September 1914, serving at Gallipoli from March until November 1915 when he was medically evacuated to Alexandria, suffering from pyrexia, or trench fever. On his return to the United Kingdom, he applied for a commission, being appointed Second Lieutenant in December 1916. On 3 August 1917, Second Lieutenant Cam had been wounded, but remained on duty. He has no known grave and is commemorated on the Tyne Cot Memorial to the Missing. He is also commemorated at Paulerspury War Memorial, on Dragon School War Memorial, Oxfordshire, and on the memorial plaque at the Institute of Electrical Engineers, Embankment, London.

The Artillery support to the Division fell short of what was anticipated, particularly in relation to the creeping barrage. This situation was realised before the battle commenced and was commented on by members of two of the Artillery Brigades. Lieutenant Colonel Claud Potter, commanding officer of 153rd Brigade Royal Field Artillery commented after the battle:

> I think our heavy artillery preparation was insufficient and the concrete dugouts containing machine guns were not done in. Barrage came down beautifully at zero hour. Hun retaliation

---

81　Stuart White, *The Terrors: 16th (Pioneer) battalion Royal Irish Rifles* (Belfast: Somme Association, 1996), p. 163.
82　TNA WO 95/2497/3: 150th Field Company Royal Engineers War Diary.

was very rapid but not particularly heavy. I saw our fellows get Hill 35 apparently going strong under our barrage. An hour later saw then come streaming back from Somme and Gallipoli, the Hun reoccupying the Hill at under 3000 yards range, the whole thing very plain through glasses. In afternoon observation very good and could see Hun moving about everywhere. In morning, saw their reinforcements marching down from Passchendaele Ridge and along Hill 35 from Zonnebeke direction. Infantry lost very heavily, probably 50-60 per cent nearly all from MG's. Back areas little strafed and we got off very lightly. A total of six wounded only. A bad day I fear.[83]

The 108th Army Field Artillery Brigade war diarist corroborated the claim over the failure to neutralise the machine-gun bunkers and strongpoints:

> The attack was not a success. The infantry 108th and the 109th Bdes suffered heavy casualties and were forced to retire to the *Stutzpunkt* or Black Line, the line from which they had advanced. Failure to maintain any of their objectives and their subsequent retreat was due to heavy MG fire which prevented the infantry from keeping up to the barrage and this could not be stopped owing to all lines of communication being cut. In consequence, the Bde did not move to its forward positions as per programme.[84]

The simple fact was that the infantry had to deal with each of the strongpoints individually as they advanced. This was costly in terms of time and manpower and meant that the creeping barrage soon left them behind to deal with the bunkers and strongpoints without Artillery cover. This indicates a failure to appreciate the reality of the situation on the ground in formulating the plan of attack. This will be analysed further in the next chapter.

Given the nature of what transpired, the officers and men of the Royal Army Medical Corps were always going to be busy. The battalion war diary entry of 108th Field Ambulance based at Red Farm is by necessity, brief: '16 August, Division attacked. Casualties heavy, busy day and night.'[85] As previously mentioned, the unit's Captain Horace Dorset Eccles, attached to 13th Royal Irish Rifles, was killed.

The 109th Field Ambulance were based in appalling conditions at Wieltje Mine Shaft. Sergeant Robert McKay recalled the events of 16 August in his diary:

> The 36th (Ulster) Division attacked this morning at 5:00 a.m. Owing to the state of the ground, tanks were unable to move…The infantry took a few pill-boxes and a line or two of trenches from the enemy, but at a fearful cost. It is only murder attempting to advance against these pillboxes over such ground. Any number of men fall down wounded and are either smothered in the mud, or drowned in the holes of water before succour can reach them. We have been working continually now since 13th inst. And resulting from the renewal of the attack, more wounded are coming down than any day since I came up. Wounds are nearly all bad. The Stretcher Bearers are done up completely. Owing to the constant walking in the mud towards the line and then in the water in the mine shaft,

---

83   John Potter, *Scarce Heard Amid the Guns* (Belfast: Northern Ireland War Memorial, 2013), p.114.
84   TNA WO 95/456/3: 108th Army Field Artillery Brigade War Diary.
85   TNA WO 95/2499/1: 108th Field Ambulance RAMC War Diary.

many of the men's feet are swollen and blistered and if one takes off his boots, he finds it almost impossible to get them on again. Luckily the weather is warm indeed, down in the mine shaft the heat is oppressive owing to bad ventilation. The 109th Field Ambulance has suffered many casualties here. Today the enemy put a shell through the door of a pillbox, killing practically all inside. Cpl Greenwood, Private Barrett and Private McCormick were all killed. The enemy have nothing but pillboxes on this front. As soon as the infantry capture one they find themselves faced by another.[86]

The Field Ambulance war diary for 16 August records 76 wounded being treated on that date, far outnumbered by those sick at 149. The following day however, 89 sick cases were treated as opposed to 882 wounded. These figures are indicative of the serious difficulties the walking wounded had in returning from the battlefield and that the stretcher bearers had in retrieving non ambulant cases.

Sergeant McKay's account highlights another problem which faced the attacking troops. Once a pillbox had been captured, it could be utilised however, the doors all were in full view of the Germans and, as they had built them, they had the exact coordinates of each, which the German Artillery made full use of. The three men identified by Sergeant McKay as having been killed at Bank Farm were all from Belfast and two were holders of the Military Medal. All three are commemorated on the Tyne Cot Memorial to the Missing.

Corporal John Edwin Greenwood MM was born in Belfast in 1895, the eldest son in a family of 10 children. Prior to the war, John worked for the Linen firm of John Stewart Brown and Sons, Dublin Road, Belfast and was also a member of North Belfast Ulster Volunteer Force. He enlisted shortly after the outbreak of war, along with his younger brother, Albert Victor, who was also attached to 109th Field Ambulance. John was awarded the Military Medal for gallantry in the field for an incident at Bailleul, northern France on 5 June 1917. The unit war diary described the circumstances:

> 5 June 1917 8.00 pm. Whilst on parade in camp field close to Duke of York siding, an enemy aeroplane dropped bombs on ammunition trains standing in the siding. A truck immediately took fire and explosions began to take place. As the camp was 200 yards from the siding, the parade was immediately dismissed and all the patients and personnel as well as the horses were hurried out of camp out of danger. No casualties were caused although shells and fragments were falling thickly on the camp. Sergeant Major Harland collected a small party and succeeded in salving eight trucks from the end of one of the burning trains. The members of the party were, Sergeant Major Harland, Sergeant Hall, Corporal Greenwood and Private Feely all of 109th Field Ambulance, also Private Glynn of 8th Royal Inniskilling Fusiliers.[87]

Following his death, Corporal Greenwood's mother, Annie, was awarded a Dependant's Pension of five shillings per week for life.

---

86 IWM: Doc. 22065 Sergeant Robert McKay papers.
87 TNA WO 95/2499/2: 109th Field Ambulance RAMC War Diary. For his role in leading the party, Sergeant Major Thomas Harland was awarded the Military Cross, notice of which appeared in *The London Gazette* of 14 August 1917.

Private William McCormick MM was aged 21. He had been born at Partick, Lanarkshire, but was raised by his adoptive parents at Beverley Street, Belfast. By 1911, he had completed his education and was employed in a Spinning Mill. He was awarded the Military Medal for gallantry in the field, notice appearing in divisional orders on 22 October 1916.

The third member of the party to be killed was nineteen years old Private John Henry Barrett from Southland Street in the Shankill area of Belfast.

The third Field Ambulance attached to the Division, 110th, was kept to the rear, near Poperinghe, however, they did supply officers to replace those of 108th and 109th Field Ambulances who had been wounded or killed. One of these was Captain John Bromley Rawlins, aged 27 and from Erdington, Warwickshire, who was attached to 12th Royal Irish Rifles on the evening of 15 August and was killed soon after his arrival with them. His remains were recovered and identified in January 1920 along with those of two other unidentified RAMC members near Bank Farm, close to where the men named above were killed.

Corporal John Greenwood MM. (Great War Ulster Newspaper Archive)

Apart from the small gains made by 109th Brigade on the very left of 36th Divison front, the remainder of the attack failed to make any ground whatsoever. Having attacked at 4:45 a.m. by 10:00 a.m. the advance was over.

As highlighted previously, a message was sent by Fifth Army HQ to XIX Corps HQ at 2:08 p.m. It is transcribed verbatim below:

> Following orders are passed in confirmation of instructions telephoned. II Corps will make every effort to clear up situation on his right flank. Meanwhile XIX Corps will capture line BORRY FARM – HILL 35 – HINDU COT and will get in touch with 18 Corps at Winnipeg. With views to advance at earliest possible moment.[88]

This order showed an astounding lack of knowledge of firstly, the battlefield conditions, and secondly the strength of the attacking forces after the first advance. These orders were passed

---

88 TNA WO 95/969/3: XIX Corps War Diary, Appendix 272.

to the Headquarters of both divisions at 4:00 p.m. To his credit, Major General Hickie of 16th Division described it as impossible. There is some evidence that the proposal was given some consideration by 36th Division as the divisional narrative of the battle stated:

> The advisability of attempting another attack later in the day was fully considered but reports of Brigadiers and Staff Officers who visited the line made it clear that the troops in the line were incapable of doing any more.[89]

This information was relayed to XIX Corps headquarters and the projected attack was cancelled at 8:00 p.m.

Arrangements were then made to relieve the remnants of 108th and 109th infantry brigades as the contemporary divisional narrative continued:

> The disorganisation owing to casualties was considerable and the men were exhausted. Losses in officers had been heavy and of the two attacking brigades, less than 1,000 men were available. It as decided therefore to relieve the troops in the line and the 107th Infantry Brigade accordingly took over the front on the night of 16th/17th, the 108th and 109th Infantry brigades being withdrawn behind the old British front line.[90]

The divisions remained holding the Black Line on 17 August, sending out probing patrols to assess the extent of the German counterattack. Many wounded were assisted to the rear by these patrols. One patrol from 48th Brigade established a post in a derelict house in front of the Black line and could observe the Germans consolidating their positions at Vampir and Potsdam. Otherwise the day was quiet. One incident of note was a British plane being brought down in flames near Spree Farm at 10:10 a.m.[91]

Both divisions were relieved in the early hours of 18 August, 16th Division at 4:10 a.m. by 15 (Scottish) Division and 36th Division at 3:40 a.m. by 61st (2nd South Midland) Division, a Territorial unit which had been held by VIII Corps as reserve. So ended the Battle of Langemarck for the Irish divisions. Fortunately, many conclusions as to the final outcome are available from those at the sharp end and up the chain of command. The following chapter will discuss these conclusions in detail.

---

89   TNA WO 95/2492/1: 36th (Ulster) Division War Diary.
90   TNA WO 95/2492/1: 36th (Ulster) Division War Diary.
91   Almost certainly FE2D B1891 piloted by 24-year-old Canadian Lieutenant Harold Waddell Joslyn, 20 Squadron and Observer, 23 years old 2nd Lieutenant Alexander Urquhart from Inverness, shot down over St Julien 10.10 am by Leutnant Franz Xavier Dannhuber of *Jasta 26* who reported shooting down an aircraft near St Julien at 10.10 am 17 Aug. Dannhuber was a German ace with 11 victories and ended the war in command of *Jasta 79b*. Both pilot and observer are commemorated on the Arras Memorial to the Missing. See *The Aerodrome* <www.theaerodrome.com>

8

Aftermath

The story of the two Irish Divisions in their fighting on August 16th is black in tragedy.
Philip Gibbs[1]

As I researched and began to write this account, what struck me was not just the number of fatalities in what was largely for the Irish divisions a one day battle, but the number of men who have no known grave. Time and again as I was typing the account of a serviceman, the phrase, 'has no known grave and is commemorated on the Tyne Cot Memorial to the Missing' was the case. More so than in any other action of the Great War that I have researched were the dead basically unrecoverable. From men atomised by shell fire, to those wounded by the ruthless efficiency of the German machine gunners and who succumbed and slipped into the morass that the battlefield had been turned into.

The image overleaf was taken of the battlefield on 9 August and gives some idea of the conditions the officers and men of both Divisions were existing and fighting in before the attack of 16 August. On my research visit to the battlefield, I found it harder than on any other part of the Western Front to reconcile my view of the battlefield from the various accounts, with the image overleaf which is a view from the Black Line towards Hill 35. The knowledge that countless Irishmen, and others, still lie in these fields of oilseed rape, I found unsettling.

The casualties sustained by each of the Irish divisions were indeed, horrendous.

As always, working out the exact number of casualties is a virtually impossible task, particularly given the numbers who were reported as missing and simply vanished without trace. In addition, it is exceptionally difficult to quantify those who were wounded and succumbed to those wounds at a later date. The British official history of the Third Ypres campaign mentions the casualties of both divisions although for different time periods:

> The casualties of the 16th Division during the period 1st-20th August were 221 officers and 4064 other ranks, of which 115 officers and 2,042 other ranks occurred during the battle period 16th-18th August (26 officers killed, 61 wounded, 28 missing; 254 other ranks killed, 1098 wounded, 690 missing).

---

1   Gibbs, *Realities of War*, p.388.

Aerial photograph, 9 August 1917. (Inniskillings Museum ID 353)

Black Line to Hill 35 vista. (Author)

186   A Bad Day I Fear

> The 36th Division lost 144 officers and 3,441 other ranks during the period 2nd-18th August, of which total 81 officers and 1955 other ranks occurred during the battle period 16th-18th August (19 officers killed, 55 wounded, 7 missing; 299 other ranks killed, 1203 wounded, 453 missing)[2]

The figures from the *Official History* are definitely of value, particularly in relation to those wounded. The figures for fatalities for each Division for the period 16-18 August are also of interest. If it is assumed that all those missing were killed (an unlikely scenario) this would give the fatalities by Division as 998 for 16th Division and 778 for the 36th Division. As has been mentioned, the *Official History* was published in 1948, over 30 years after the battle and it would be expected that the figures would be close to correct, given the assumption of death for many of the Missing for whom no other explanation could be found.

I have carried out my own research on fatalities sustained by each division by perusal of the Commonwealth War Graves Commission records. It should be stated that these figures cannot be taken as exact, due to men appearing on the records as belonging to a parent unit, when they were in fact attached to another unit, perhaps only temporarily. With further developments to this research, they are however more accurate than those published in the *Official History*.

I have divided the figures into two periods – 31 July to 15 August, to cover the period when the first units became attached to 55th and 15th Divisions, and 16-18 August, to cover the period of involvement in the battle and to capture details of some of those who may have died of wounds post battle. The figures in Table 1 combine officer and men fatalities:

Table 1.

	31 July to 15 August	16-18 August
16th (Irish) Division	445	624
36th (Ulster) Division	414	622[3]

The similarity between these figures is remarkable and is an indication of the efforts and sacrifice of the Irish divisions against overwhelming odds.

Further analysis of the CWGC figures provides some interesting statistics:

- The battalion with the greatest number of fatalities across both divisions were 8th Royal Inniskilling Fusiliers in 16th Division, with 154.
- The battalion with the greatest number of fatalities in 36th Division were 9th Royal Irish Fusiliers with 144.
- The attacking battalions of 49th Infantry Brigade – 7th and 8th Inniskillings and those of 108th Infantry Brigade – 9th Royal Irish Fusiliers and 13th Royal Irish Rifles who attacked alongside each other in the centre of the Irish Division's front sustained 517 fatalities, just over 41 percent of the total. This fact shows that the strength of the German defences in the

---

2   Edmonds, *Military Operations France and Belgium 1917*, Vol. II, p.197, fn. 1. The figures for 36th Division during 2nd-18th August are gleaned from the the its operations narrative found in the war diary.
3   Casualty figures obtained from CWGC <www.cwgc.org> (accessed 6 May 2022).

line including Borry Farm, Iberian, Hill 37, Hill 35 and Gallipoli were the most formidable on the 5th Bavarian Division Front.
- The Royal Irish Rifles had the most battalions involved in the battle with 10 and unsurprisingly suffered the greatest number of fatalities at 641.[4] The Royal Inniskilling Fusiliers had five battalions in the field and suffered 540 however, the Royal Irish Fusiliers with two battalions, one in each Division, suffered 230 fatalities.[5]
- The most shocking statistic and one that bears out the testimonies regarding ground conditions and the difficulties of recovering the fallen, is that of the 1246 fatalities, 979 are commemorated on the Tyne Cot Memorial to the Missing and a further four on the Ypres (Menin Gate) Memorial. This is just under 80 per cent of the fatalities incurred by both Divisions. The agony of families across Ireland can only be imagined.

A suspicion has existed and which I have heard mentioned on occasion is that the Irish divisions were sacrificed for political reasons. With the Easter Rising having taken place in Dublin some 15 months previously, the theory promoted was that placing the Irish divisions in the most difficult part of the front would solve any future problems of discipline and morale. To investigate this further, I have considered the casualty rates of other units in the same area. The 145th Brigade of 48th (South Midland) Division was to the left of 109th Brigade of 36th Division and attacked at the same time with their objective being the village of St Julien. In the attack they suffered 911 casualties.[6] No exact comparable figure is available for 109th Brigade however, 145th Brigade suffered 267 fatalities and the Division as a whole suffered 2036 casualties in the period. I would contend therefore that for these two brigades, the casualty rates were similar.

To the right of 16th Division was 8th Division. This formation had participated in the opening phase of the offensive, the Battle of Pilckem Ridge, where they had sustained over 3,000 casualties. Astonishingly, they were back in the same sector from 14 August and took part in the advance on 16 August, where they sustained a further 2,111 casualties.[7] In a similar position were the 15th (Scottish) Division, in XIX Corps along with the Irish divisions. They had, as already highlighted, participated in the Battle of Pilckem Ridge, and had to be replaced due to exhaustion and casualties on 4 August by 16th Division. From 29 July to 4 August, they sustained 3,580 casualties.[8] On the night of 17 August, they relieved the 16th Division in the same sector they had been in at the beginning of the month. Records indicate that from 5-31 August, they sustained a further 2,888 casualties.[9] Following the action of 16 August, both 16th and 36th divisions were withdrawn from the line and given time to reorganise before being transferred to a quieter part of the line in the Somme area. The 8th and 15th (Scottish) divisions were not afforded that luxury. Any suspicion that the Irish divisions were treated

---

4   7th battalion in 16th Division, 8th, 9th, 10th, 11th, 12th, 13th, 14th, 15th and 16th in 36th Division.
5   7th and 8th battalions Royal Inniskilling Fusiliers in 16th Division, 9th 10th and 11th battalions in 36th Division. 7/8th Royal Irish Fusiliers in 16th Division, 9th battalion in 36th Division.
6   TNA WO 95/2761/4: 145th Infantry Brigade War Diary. The casualties were 38 officers and 873 other ranks.
7   Edmonds, *Military Operations France and Belgium 1917*, Vol. II, p.194, fn. 2.
8   Lieutenant-Colonel J Stewart DSO & John Buchan, *The Fifteenth (Scottish) Division 1914-1919* (Edinburgh: Blackwood & Sons, 1926), p.177
9   Stewart & Buchan, *The Fifteenth (Scottish) Division 1914-1919*, p.195.

unfavourably does not stand up to scrutiny. The main issue would appear to be the mismanagement of resources within Fifth Army, of which more later.

The Germans did not however have things all their own way with losses from the Artillery bombardment being particularly severe. The German 3rd (Reserve) Division, the 49th and 2nd Reserve Infantry Regiments of which had initially been facing 16th Division suffered so severely that they were withdrawn from the line by late afternoon on 16 August.

It is fortunate that accounts exist within the various war diaries which analyse the reasons why the attack failed. Accounts from eight separate sources including battalions, brigades and divisions were identified and examined for common themes which are considered below.

The primary reason identified across all accounts was the state of the ground. The inability of the attackers to negotiate the quagmire that the battlefield had become meant that any cover provided by the creeping barrage was lost soon after the advance began. One of the accounts commenting that it would have been hard to keep up with the barrage even if no opposition had been met.[10] This factor was acknowledged by the Commander in Chief, Field Marshal Sir Douglas Haig in a progress report to the War Cabinet on 21 August 1917:

> A few days of fairly fine weather had dried the ground a good deal, but a heavy rainstorm on the previous evening had again rendered it very difficult and the advance was made under more unfavourable conditions than had been hoped for. In may places the men could only get forward by assisting each other out of breast-high mud and water in the shell holes.[11]

This factor dovetails neatly with another which was commented on by the majority of accounts, namely, the exhausted state of the troops. This situation was summed up succinctly in the 36th Division narrative:

> The state of the trenches and the bad weather made frequent reliefs essential if the men were to be kept even reasonably fit. To cope with the work in the forward area, principly the making of tracks, roads and gun emplacements, large working parties running into close to 1,000 men a day had to be furnished. It was thus impossible to keep any troops fresh for the attack and all had to take their turn in the line and do their share of the work. The consequence was that the men were undoubtedly not at their best on Zero day.[12]

The constant attrition of the officers and men from particularly of the infantry battalions, from when both divisions took over the front line ensured that at the time of the advance, few were over half strength and there were little or no reserves to call on. In these circumstances there was no likelyhood of success from the outset and for the battalions to make the efforts that they did is admirable.

The performance of the Artillery is commented on both positively and negatively. The positive comment indicated that the artillery support once the advance commenced was good however, this comment is caveated by the fact that the creeping barrage went too fast. The negative reports concentrate on the failure of the Artillery to deal with the many reinforced concrete

10 TNA WO 95/2510/5: 11th Royal Inniskilling Fusiliers War Diary.
11 TNA CAB/24/24/15: Report to War Cabinet, 21 August 1917.
12 TNA WO 95/2492/1: 36th (Ulster) Division War Diary.

bunkers and pillboxes and also to neutralise the German artillery on the Gheluvelt Plateau. Major General Uniacke was satisfied with the progress of the artillery bombardment prior to the opening offensive on 31 July however, it is evident that this bombardment had failed to deal with the concrete bunkers, primarily due to the fact that Howitzers of six inches or above were required to ensure their destruction, but these were in short supply and moving them forward into range through a quagmire was in many cases not possible. The German artillery batteries also had not been dealt with satisfactorily, leaving them able to put down a heavy barrage on the Black Line which hampered the movement of the support battalions and the movement of supplies to sustain the advance. The history of the Royal Regiment of Artillery acknowledged the deficiencies:

> The battle was not a success from an artillery point of view. Since the tactics of the day demanded a thorough fireplan, it was essential to have time to prepare and this was not given. The result was that many key points in the bombardment were not dealt with.[13]

The poor performance of the artillery can be laid directly at the door of General Gough, who had been ordered by Field Marshal Haig not to contemplate further advances until the enemy artillery had been dominated.[14]

Another comment which touches on the performance of the artillery was that of communication. An age old problem in that once the troops advanced, it was exceptionally difficult to get accurate information as to what was happening. This factor was exacerabated by firstly, the state of the ground, and secondly by the smoke from the artillery which shrouded the battlefield. The state of the ground accompanied by the German counter bombardment ensured that communication by telephone was not possible with many signallers perishing whilst trying to run forward telephone lines. This meant that commanders at the front had to rely on runners, a thankless task in the quagmire that the battlefield had become, and again many of these brave men fell. The smoke generated by the artillery on both sides rendered the job of the Forward Observers whose task it was to coordinate between Infantry, Royal Flying Corps and Artillery, impossible.

The smoke on the battlefield hindered the work of the Royal Flying Corps who come in for criticism in some accounts, with one observing:

> The troops all complained that sufficient protection was not afforded by our aircraft. Hostile aeroplanes were the first on the scene in the morning and the last at night.[15]

This criticism was not confined to the Irish divisions. On the right of 16th Division, the 8th Division's 23rd Infantry Brigade commented in their after action report:

> Aeroplane work was not good. They should be specially employed in looking for hostile troops massing and for passing back the information to the artillery for necessary action.

---

13 Farndale, *History of the Royal Regiment of Artillery: Western Front 1914-18*, p.204.
14 Blake, *The Private Papers of Douglas Haig 1914-1919*, p.250.
15 TNA WO 95/1973/3: 48th Infantry Brigade War Diary.

As far as could be seen this was not once done, the result being that hostile counter attacks had deployed by the time our SOS barrages were put down.[16]

The duties of the Royal Flying Corps during the battle were artillery cooperation, contact and counter attack patrols. In the case of XIX Corps, 21 Squadron were supplying air cover. Contrary to the complaint above, British planes were in the sky although by their own admission, were less than effective:

Flight from 5:10-7:35 a.m. No movement of enemy troops seen. MG's firing on plane from Zonnebeke. Comment: This machine was flying at about 3000 ft making it impossible with the smoke and cloud to see any movement. Lts Jones and Wallace 21 Sqdn RFC.[17]

This was also commented on in more general terms across the Fifth Army front:

Low clouds, mist and smoke drifting over the battlefield on the 16th, especially in the morning, made observation difficult and the counterattack concentrations, except in rare instances, escaped the notice of the air observers.[18]

This was certainly the case for both 16th and 36th divisions whose first inkling of a counter attack was when they observed the Germans in great numbers swarming over Hills 35 and 37 towards them.

The final point which most of the accounts commented on was the resilience of the German defenders. Perhaps buoyed by the security afforded by the well constructed pillboxes and strongpoints, the defenders fought tenaciously and any ground gained was hard won:

The resistance encountered was very stubborn with MG and rifles, enemy only retired when almost surrounded. Very few allowed themselves to be taken prisoner. They fought practically until every man was killed on Hill 35. Positions were held until the men were right into them.[19]

It is only natural in circumstances where failure has occurred to look for a source of blame – someone other than your own. Some accounts from 49th Infantry Brigade lay the blame for the retirement on 108th Brigade across the divisional boundary. Evidence does indicate that 9th Royal Irish Fusiliers and 13th Royal Irish Rifles did retire just over an hour after the advance began and certainly before any German counterattack was mounted. This action made the positions of 49th Infantry Brigade battalions untenable due to enfilade fire and caused them to withdraw also. The criticism does not take into account however, the conditions which these battalions met with, particularly the double belt of barbed wire which ran at an angle in front of Gallipoli Farm, the few gaps in which were covered by machine guns, channelling the attackers into a killing zone which was certain death to negotiate, as is evidenced by the 144 fatalities the

---

16   TNA WO 95/1710/1: 23rd Infantry Brigade War Diary.
17   TNA WO 95/960/1: XIX Corps War Diary, Appendix 263.
18   Jones, *The War in the Air,. Volume IV*, p.173.
19   TNA WO 95/2505/2 9th Battalion Royal Irish Fusiliers War Diary.

9th Royal Irish Fusiliers sustained. Long range machine gun fire from Hill 37 also pinned down the men of both divisions and the men of 9th Royal Irish Fusiliers covered the 7th Inniskillings and 7/8th Royal Irish Fusiliers as they retired to the Black Line. It is not possible to compare like with like as far as the battlefield is concerned. If the artillery had been more effective in their destruction of the German defences, the story of the advance might have been different.

Further up the command chain GOC 36th Division Major General Nugent was aghast at the days events and he poured out his thoughts to his wife, in an emotional letter:

> It has been a truly terrible day. Worse than the 1st July I am afraid. Our losses have been very heavy indeed and we have failed all along the line, so far as this Division is concerned and the whole Division has been driven back with terrible losses … Tomorrow we have to make another attack at dawn and I have no men to do it with. It is a ghastly business. Our failure has involved the failure of the Divisions on both sides of us and that is so bitter a pill. In July of last year, we did our work but failed because the Divisions on either flank failed us. This time it is the Ulster Division which has failed the Army. I am heartbroken over it and I fear that we shall be absolutely wiped out tomorrow. We have not enough men left to do the attack or to hold the line we are to hold, even if we get it. My poor men.[20]

The interesting point about this letter is that it appears to have been written in the afternoon of 16 August, before the decision to abandon the attack was made at 8:00 p.m. With the benefit of further information regarding the attack across the Fifth Army front, he wrote again to his wife the following day, giving a more measured assessment:

> My Division did not make any further attack. When we went into the numbers available, it was realised how serious the losses had been and I pointed out that it was out of the question. Other Divisions on my right and left all agreed as to their own men. The losses had been so heavy that there was nothing more to be done. I thought my Division was the only one to fail but it isn't so, On the left, the Guards and the French and two other Divisions got where they were supposed to go, but it was recognized that they had a comparatively easy job and that they are not in touch yet with the main German position. On the right we are right up against it and no one got on. It was not only the Ulster Divn which failed but nearly all. A poor satisfaction certainly but still some. It was machine guns which did us. We had Bavarians against us and they were magnificent fighters. We hardly saw any of them. They were snug in concrete emplacements so strong that our Artillery failed to smash them in and they just mowed down our attack. We are coming out tonight and go back into rest to reorganise and receive reinforcements.[21]

This was the last action that both Irish divisions were to have with XIX Corps due to their seriously depleted nature. On 19 August Operational Order No 83 was issued by XIX Corps Headquarters detailing the transfer of 16th and 36th divisions from Fifth Army to Third Army,

---

20 Perry (ed.), *Major General Oliver Nugent and the Ulster Division 1915-1918*, p.166.
21 Perry (ed.), *Major General Oliver Nugent and the Ulster Division 1915-1918*, p.167.

16th Division to move on 21/22 August and 36th Division to move on 23/24 August. The artillery of both divisions was to follow a week later.

Prior to leaving XIX Corps, Major General Nugent went to visit General Gough on 21 August and shared his thoughts in a letter to his wife:

> I went to see Gough this afternoon. He was very pleasant and is a charming person as he always is, but my dearest, no one can talk to him and come away thinking that he is mentally or intellectually fit to command a big Army. He isn't and it is wrong that the lives of thousands of good men should be sacrificed through want of forethought and higher leading. Being a good cavalry soldier and a good fellow are not the only qualifications for the command of great armies in which Cavalry takes no part…Two fresh Divisions attacked the same ground that we and the 16th attacked over, they attacked yesterday and I heard that the attack was a complete failure. They could do no more than we could. If this is so, it means that six Divisions have now been wasted over the same piece of ground and so far as I can see, the Corps have learned nothing from our experiences, nor from the experiences of the Divisions that attacked before us. Neither apparently has the Fifth Army.[22]

This letter shows a hardening of attitude on behalf of Nugent against Gough personally and the Fifth Army in general. Less than two weeks previously, he had met Gough for the first time and stated:

> Gough the 5th Army Commander came to see me yesterday and stayed quite a long time. I liked him as far as one can judge from a first impression.[23]

This antipathy towards Gough remained with Nugent for the rest of his military career. Even though 36th Division under Nugent's command was to fight as part of Gough's Fifth Army in the German Spring Offensive of March 1918, Nugent always held Gough responsible for the losses suffered on 16 August 1917, as he commented in late March 1918:

> Gough has gone home or at any rate has been relieved from command of 5th Army. If only it had been done six months earlier.[24]

It may be that when he penned his letter on 21 August, Nugent was aware of comments made by Generals Watts and Gough following the attack of 16 August.

On the afternoon of 17 August, Field Marshal Haig visited General Gough as part of a factfinding trip to the Corps and Army Headquarters to assess how the offensive was progressing. He later wrote in his diary;

> He [Gough] was not pleased with the action of the Irish divisions of the XIX Corps (36th and 16th). They seem to have gone forward, but failed to keep what they had won. These two Divisions were in the Messines battle and had an easy victory. The men are Irish and

---

22 Perry (ed.), *Major General Oliver Nugent and the Ulster Division 1915-1918*, p.169.
23 PRONI: D3835/E/2/14/5 Letter to wife, 8 August 1917.
24 Perry (ed.), *Major General Oliver Nugent and the Ulster Division 1915-1918*, p.219.

did not like the shelling, so Gough said. At HQ XVII Corps I was told that only the left of 11th Division got forward… Most of the concrete farms and dugouts had not been destroyed by our bombardment and held up the attack. At XIX Corps I saw General Watts who gave a bad account of the two Irish divisions (36th and 16th) Nugent and Hickie are the respective GOC's. But I gather that the attacking troops had a long march up the evening before through Ypres to the front line and then had to fight from zero 4.45 am until nightfall. The men could have had no sleep and must have been dead tired. Here also a number of concrete buildings and dugouts were never really destroyed by artillery fire and do not appear to have been taken. So the advances made here were small.[25]

Gough's comments were and are regarded as an affront to the fighting capabilities of Irishmen and require further investigation. They are all the more surprising as although born in London, Hubert Gough was brought up mainly in County Tipperary.[26] There are two points which can immediately be identified from the diary entry, firstly, Field Marshal Haig was sympathetic to the situation that the Irish divisions found themselves in and secondly, the reference to 11th Division shows that small gains were not unique to the Irish divisions.

General Gough's comments show an inclination to apportion blame to avoid further scrutiny of his own performance and appear to have been a characteristic of Gough's personality. In 1915, during the Battle of Loos, he apportioned blame to 28th Division and its commander, Major General Sir Edward Bulfin, over failure to prosecute an attack which Gough himself had interfered in the tactical planning of. Following this failure, Gough approached the then General Haig and told him that Bulfin should be sacked citing:

> That he considered the staff work of the Division was bad and that several operations had failed through ignorance and bad management on the part of Brigadiers and Divisional Staff.[27]

General Haig appreciated the efforts General Bulfin had made and asked him to consider remaining however, a man of integrity, Edward Bulfin declined, citing complications from an earlier injury. He had had however, enough of General Gough.

A similar situation occurred in 1916 following an abortive attack during the Battle of the Somme. As Haig remarked in his diary:

> I visited Toutencourt and saw General Gough. The failure to hold the positions gained on the Ancre is due, he reported, to the 49th Div (Percival). The units of that Division did not really attack and some men did not follow their officers. The total losses of this Division is under a thousand! It is a Territorial Division from the West Riding of Yorkshire.[28]

---

25 Sheffield & Bourne (eds). *Douglas Haig. War Diaries and Letters 1914-1918*, p.317.
26 A comprehensive account of his early life is outlined in his 1954 memoirs, *Soldiering On*.
27 John Powell, *Haig's Tower of Strength. General Sir Edward Bulfin: Ireland's Forgotten General* (Barnsley: Pen & Sword Military, 2018), p.140.
28 Blake, *The Private Papers of Douglas Haig 1914-1919*, p.163.

It was a fact that the Dominion troops of Canada and Australia had made it clear to Field Marshal Haig that they would not serve under General Gough again following severe casualties suffered by the former at the Somme and the latter at Bullecourt in April 1917. These instances suggest that there were issues within Fifth Army which made it an unhappy place in which to serve. Prior to analysing Fifth Army more deeply, the relationship between General Gough and the Commander XIX Corps, General Herbert Watts is relevant, as Watts also apportioned blame to the 16th and 36th Divisions.

It is an unfortunate truth that General Watts was not highly regarded throughout the Army. In an early encounter with him in February 1915, the then Army Commander General Douglas Haig noted:

> We went to Fleurbaix to HQ 21 Bde, Brig Gen Watts. A plucky hard little man, with no great brains, I should judge from his doings at Ypres last November.[29]

Herbert Watts was born at Wisbech, Cambridgeshire in 1858, the son of a Vicar. He was commissioned into the 14th Regiment of Foot in 1880 and served with it for 30 years before retiring in the rank of Colonel in 1914 when he was 56.[30] To employ contemporary Army parlance, he was 'dug out' at the outbreak of war to command 21st Brigade, 7th Division. The Brigade suffered heavily at Ypres in October 1914 and ironically, Watts' divisonal commander for most of 1915 was the then Major General Hubert Gough. Watts himself commanded 7th Division temporarily in late 1915 before being brought in for a short time to command 38th (Welsh) Division in July 1916 following the sacking of their previous commander, Major General Ivor Phillips, after the Division's failure at Mametz Wood on the Somme. By then in the rank of Major General, he successfully sorted out the issues with 38th Division before returning to 7th Division where he remained until his promotion to Corps Commander. He was well regarded within 7th Division and his promotion was seen as a loss. He was however, not seen as an asset within Fifth Army.

Of the four Corps Commanders, General Watts as an officer recalled at the outbreak of war, was the odd man out. The other three Corps Commanders, General the Earl of Cavan, General Sir Ivor Maxse and General Sir Claud Jacob were all younger and had had unbroken service. They were all supremely confident men and it may be that as an older and less experienced officer, General Watts did not fit into this pattern. The fact that he was not equally highly regarded indicates that there was something amiss within the management of Fifth Army.

The view that Major General Nugent initially had of General Gough that he was amiable and likeable, is corroborated by other accounts. He did however have a reputation for sacking those that he considered inefficient or disloyal. This could be seen as instilling a certain amount of trepidation within his subordinates. General Gough however, did not run Fifth Army himself. As he rose through the ranks of command, he established a close knit team around him to advise and assist in decision making. Two of these individuals are of great importance in understanding how Fifth Army operated.

---

29 Sheffield & Bourne (eds.) *Douglas Haig. War Dairies and Letters 1914-1918,* p.103.
30 The 14th Regiment of Foot later became the Prince of Wales's Royal Regiment of Yorkshire.

The first was Gough's Chief of Staff, Major General Neil Malcolm, who joined Gough's staff at the beginning of June 1916. Aged 46, he had been a boyhood friend of Hubert Gough and his brother, Johnny. An old Etonian, he had been commissioned into the Argyll and Sutherland Highlanders in 1889 from the Royal Military College, Sandhurst, and had been wounded during the Boer War. He had served on the staff of the Mediterranean Expeditionary Force at Gallipoli and had been specifically requested by Gough as Anthony Farrar-Hockley mentioned in his excellent biography:

> Hubert had asked for his services in May and he was to prove a loyal subordinate. Loyal as it turned out, almost to the ruination of his chief.[31]

Fiercely loyal to Gough, Malcolm was highly intelligent and exuded supreme confidence and expected others to have the the same capabilities, as Farrar-Hockley commented:

> It was Malcolm's view that whereas they had certain first rate Corps and a number of dependable Divisions, too many of the remainder were commanded and staffed by time servers who were letting his Army Commander down. He began to bear down on those he believed to be failing in their duty. 'If you'd spend less time worrying who is going to be hit by the next shell or bullet' he remarked to a timorous GSO1 he encountered at one of the Corps HQ, 'you might have got your brigades onto their objectives today.' When he believed that a division or Corps had not tried hard enough in an operation, he threatened that their relief would be postponed until the task had been achieved.[32]

It was the case that Malcolm ruled by fear and corps commanders and other subordinates were afraid to approach him or express dissatisfaction with any aspect of planning due to the fear of retribution. Gough therefore may have been unaware of any dissent and believed that all was well, whilst his Chief of Staff ruled with an iron fist. In his excellent essay, Ian Beckett observes:

> Gough specifically stated that he held conferences on the evening of every major attack and he could not recall any occasion when the decision was not unanimous. Malcolm wrote similarly. Obviously one explanation might be that since dissent was unacceptable, none was offered, but with the exception of LG Sir Herbert Watts of XIX Corps, Gough and Malcolm appear to have had the greatest respect for their other Corps Commanders.[33]

The second person of importance and the antidote to the unremitting harshness of Neil Malcolm was Brigadier General Sir Edward Henry Lionel Beddington.[34] Aged 36 and a Cavalryman like General Gough, he had been a Squadron Leader in the 16th Lancers when Gough was his commanding officer and he was in the rank of Captain on Gough's staff in 1916 where he operated as Gough's troubleshooter. Any problems which arose would be sorted out by

---

31 Farrar-Hockley, *Goughie*, p.183.
32 Farrar-Hockley, *Goughie* p.227.
33 Ian Beckett, *Gough*, 'Malcolm and Command on the Western Front' in Brian Bond et al, *Look to Your Front: Studies in the First World War* (Staplehurst: Spellmount, 1999) p.9.
34 Beddington was known throughout Fifth Army as 'Moses' on account of his Jewish heritage.

Beddington. The other important role that he played was that he was a sympathetic ear for Corps Commanders and other subordinates who could confide in him knowing that their views would be presented to Gough, bypassing the ear of the tyrant that was Malcolm. Unfortunately for all concerned (except Beddington) he was promoted in November 1916 and left Gough's staff. He was not adequately replaced and this gave Malcolm a greater degree of control which he exercised with his customary ruthless efficiency.

At the time of the Third Ypres offensive, Beddington was in the rank of Major in a Staff Officer's role in 8th Division, well placed to observe the workings of Fifth Army which was a much less contented place than when he had been on Gough's Staff. Fortunately, but too late for the Irish divisions, Beddington was posted back on promotion to Fifth Army Staff at the beginning of December 1917. His papers exist and it is worth reproducing his comments following his return in full:

> I motored south to Fifth Army and got there in the afternoon, picked up the situation and in the evening before dinner went round the offices and saw all the Major Generals who were the same people whom I had known a year previously when I had been G2 of the Army. To my surprise, I had a tremendous welcome from everybody, so much so that I asked the Gunner General, Uniacke, why this was. He was gloriously outspoken as usual and said, 'We all know we can get on with you from previous experience, not that you are anything extraordinary. But we could none of us work with your predecessor, whom we found quite intolerable.' I also saw the MGGS, Neil Malcolm, who looked to me very tired. He said he was sorry for my sake that I could not stay with 8th Division, where he knew that I was very happy, but GHQ had made the appointment, merely asking them if I was acceptable. I asked for Goughy but I was told he was on leave and would be back the following night.
>
> So two days afterwards, I saw Goughy and after we had greeted each other, I asked him if I could go and fetch Neil Malcolm as there was something I wanted to say to both of them. Goughy said 'of course' so I went to Neil and brought him back with me to Goughy. I then somewhat nervously began to tell them that Fifth Army was very unpopular with Divisions and that only Divisional Commanders who were quite confident in themselves and their Divisions were happy to serve in it, others all dreaded it, especially those whose nerves were not strong and those who were not sure that they were filling the bill or were doubtful of the efficiency of their Divisions. I could see Neil Malcolm getting very angry, but Goughy seemed to be his normal self and told me to go on. I said there seemed to be a lack of sympathy and help from Army HQ to Divisions, and Commanders seemed to feel that unless they put up a first-class show they would be outed. I continued that, having been away from them for a year and spent the whole year with a Division – fortunately one which had received nothing but praise and kindness from Fifth Army – I could not fail to know the feeling of Divisional Commanders and that I felt that I should be failing in my duty, whatever the personal consequences were, If I did not tell them at the first opportunity what I believed to be the general feeling about Fifth Army amongst Divisions.
>
> Neil Malcolm then started to explode, but Goughy told him to be silent and said, 'I thank you very much for telling us this and I think you were quite right to do so and there won't be any personal consequences. As a matter of fact I heard very much the same thing the night before last.' I said 'may I ask who from Sir?', he answered, 'Certainly, it was the

> Commander in Chief with whom I stayed the night before last' I thanked him very much and left Goughy and Neil Malcolm together. Presently, Neil Malcolm came into my room to tell me that the next day he was going to take over command of 66th Division and would therefore be leaving us: he added that he had been originally quite shocked at what I had said to him and Goughy, but on thinking it over, agreed that it was the right thing to do.[35]

Rumours of unease with Fifth Army had also obviously reached the ears of the commander in chief as he noted in his diary on 14 December:

> General Gough called on return from leave. I spoke to him about General Sargent, DA and QMG of Fifth Army. I was not able to recommend him for promotion; and as regards his MGS (Neil Malcolm) I proposed to transfer him to the Command of a Division. I mentioned to Gough, how many Divisions had hoped that they would not be sent to the Fifth Army to fight. This feeling I put down to his Staff. I had not told him before because it might have had effect on his self-confidence during the battle. It was of course a surprise to Gough to learn this, but from the facts which I gave him, he realized that there were cases bearing out what I had told him.[36]

If it was a surprise to General Gough, Malcolm must have been doing his job exceptionally well to shield him from any adverse comments. It would also appear that it was not only Malcolm, but some of his acolytes who were regarded as unapproachable. As close as possible to an independent observer was the war correspondent Philip Gibbs, who observed:

> I found a general opinion among officers and men, not only of the Irish divisions, under the command of the Fifth Army that they had been the victims of atrocious Staff work, tragic in its consequences. From what I saw of some of the Fifth Army staff officers I was of the same opinion. Some of these young gentlemen, and some of the elderly officers were arrogant and supercilious without revealing any symptoms of intelligence. If they had wisdom, it was deeply camouflaged by an air of inefficiency. If they had knowledge, they hid it as a secret of their own. General Gough, commanding the Fifth Army in Flanders was extremely courteous, of most amiable character with a high sense of duty. But in Flanders, if not personally responsible for many tragic happenings, he was badly served by some of his subordinates, and battalion officers and divisional staffs raged against the whole of the Fifth Army organization or lack of organization with and extreme passion of speech. 'You must be glad to leave Flanders' I said to a group of officers trekking towards the Cambrai Salient. One of them answered violently, 'God be thanked we are leaving the Fifth Army area.'[37]

In the poisonous atmosphere that prevailed within the Headquarters of Fifth Army, it is easy to see how when a scapegoat was required, Watts and his XIX Corps was tailor made for it. As Lynn Lemisko highlighted in her article, *A Dubious Reputation – 16th (Irish) Division 1916-1918*:

---

35 Liddell Hart Centre for Military Archives, GB 99 KCLMA Beddington, pp.120-22
36 Blake, *The Private Papers of Douglas Haig 1914-1919*, p.272.
37 Gibbs, *Realities of War*, p.389.

Why did Gough chose to single out 16th and 36th divisions as poor performers in his report to Haig? The answer may lie in Gough's perception of the offensive spirit of the two Divisions rather than in their actual performance.[38]

When Watts informed Fifth Army HQ on the evening of 16 August that the planned resumption of the attack could not take place, you can imagine that it was with some trepidation, given Malcolm's reputation. Whether Gough made the comments blaming the Irish divisions of his own volition, or whether they were as the result of seeds planted by Malcolm, they caused, and continue to cause great offence.

There is evidence that Gough did however continue to regard 16th Division in an unfavourable light. In the process of the preparation of the long delayed official history of the Third Ypres campaign, Gough was in correspondence with the series editor, Brigadier General Sir James Edmonds.[39] Having been sent some draft chapters, Gough replied to Edmonds on 3 May 1944 with the following observations:

> The enquiry on the action of the 16th Division was initiated by Fifth Army Headquarters (not by GHQ or XIX Corps) with the definite intention, not of fixing blame on any one, but of ascertaining the truth as far as possible and learning from mistakes … As a matter of fact which I would not like to record against the Division in any official document, I was aware that the Division was not of the highest standard, and Watts [Commander XIX Corps] was equally aware of this fact.[40]

If this was the case, why did Gough specifically ask for both Irish divisions for his Ypres offensive? This is further evidence that General Gough was keen to avert any blame being attached to his own actions.

Following the debacle of 16 August, General Gough appears to have finally appreciated the reality of the situation. The ground conditions militated against any further immediate advance, a situation that he was late to realise:

> The state of the ground was by this time frightful. The labour of bringing up supplies and ammunition, of moving or firing the guns which had often sunk up to their axles was a fearful strain on the officers and men, even during the daily task of maintaining the battle front. When it came to the advance of infantry for an attack across waterlogged shell holes, movement was so slow and fatiguing that only the shortest advances could be contemplated. In consequence I informed the Commander in Chief that tactical success was not possible, or would be too costly, under such conditions and advised that the attack should now be abandoned. I had many talks with Haig during these days and repeated this opinion frequently, but he told me that the attack must be

---

38 Lynn Speer Lemisko, 'A Dubious Reputation: 16th (Irish) Division 1916-1918' in *The Journal of the Military History Society of Ireland*, Volume XXII Summer 2000, p.75
39 The Third Ypres volume was not published until 1948 or over three decades after the event. It is fair to say that Gough was not in favour of the draft which he believed depicted him unfavourably.
40 TNA CAB 45/140: Official War Histories and Correspondence.

continued. His reasons were valid. He was looking at the broad picture of the whole theatre of war.[41]

The commander in chief, Field Marshal Sir Douglas Haig had no option but to insist that the offensive must continue, his rationale being that the French were not able to contribute in any meaningful way and any United States assistance was some months off, so the British must continue in an attritional war against the Germans, wearing down their resources and fighting spirit. There is some evidence that Haig's strategy was working but at a terrible cost in manpower. The *Official History* records that:

> From 25th July to 28th August, 23 German divisions had been exhausted and withdrawn out of the 30 that had been engaged opposite the Fifth Army alone.[42]

The controversy surrounding the conduct of the offensive continued to bedevil General Gough post war. In 1958, in a conversation with the noted military historian, John Terraine, Gough stated that:

> He attributed much of the reproach subsequently levelled against him and his Army to the unfortunate manner of his Chief of Staff, Major General Neil Malcolm. Inasmuch as a Staff takes a large part of its 'tone' from the Chief Staff Officer, this would appear to be true. General Malcolm was a Military intellectual, with a share of the impatience and arrogance that often go with this quality, both in the Army and in civilian life.[43]

Further evidence if any was needed of the supreme self-confidence bordering on narcissism which characterised General Sir Hubert Gough.

Whilst Fifth Army was preparing for its next attempt to batter against impervious German defences, the Irish divisions were preparing to leave XIX Corps in a spirit of relief rather than sadness. On the occasion of their departure, the following message was promulgated from XIX Corps:

> In bidding goodbye to the Division, the Corps Commander wishes to express his deep appreciation of the fine work done by all ranks during the time the Division has been with XIXth Corps. It was unfortunately necessary for the Division to take over the line and hold it for over a fortnight in the worst of weather under constant shelling and nightly gas attacks. But in spite of all the hardships and very large casualty lists, the Division carried out its preparations for the offensive without a pause and although the attack when it took place was not successful – very possibly due to the previous hardships undergone by the troops – it was an attack over very difficult country against the best troops in the German army and against a hitherto untried system of defence and the Division may well be proud of the many gallant and heroic acts performed by so many of its officers and men.

---

41 General Sir Hubert Gough, *The Fifth Army* (London: Hodder and Stoughton, 1931), p.204.
42 Edmonds, *Military Operations France and Belgium 1917*, Vol. II, p.210.
43 John Terraine, *Douglas Haig: The Educated Soldier* (London: Hutchinson & Co, 1963), p.337.

> Their efforts were not thrown away as the experience gained should prove of great value in coming attacks.[44]

It was pleasing that recognition was given to the efforts, particularly in holding the lines in the pre battle period however, the final line was scant consolation to those who had lost so many comrades and friends. As the direct result of casualties suffered during the battle, 7th and 8th battalions Royal Inniskilling Fusiliers of 16th Division were amalgamated on 23 August, becoming 7/8th battalion. In the 36th Division, for the same reason, 8th and 9th battalions Royal Irish Rifles amalgamated on 28 August becoming 8/9th battalion.

The role of newspapers in relating details of the action was in the vast majority of cases the sole means for families of obtaining information on the whereabouts, and all too frequently the fate of loved ones. The newspaper content and style of reporting had changed dramatically from the early months of the war, when letters home from soldiers at the front were shared by family and friends with local newspapers as a means of bringing news to a wider audience. The military authorities realised the dangers inherent in this form of free for all and had clamped down on what could or could not be published.

What we had in 1917 therefore is a much more sanitised, and it could be suggested much less interesting, version of events strictly controlled by the military authorities. There were five War Correspondents appointed by the War Office, three of whose work appears in many of the newspaper titles. They were Percival Phillips, a United States citizen, William Beach Thomas and Philip Gibbs. These three were newspaper journalists and provided accounts for their own and other newspapers although subject to the British Military Censor, a bone of contention with them all.

From research of available titles, It appears that the practice was for an article to be written for a national newspaper and then syndicated to provincial and local papers. Obituaries, principally for officers and details of rank and file soldiers with perhaps a place of employment or affiliation to a sporting or cultural society are still evident as are short biographies where a gallantry award was won.

Geographically across the island of Ireland, post 1916 there are many fewer accounts in newspapers in southern counties and unfortunately, some accounts highlight religious and political differences. Even the official War Correspondents were not immune from this with Philip Gibbs erroneously referring to the 16th Division on occasion as the Catholic Irish.

Interestingly, in addition to the official British accounts, many newspapers published accounts from the German general headquarters, which often countered the jingoistic articles emanating from official British sources and in hindsight, were often more accurate.

Notwithstanding this and bearing in mind the controlling eye of the censor, some of the articles are remarkably detailed. Philip Gibbs wrote articles which appeared in the *Daily Chronicle*. Following the battle, he wrote an article titled, 'The Irish in the Swamps' which appeared in the paper on August 21. In this sympathetic article he highlights the conditions which the men of both divisions faced:

---

44   TNA WO 95/1977/2: 7th Royal Inniskilling Fusiliers War Diary.

> Let me tell you first the happenings of the Irish troops on the right, the Catholic Irish, whose own right was on the Roulers railway, going up to the Pommern Redoubt. An hour or so before the attack the enemy, as though knowing what was about to come, flung down a tremendous and destructive barrage, answered by our own drum-fire which gave the signal for the Irish to advance. The Dublin Fusiliers and the Royal Irish Rifles went forward on the right and the Inniskillings on the left. In front of them were numbers of German strongpoints, the now famous pill-boxes, or concrete blockhouses which the enemy has built as his new means of defence to take the place of trench systems. They were Beck House, Borry Farm and the Bremen Redoubt – sinister names which will never be forgotten in Irish history. There were also odd bits of trench here and there for the use of snipers and small advanced posts. As the first wave of assaulting troops advanced, Germans rose from these ditches and ran back to the shelter of the concrete works, and immediately from those emplacements and from other machine gun positions echeloned in depth behind them swept a fierce enfilade fire of machine gun bullets, even through the barrage of our shellfire which went ahead of the Irish line. Many men in the first wave dropped, but others kept going and reached almost as far as they had been asked to go …

The article continues with further detail of the attack and then describes the advance of the Ulster Division:

> Meanwhile, the men of the Ulster Division were fighting just as desperately. They had ahead of them one of the concrete forts, one of which near Pond Farm was a strong defensive system with deep dugouts and overhead cover proof against shell-fire. This and other strongpoints had wooden platforms above the concrete walls, on which the gunners could mount their machines very quickly, firing from behind two yards thickness of concrete. Opposite the Pommern Redoubt stands a small hill which the enemy has used for a long time as one of his chief observation posts, as it gives a complete view of our ground [Hill 35]. Beyond that the country rises to a saddleback ridge with double spurs guarded on the lower slope by a small fort called Gallipoli and from these spurs he could fling a machine gun barrage across the low ground. An ugly position to attack. It was worse for the Ulster men because of the state of the ground which was a thin crust over a bog of mud. On the left, some of the Inniskillings and Irish Rifles rushed forward as far as a network of trenches and wired defences, which they took in a fierce assault against a Bavarian garrison, who fought to the finish. Here they recaptured one of our Lewis guns lost in the fighting on July 31 …

The article concludes:

> The Irish troops had no luck. It was a day of tragedy. But poor Ireland should be proud of these sons of hers, who struggled against such odds and fought until their strength was spent, and, and even then held on in far posts with a spirit scornful of the word, 'surrender'.[45]

---

45   Gibbs, *From Bapaume to Passchendaele* p.251-55.

As the reality of the events of 16 August began to be circulated, some local papers sought to compare the battle with the events on the Somme the previous year. The headline of the *Belfast Weekly Telegraph* described the battle as Ulster's Second Thiepval. The article goes on to prepare the reader for news of many casualties stating:

> The long drawn struggle on the Western Front has brought another dark and fateful day to Ulster whose soldier sons again passed through a fearful ordeal, rivalling if not indeed eclipsing in point of seemingly overwhelming bloody sacrifices, the opening of the Somme offensive on 1 July 1916.[46]

The article uses much of Philip Gibb's article however, it reproves him over his description of the composition of the Irish Division, believing it to sow confusion. It sought to set the record straight for its largely Unionist readership:

> Even as related by the correspondents, the narratives tend to be somewhat confusing owing to the unfortunate naming of the Irish Regiments, as in the public mind the regimental composition of the Divisions from Ireland has never been clear. It being too often overlooked that in the Division generally known as the Irish and frequently alluded to as the Southern or Catholic Irish, there are five battalions of the Ulster regiment's battalions of the Royal Irish Rifles, Royal Irish Fusiliers and Royal Inniskilling Fusiliers.[47]

The tone of this part of the article was to ensure that credit for gallant acts was credited in what was perceived as the 'right' quarter. In reality there seemed little need for this attempted clarification.

The initial report in *The Irish Times*, of 17 August, carries an account from a Press Association journalist which gives a general overview of the events of 16 August, but does not refer to either Irish Division.

The Dublin Daily Express of 23 August, carries an article syndicated from *The Daily Mail* by Beach Thomas, which carried the sub-headings, *Glorious Irish Bravery*, and *North and South in a Charge*. This article gives a general description of the attacks made by both divisions although not in the same detail as that by Philip Gibbs, and mentions a heroic Roman Catholic Padre, without naming him.

An interesting article appeared in *The Northern Whig* of 23 August, quoting from the *Pall Mall Gazette* and showing that making assumptions without checking facts left one open to potential ridicule:

> The *Pall Mall Gazette* notes with surprise that the operations in Langemarck and the vicinity were directed by General Gough, for Sir Hubert had previously been employed in a southerly sector. If the announcement is correct, Sir Hubert's transference is probably due to his knowledge of the terrain.[48]

---

46 *The Belfast Weekly Telegraph*, 25 August 1917.
47 *The Belfast Weekly Telegraph*, 25 August 1917.
48 *The Northern Whig*, 23 August 1917.

By the week following the battle, the War Correspondents accounts began to appear in Provincial papers throughout Ireland, the majority focusing on Irish tenacity in the face of overwhelming odds. At the same time, officer's deaths began to be reported with short obituaries, Details of rank and file men known to be killed began to appear in the following week, such as that of 25 years old Serjeant Richard Owens 9860, 11th Royal Inniskilling Fusiliers, whose death was notified in *The Londonderry Sentinel* of 28 August 1917:

> Mrs Owens, 80 Fountain Street, Londonderry has been notified that her husband, Serjeant Richard Owens Royal Inniskilling Fusiliers (attached Donegal and Fermanagh Volunteers) has been killed in action. Rev. Alexander Spence writing to Mrs Owens says, 'Serjeant Owens led his platoon with the greatest determination against the enemy on 16th August, in the face of extremely heavy shell and machine-gun fire. After a short time your husband was severely wounded by a machine-gun bullet. A couple of his comrades were carrying him to the safety of a dugout when a heavy shell landed beside them and killed all three. I need not say how keenly I feel the loss of your gallant husband. I knew your husband very well indeed, probably better than any other man in the battalion. We have been friends for a long time. At the sports which we held on 12th July, he won nearly all the distance races. He was an advocate of total abstinence and had been so both here and during his service in India. In everything he was a splendid example of Christian manhood, and now he has put a crown of honour on a complete life by dying for the great cause for which we fight. Your husband has done the greatest thing a man can do by dying as he did. He is safe with God where there is no war or sorrow and you and those who love him must remember him, not always with sorrow, but with great pride. Though I shall always miss him, yet I cannot regret what has happened, for if ever a man was ready to die and worthy to die, it was your husband.[49]

Whether or not Mrs Owens would have agreed with the sentiments in the last line of the letter is uncertain. Serjeant Owens like so many, has no known grave and is commemorated on the Tyne Cot Memorial to the Missing. Mrs Owens at least was informed as to what had happened to her husband. For so many, they joined the ranks of those Missing, that were published in Newspapers throughout September. *The Portadown News* of 8 September 1917, published a list of local men killed, wounded and missing from 16 August. The fact that the list of those recorded as missing was triple that of those killed showed that the agony of waiting continued for many families, few of whom would receive good news.

---

49 *The Londonderry Sentinel*, 28 August 1917. The Reverend Spence MC was himself killed during the German Spring Offensive on 31 March 1918.

Retrospective

For the officers and men of the Irish divisions the desperate fight for survival in the quagmire the battlefield had been turned into, was the tangible manifestation of many factors which were totally beyond their control. Decisions made at the highest level placed the Irish formations in an impossible situation and, over a century later and in a completely different social and cultural environment, it is of value to re-examine the factors which needlessly caused the deaths of so many.

At the strategic level, the dysfunctional, fractious, and at times openly hostile relationship between Prime Minister David Lloyd George and Field Marshal Sir Douglas Haig contributed to a situation where the national war effort at that time was disjointed.

A Victorian officer and gentleman, Haig expected others to adhere to the same values and standards and was aghast at the duplicity, deceit and dishonesty displayed by the Prime Minister, the consummate politician. There are numerous examples of Lloyd George going behind Haig's back, with other politicians and with the French allies. There is no doubt that Lloyd George was a patriotic man and he believed in achieving victory. He was, however, appalled at the casualties suffered on the Somme in 1916 and was wary of Haig's intentions surrounding Third Ypres as, correctly as it transpired, he predicted heavy casualties. To mitigate against these he proposed stalling on the Western Front and exploring other strategic options such as supporting Italy or attacking Germany allies on another fronts. In reality, this was not a realistic proposition. High ranking British commanders recognised that Germany could only be defeated on the Western Front and it was to the detriment of the war effort that the civil–military relationship remained problematic.

One consequence of the Third Ypres offensive is that Lloyd George held back much needed reinforcements from Haig at the end of 1917 and beginning of 1918, which necessitated a reorganisation of the infantry, resulting in the disbandment and amalgamation of over 140 battalions. This vindictive move undoubtedly contributed to the initial German success in the opening stages of their Spring 1918 offensive.

Faced with the continuing effects of the mutiny in the French Army, which left them only able to play a supporting role in the Third Ypres offensive, Haig realised that the British were on their own on the Western Front. The United States would be unable to take the field in any meaningful way for another nine months, so he was really left with no option but for the British to bear the brunt of operations on the Western Front. In this circumstance he was correct in his analysis however, it was the method of prosecuting that war at that time which remains open to question.

Without doubt, Haig's greatest mistake at that time was in appointing General Hubert Gough to undertake the northern part of the offensive. Numerous publications refer to Gough as a 'thruster' and it may have been this characteristic that persuaded Haig to chose Gough over Plumer. The flaw in the judgement was predicated on knowledge of the battleground, Gough had last been in the area in the latter days of 1914, and the conduct of the war had changed immeasurably since then. However, as Plumer had been in the Ypres salient for over two years, Haig saw the opportunity to provide new impetus with a man younger than his contemporaries, who had a reputation gained at the Somme and latterly Arras of making progress in difficult circumstances.

Having appointed Gough, Haig should have realised that his reputation was also based on impetuosity, which had been evident throughout his military career. Haig's style was to give his commanders a broad outline of objectives and then let them get on with it. With Gough's character, this was a fatal mistake, evidenced by Gough's repeated failure to capture the Gheluvelt plateau despite repeated orders, and his rash decision to continue with repeated attacks (including Langemarck) before waiting for sufficient artillery to support the infantry attack, and for the ground to have a chance to dry. If Haig is to be castigated, it was for not keeping a tighter reign on Gough and insisting that he followed orders. However, as a fellow Cavalry officer, it is possible that Haig did not wish to curb Gough's enthusiasm as he fervently hoped for a long awaited breakthrough.

When he belatedly decided to transfer responsibility for the main offensive to Plumer's Second Army from Gough's Fifth at the end of August 1917. Plumer asked for, and was granted three weeks to get sufficient artillery into position. It is worthy of note that when Haig visited Second Army and Fifth Army HQ's to discuss plans prior the the recommencement of the offensive in September, he noted that all was satisfactory with Second Army plans and preparations however, following his visit to Fifth Army he noted:

> I am inclined to think that the Fifth Army staff work is not as satisfactory as last year.[1]

When the attack commenced in what is known as the Battle of Menin Road Ridge on 20 September, it was only then that the German strongpoint at Borry Farm which had cost so many lives was captured. Evidence therefore of what careful and considered planning is capable of, instead of rashness in seeking to advance too far without adequate preparation. Therein lay the problem.

The primary reason why Fifth Army performed badly in the offensive is that by 1917 it had become a dysfunctional organisation. Unfortunately, this was to cost the lives of thousands of its own men including the Irishmen who fell on 16 August.

As previously mentioned, General Gough himself had an impulsive character, he was also, however, well regarded personally by officers and men, made them feel at ease and came across as a cordial individual. It is well documented that as a relatively junior officer, he took great pains to visit the troops in the front line regularly to gain their opinions and to offer support, which was well received. As his meteoric rise through the ranks advanced, he found less time to be able to do this and as a consequence, may have lost sight of the situation on the ground.

One of his major failings however, was in the control of his staff. Throughout 1917, Fifth Army operated with a culture of fear, where any deviation from orders or failure to achieve goals

---

1   Sheffield & Bourne (eds.) *Douglas Haig. War Dairies and Letters 1914-1918*, p.328.

was harshly dealt with. Astonishingly, General Gough appears to have been oblivious to this ethos at that time. It is only when it was brought to his attention by his commander in chief on the one hand and a relatively junior, but plain speaking officer on his staff on the other, that he realised that something was amiss.

Overreliance on the undoubted but flawed skills of Major General Neil Malcolm meant that Fifth Army effectively became a dictatorship throughout 1917. Although he led a tyrannical regime, Malcolm appears to have influenced, and drawn others of a similar mien to him. The highly critical comments of Philip Gibbs are worth repeating here:

> I found a general opinion among officers and men, not only of the Irish Division, under the command of the Fifth Army that they had been the victims of atrocious Staff work, tragic in its consequences. From what I saw of some of the Fifth Army staff officers I was of the same opinion. Some of these young gentlemen, and some of the elderly officers were arrogant and supercilious without revealing any symptoms of intelligence. If they had wisdom, it was deeply camouflaged by an air of inefficiency. If they had knowledge, they hid it as a secret of their own.[2]

Unfortunately, even after Malcolm's departure, the Fifth Army would take time to recover from this dent in their reputation and time was not on their side as they bore the brunt of the German Spring Offensive. In the midst of this, Gough was sacked. A decision that he felt was harsh. In a conversation with another senior Irish officer, Major General Ladislaus Herbert Richard Pope-Hennessy in 1933, Gough complained of being sacked in 1918 and admitted that he ought to have been sacked for Passchendaele.[3]

The conduct of Fifth Army operations from the opening of the offensive is lamentable and much culpability must lie with preparations and assessments carried out by the Headquarters staff. The coming of torrential rain on the afternoon of 31 July should have been a red light to consider halting the offensive until the ground dried. Perhaps as was the case with the then Brigadier General Davidson at GHQ, no-one from Fifth Army HQ had ever visited the battlefield to establish conditions for themselves. If they had done so an appreciation of the situation would at least have provoked discussion as to how to proceed. As it was, the decision to continue compounded the problems.

The relief of 55th and 15th divisions from 1-4 August by 16th and 36th divisions was the death knell for any chance of a positive outcome for the Irish Division. Both the relieved divisions were exhausted and had suffered heavily, so much so that 55th Division were withdrawn from the line for five weeks to recuperate and reorganise. The 15th Division were unlucky, in that although they had suffered equally heavily, they were back in the front line, relieving 16th Division on 18 August. The same experience befell 8th Division of neighbouring II Corps, who were given two weeks to recover from the mauling they had received on 31 July before taking part in the Battle of Langemarck. This mismanagement of resources ensured that little progress could be made, and was especially harsh on the Irish divisions.

---

2   Gibbs, *Realities of War*, p.389.
3   GB 99 KCLMA Liddell Hart Centre for Military Archives. LH 11/1933/23.

To ensure any chance of success, the Irish divisions were required to be up to strength and fresh for 16 August. The fact that they had to relieve the other divisions and hold the front line for two weeks before the assault, ensured that they had no chance to succeed and were beaten before they started.

Existing in a swamp with little cover and under continual German artillery fire led to steady degradation of their fighting strength, to the extent that when the advance commenced, some battalions comprised a third of their fighting strength. The *Official History* states that some battalions were down to half their establishment however. Further research demonstrates that some figures were lower than that and it was commented that:

> The waves of the assaulting troops were so thin that, in the words of a participant, the operation looked more like a raid than a major operation.[4]

The effect of the conditions on his troops has been sympathetically remarked upon in Major General Nugent's correspondence:

> It is a horrible wearing form of fighting having to sit still and be shelled night and day.[5]

The problem for both Irish divisions was that any representation to their Corps Commander for respite was likely to go no further, as General Watts was unlikely to approach Fifth Army given the fearsome reputation of Major General Malcolm.

Having left both divisions in appalling conditions for many days, the sensible thing to do would have been to wait until drier conditions prevailed as had been directed by Field Marshal Haig. This would have had a number of benefits:

- With firmer ground, Artillery assets could have been moved forward to accurately target German batteries on the Gheluvelt plateau. Drier conditions would also have made the battlefield firmer underfoot and enabled the infantry to advance within the protective blanket of the creeping barrage.
- Firmer ground would also have ensured that Tanks could have been utilised to their full potential. The outcome of the battle may have been very different if the tanks had been used as an asset to support the infantry at close quarters against bunkers and pillboxes.
- A pause in proceedings would have meant that 16th and 36th Divisions would not have had to replace 55th and 15th Divisions in the front line, and would have been able to spend valuable time training and resting before being pitched into battle.

Once the advance started, evidence indicates that the officers and men of each of the infantry battalions showed outstanding bravery against overwhelming odds. It must have been a daunting task to advance through in places waist high mud, to attack well fortified German positions.

The attack began to fail around one hour after Zero hour, when 9th Battalion Royal Irish Fusiliers came up against impenetrable barbed wire defences in front of the German strongpoint

---

4 Edmonds, *History of the Great War based on Official Documents, Military Operations France and Belgium 1917* p.195.
5 PRONI D/3835/E/2/14 Farren Connell papers.

of Gallipoli Farm. This barbed wire had not been adequately dealt with by Artillery fire and the infantry were funnelled into a killing zone covered by machine guns from in front and on both sides, a fact borne out by the high number of fatalities suffered by the battalion. When the Fusiliers began to retire, the positions of the battalions on either side of them became untenable and they were forced to withdraw also. This action had a ripple effect along XIX Corps front and was compounded by the German counter attack which meant that with the exception of 11th Royal Inniskilling Fusiliers on the far left of 36th Division front, no ground was gained whatsoever.

That the massing of German counter attack troops was not observed and prior warning given, indicates a failure on the part of the Royal Flying Corps. Several accounts from the infantry battalions of both divisions indicate that the sky was empty of British aircraft however, although there were difficulties with low cloud and smoke from the battle, records indicate that aircraft from 21 Squadron were in the air from just after 5:00 a.m. With the weight of the counter attack, it is commendable that the Black Line was able to be held with composite units and stragglers hastily assembled.

The medical evacuation chain appears by all accounts to have worked exceptionally well under trying circumstances. The retrieval of the wounded from the battlefield was a gruelling task in horrendous conditions and the Royal Army Medical Corps stretcher bearers supplemented by those from other units, performed heroically. Testament to this is the fact that despite many other worthy cases, the only Victoria Cross earned by the Irish divisions on 16 August was awarded to a stretcher bearer.

To say that the German defensive system was not given sufficient attention by Fifth Army planners would be something of an understatement. The architect of the system, Generalmajor Fritz von Lossberg had designed a defensive system of mutually supporting strongpoints garrisoned by many machine guns, the defensive principle being that attacking troops would make some progress and that when they had been thinned out by machine gun fire from the pillboxes and bunkers, they would then be attacked in overwhelming force by the *Eingreif* divisions. That the design of such a defensive system was entrusted to a relatively junior officer is indicative of German military thinking of the time which was innovative and depended on skills rather than seniority. Fifth Army staff were aware that the pillboxes and bunkers had not been neutralised by the artillery bombardment as pre-battle reports indicated that any camouflage had been swept away by exploding shells to reveal white concrete structures which were evidently impervious to the artillery available.

Thursday 16 August 1917 was a dark day for Ireland. The 16th (Irish) and 36th (Ulster) Divisions) having triumphed together at Wytschaete 10 weeks earlier, were neglectfully thrust into an attack which had no prospect of success from the outset. They were disadvantaged by weak leadership at Corps level and by an uncaring and incompetent Fifth Army, the staff of which neither knew nor cared of the conditions that men were being sent to fight in.

The deaths of over 850 men in the period 31 July to 15 August and over 1240 during the subsequent battle and the days immediately afterwards, cast a dark shadow across the country, especially as so many of those who fell were reported missing. The impact of such losses was equated by the *Belfast Weekly Telegraph* to the Somme battles of 1916. There are many accounts of the Battle of the Somme in print. Hopefully, this account will go some way to tell the story of those who fought during the Battle of Langemarck.

Appendix I

Infantry Battalions of 16th (Irish) and 36th (Ulster) Division
Orders of Battle
Langemarck, 16 August 1917

16th (Irish) Division

47th Infantry Brigade
1st Battalion Royal Munster Fusiliers
6th (Service) Battalion Royal Irish Regiment
6th (Service) Battalion Connaught Rangers
7th (Service) Battalion Leinster Regiment

48th Infantry Brigade
2nd Battalion Royal Dublin Fusiliers
7th (Service) Battalion Royal Irish Rifles
8th (Service) Battalion Royal Dublin Fusiliers
9th (Service) Battalion Royal Dublin Fusiliers

49th Infantry Brigade
2nd Battalion Royal Irish Regiment
7th (Service) Battalion Royal Inniskilling Fusiliers
7/8th (Service) Battalion Royal Irish Fusiliers
8th (Service) Battalion Royal Inniskilling Fusiliers

Divisional Troops
11th (Service) Battalion Hampshire Regiment (Pioneers)

36th (Ulster) Division

107th Infantry Brigade
8th (Service) Battalion Royal Irish Rifles (East Belfast Volunteers)
9th (Service) Battalion Royal Irish Rifles (West Belfast Volunteers)
10th (Service) Battalion Royal Irish Rifles (South Belfast Volunteers)

15th (Service) Battalion Royal Irish Rifles (North Belfast Volunteers)

108th Infantry Brigade
11th (Service) Battalion Royal Irish Rifles (South Antrim Volunteers)
12th (Service) Battalion Royal Irish Rifles (Central Antrim Volunteers)
13th (Service) Battalion Royal Irish Rifles (1st County Down Volunteers)
9th (Service) Battalion Royal Irish Fusiliers (Armagh, Cavan and Monaghan Volunteers)

109th Infantry Brigade
9th (Service) Battalion Royal Inniskilling Fusiliers (Tyrone Volunteers)
10th (Service) Battalion Royal Inniskilling Fusiliers (Derry Volunteers)
11th (Service) Battalion Royal Inniskilling Fusiliers (Donegal and Fermanagh Volunteers)
14th (Service) Battalion Royal Irish Rifles (Young Citizen Volunteers of Belfast)

Divisional Troops
16th (Service) Battalion Royal Irish Rifles (2nd County Down Volunteers) (Pioneers)

Appendix II

**Group Ypres, Fourth Army
Orders of Battle
16 August 1917**

79th Reserve Division
261st Reserve Infantry Regiment
262nd Reserve Infantry Regiment
263rd Reserve Infantry Regiment

5th Bavarian Division
7th Bavarian Infantry Regiment
19th Bavarian Infantry Regiment
21st Bavarian Infantry Regiment

3rd Reserve Division
2nd Reserve Infantry Regiment
34th Fusilier Regiment
49th Reserve Infantry Regiment

54th Division
27th Reserve Infantry Regiment
84th Infantry Regiment
90th Infantry Regiment

In Reserve
56th Division
183rd Division

Appendix III

(Annexe to Fifth Army Summary of the 17th August, 1917).

Translation of captured order issued by German Fourth Army, dated July, 1917.

1. The construction of defensive positions has been radically altered in character by the experience of the fighting of the year 1917. The positions of the Fourth Army are henceforward to be constructed on the principles which follow.

The nature of the construction is to be divided into :-

(a) Construction of positions on the battlefield.
(b) Construction of fresh positions.
(c) Modification of old positions.

(a) Construction of positions on the battlefield.

2. In the case of the positions constructed hitherto with several continuous lines, the plan of the enemy is to destroy them at the beginning of a battle by the expenditure of great quantities of ammunition. The dugouts situated in old trenches, principally in the first and second lines, were man-traps and have often led to the loss of a large number of prisoners. These circumstances prove the weakness of the rigid methods of defence practised hitherto, shortly before and during the battle.

The strength of the defence must lie in the concealment of our fighting force from the enemy's observation - trenches, dugouts, machine guns, military organizations and battery positions which appear on the enemy's aeroplane photographs, will be sacrificed to the enemy's artillery.

The severity of the enemy's fire makes any effort to keep our trenches in repair impossible. Any attempt to do so exhausts the fighting strength of the troops prematurely, while it is impossible to keep pace with the work of destruction.

Another method of construction must therefore be put in hand at the beginning of the battle. That is to say there must be a deliberate transition from the old pattern of position which is visible and will be shot to pieces by the enemy, to a zone of defence fortified in depth. This must allow of offensive action by the defence from positions concealed as far as possible, lightly manned in front and more thickly towards the rear.

3. Principles.

I. As the destructive fire of the enemy proceeds, the mass of the infantry is to be taken out of the forward visible and battered trenches and dugouts and to be echeloned in depth in the open before the first infantry attack.

In old positions completely new dispositions must be introduced without reference to existing trenches, simply according to the circumstances of the battle. It is the duty of all officers to order and carry out unhesitatingly the methodical disposal of the troops at the proper time..

II. Shell-hole nests are to take the place of a trench line and are to be occupied by squads and single machine guns arranged chockerwise over the area.

- 2 -

Care is to be taken to improve the shelter in the shell-holes by the insertion of frames or by joining adjacent shell-holes by means of tunnels supported by frames. The excavated earth is to be thrown into shell holes near by or, if the condition of the soil permits, distributed over the ground; thus in time tunnelled dugouts are formed which to outward appearance are shell holes and are invisible to aeroplane observation. If frames cannot be used for the purpose owing to water in the ground, the simplest means are to be used to give protection against shrapnel-fire.

Close behind the forward shell-hole line, strong points are to be constructed for machine guns, Assault troops and elements of the supports that have been brought forward. Wire is to be erected in front of the forward shell-hole line, irregular in trace, but connected as far as possible. It has been found useful to fill up the shell holes in front of the shell hole line with wire to prevent their occupation by the enemy.

Further back, it is best for the shell hole nests to have wire entanglements only local in extent, since continuous belts make offensive action on our part more difficult.

Wire entanglements that cause the enemy to change direction and be exposed to machine gun fire are to be frequently employed.

All work of construction must be hidden from the enemy. Conspicuous works and connected trench lines do not conform to this important condition.

III. A great part of the reserves and supports are to accommodated in the open in and near shell holes, in woods, ravines etc. wherever cover from air observation exists. Villages, which, as experience shows, draw enemy fire, must be as far as possible avoided.

Reserves and supports must work methodically at the construction of a continuous line consisting of several trenches (a reverse slope line), which must be screened from enemy observation.

This position will form a support for the echeloned defences in front of it. It must be strongly wired with gaps for the passage of troops to attack through and must have several trenches. Deep dugouts will only be constructed in the second and third line. The first line will only contain small dugouts for about one sixth of the garrison.

This position will be generally . . the position for the protection of the artillery and will be about 1½ to 2 kilometres from the forward shell-hole line.

IV. If there is sufficient labour available, further rear positions are to be constructed on these principles as support positions (Ruckhaltstellung).

(b)

- 3 -

(b). On the construction of new positions.

4. The principles laid down for the construction of a zone of defence fortified in depth will also apply to the construction of the forward position, the protective position for the artillery, and the communication trenches between them.

5. It is not sufficient that the infantry alone should be disposed in depth. The principles laid down must also be followed in the disposition of Machine Guns and trench mortars, and above all in the disposition of the artillery with its O.P's and Command posts.
   The chief strength of the position is to be sought by organisation in depth, in the proper distribution of force over the whole fortified zone and in concealment.

6. Care is to be taken that cover against air observation is ensured. Artillery positions and machine gun emplacements in the fortified zone which are located during construction, lose their value. Every single man must know this. Air photographs of our own positions must be taken to ensure that due precautions are being observed. Dummy works will be employed in order to deceive the enemy.

7. Dugouts are to be begun at once throughout the whole depth of the defensive zone. Dugouts are to be provided in the first trench for 1/6th of the garrison of the forward line (fighting troops); in the second trench for 1/3rd of the garrison; further to the rear as far as the protective position for artillery, (exclusive) for about $\frac{1}{2}$ of the fighting troops. The same principles are to be followed in the construction of the position for the protection of the artillery which is designed for occupation by the supports.
   Numerous dugouts are to be constructed outside the trenches, in readiness for the methodical distribution of the trench garrison over the intervening area at the commencement of defensive operations.

Where mined dugouts can be constructed, they are to be covered by 8 to 10 metres of earth and to have at least 2 exits. In the case of concreted dugouts, a high elevation is to be avoided. Their tops are to be kept flat.

8. The dugouts in the forward line must also be shell-proof; there must be just sufficient accommodation for the small proportion of the garrison laid down in para. 7.
   If these shell-proof dugouts can be constructed of less depth than the mined dugouts by the use of material of greater resisting power, such as concrete, iron, and beams, this is to be recommended as facilitating the rapid exit of the men.
   Long struts are to be used in the construction of deep dugouts so that the exits may be wide and high and facilitate the rapid egress of the garrison. Care is to be taken that the exit has sufficiently strong head cover.
   Besides these dugouts, each for about a gruppo (9 men), splinter-proof shelters for observation posts are necessary close beside the dugouts. From these observation will normally take place. In case of an intense bombardment, observation will be carried out by courageous men who will leave the dugouts at frequent intervals and observe over the parapet.

9.

- 4 -

9. It is of advantage to have an exit from the rear of the dugout leading back from the trench, preferably into a shell-hole, which conceals it from view.

The garrison can then leave their dugouts when the enemy has penetrated into the trench (see sketch).

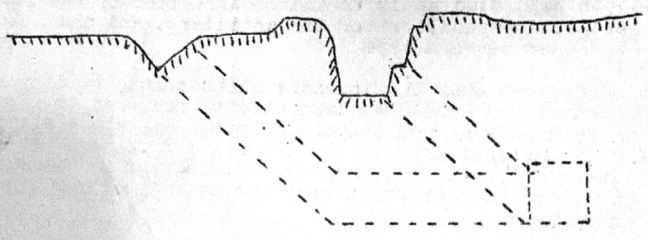

10. To ensure the certainty of the alarm being given in deep dugouts, it is recommended that several niches should be made in the entrance of dugouts and in them sentries should be posted. These sentries will be able to engage the enemy directly he enters the trench and will, by keeping the entrance free, enable the garrison to turn out. For a similar purpose it is advantageous to construct a machine gun emplacement on the flank of deep dugouts. This will make it possible to keep the entrance to the dugout under fire and prevent the enemy from entering.

11. In front of the forward trench a strong and continuous wire entanglement is necessary, consisting of 3 belts each 10 metres wide at intervals of 5 to 10 metres. It should follow an irregular trace and is not to be too high. Particular care is to be taken to ensure that the front belt of wire can be swept by flanking fire. The wire is not to be taut; otherwise it gets severely damaged by air pressure when a shell explodes. For emergency purposes strong isolated belts of wire 1 metre to 1½ metres high at intervals of 2 to 3 metres can be employed.

The first step in the construction of the position is the erection of the first belt of wire, the outer edge of which will be about 60 metres in front of the front trench. In front of the second and third trenches and, in the case of rear positions, in front of the forward trench line also, gaps for the passage of troops moving to attack are to be left. To begin with, only the posts for the wire are to be driven in, the wire is to be dumped in readiness.

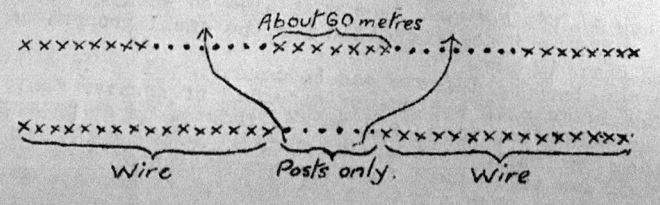

The protection of the first of the 3 belts of wire must be done from holes or portions of trench behind the first belt of wire.

In the zone fortified in depth, the wire entanglements are to be distributed over the whole area, in irregular lines about 10 metres broad, or in numerous strong belts, advantage being taken of the cover afforded by the ground, such as hedges, sunken roads, etc.

- 5 -

12. **Order of procedure in all new work.**

   Marking out - wiring - dugouts.
   Digging of trenches last, unless lack of material renders it necessary to proceed with it first.

13. The construction of a very large number of machine gun emplacements in the ground between the lines at once be begun. Machine gun emplacements will be sited not on high points but on slopes and in ravines, with the object of securing flanking fire.
   They must take the enemy by surprise. It is therefore not advisable to place these machine guns in the angles of the wire. The enemy is bound to suspect their presence there. (see sketch).

   Dummy emplacements are to be constructed at those points while the actual machine guns are concealed on the flanks or in rear. It is particularly important that machine gun emplacements should be screened from observation from the air. Accordingly the first step is to cover the excavation and the materials for construction by means of wire netting covered with brushwood. The machine gun emplacement must not be completely surrounded by high wire which gives away the emplacement to the airman. It is preferable to erect belts of wire or several wire defences so arranged that the enemy must run into them and that they can be swept along their length.

14. Here and there in the position the communication trenches between the several lines can be built obliquely without much increasing their length. (Sketches a and b). This procedure will provide a network in which the communication trenches, which are always to be provided with wire and to be organised for fire, can be utilized as switch lines.

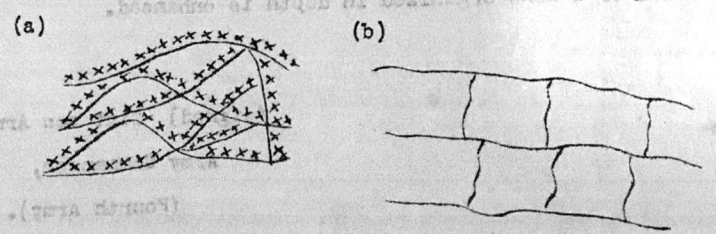

   (a)   (b)

   This arrangement has the following advantages: that the enemy cannot accurately locate our defensive system. If he intends to destroy the position he must engage the area between the 1st and 3rd lines. This will impede and tend to break up his artillery preparation. The enemy having penetrated is caught in the network and is prevented from surrounding the trench garrison which is holding out in front.

– 6 –

If the communication trenches are in straight lines (sketch b) the enemy can engage the separate lines and neglect the intermediate ground.

(c) <u>Reconstruction of old positions.</u>

15. In the old positions and also at many parts of the FLANDERN STELLUNG (ZONNEBEKE – STADEN Line) the majority of the dugouts are in the first trench and but few in the rear lines. This mistake is in future to be avoided, for it leads to crowding of the forward line of defence with the well-known disastrous consequences.

In the rear positions and in the FLANDERN STELLUNG, where the ground permits, this mistake is to be remedied by digging a new trench in front of the old first trench.

In the old forward lines, where this is out of the question the alteration is to be effected by the rapid construction of dugouts in the rear lines of the position. As this work progresses the dugouts of the forward line are to be gradually reduced. This can be done either by removing the material of superfluous dugouts and employing it for dugouts in the rear or by barricading existing concrete dugouts so that they cannot be opened except on the express order of responsible senior officers. They will possibly then afford convenient points of assembly for our own Assault troops in case of an attack by us.

When the sketch showing work done is sent in on the 25th of each month all groups and the Guard Corps are to state, with reference to local conditions, how the reconstruction of old positions has advanced.

16. In certain sectors and especially in the rearward positions, the work on positions has been chiefly directed to the upkeep of trench-lines. The fortification of the zone organised in depth has not been properly carried out everywhere. I am aware that the maintenance of positions in certain sectors has been difficult and has made very heavy demands on the troops. In spite of the great amount of work accomplished, parts of the positions, as is shown in the reports, are not capable of defence owing to the state of the ground. In such sectors the value of a zone organized in depth is enhanced.

(signed) Sixt von Arnim,

Army Commander,

(Fourth Army).

1   IWM Doc 7190. Private papers of Colonel Kenneth Charles Weldon DSO

Appendix IV

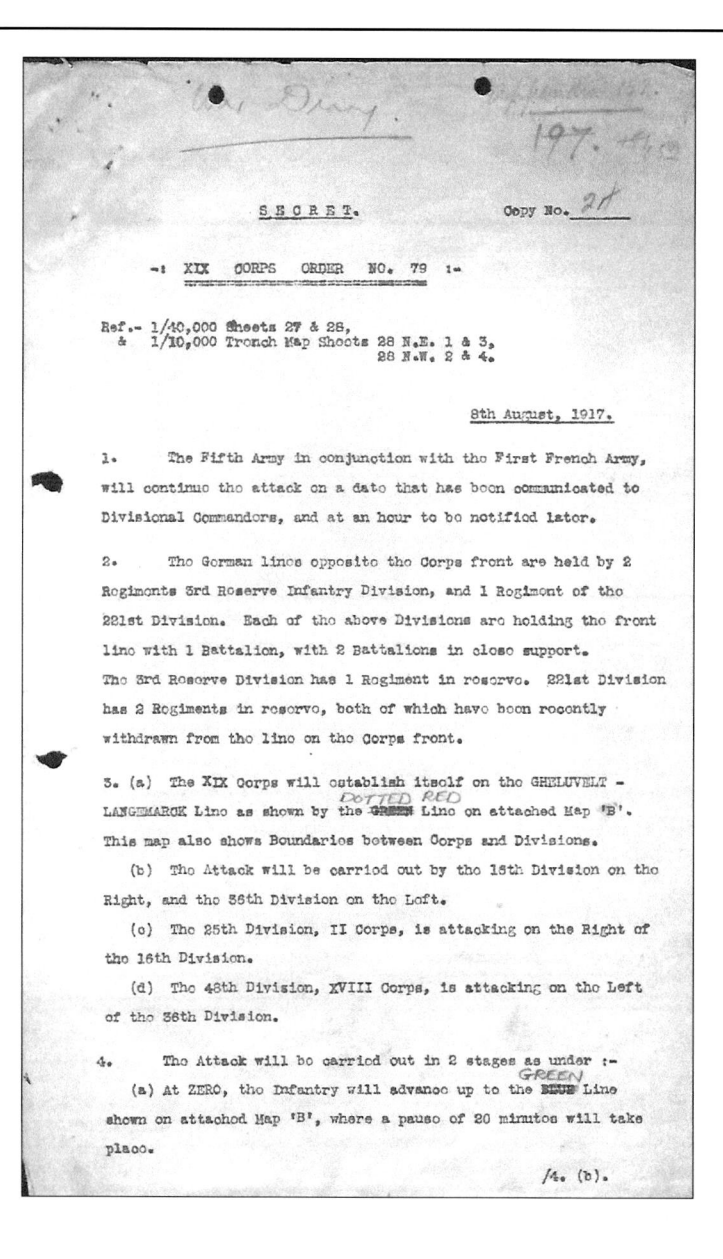

S E C R E T.   Copy No. 21

XIX CORPS ORDER NO. 79

Ref.- 1/40,000 Sheets 27 & 28,
& 1/10,000 Trench Map Sheets 28 N.E. 1 & 3,
28 N.W. 2 & 4.

8th August, 1917.

1. The Fifth Army in conjunction with the First French Army, will continue the attack on a date that has been communicated to Divisional Commanders, and at an hour to be notified later.

2. The German lines opposite the Corps front are held by 2 Regiments 3rd Reserve Infantry Division, and 1 Regiment of the 221st Division. Each of the above Divisions are holding the front line with 1 Battalion, with 2 Battalions in close support. The 3rd Reserve Division has 1 Regiment in reserve. 221st Division has 2 Regiments in reserve, both of which have been recently withdrawn from the line on the Corps front.

3. (a) The XIX Corps will establish itself on the GHELUVELT - LANGEMARCK Line as shown by the ~~GREEN~~ DOTTED RED Line on attached Map 'B'. This map also shows Boundaries between Corps and Divisions.

   (b) The Attack will be carried out by the 16th Division on the Right, and the 36th Division on the Left.

   (c) The 25th Division, II Corps, is attacking on the Right of the 16th Division.

   (d) The 48th Division, XVIII Corps, is attacking on the Left of the 36th Division.

4. The Attack will be carried out in 2 stages as under :-

   (a) At ZERO, the Infantry will advance up to the ~~BLUE~~ GREEN Line shown on attached Map 'B', where a pause of 20 minutes will take place.

/4. (b).

- 2 -

(b) At the conclusion of that period, they will advance and capture the GHELUVELT - LANGEMARCK Line. The 56th Division will also establish a post at, or near WURST FARM in order to have observation over the valley of the STROOMBEEK.

5. (a) Separate instructions for the bombardment of the positions to be attacked have been issued. (XIX Corps Artillery Instructions).

(b) Instructions and Maps regarding Barrages are also issued separately.

6. The Attack will be supported by Machine Gun Barrages, which will be carried out under Divisional arrangements.

7. 3rd Brigade Tank Corps will allot Tanks to support the attack as follows :-

    1 Section 'C' Battn. to 15th Division.

    1 Section 'B' Battn. to 56th Division.

These Tanks cannot be guaranteed owing to the uncertain weather conditions, but should be available if there is no more rain before the operation.

Tanks cannot possibly leave their Starting Points before it is light, and this will probably put them behind the Infantry. They will therefore act as "moppers up" in cases where isolated positions continue to hold out.

8. No. 21 Squadron R.F.C. will detail a Contact Patrol Aeroplane to work with the attacking Divisions during the attack.

Flares will be lit by the Infantry in the front line, and Watson Fans waved.:-

(a) When called upon to do so by the Contact Aeroplane, by means of Klaxon Horns and Very Lights.

This call will, if the attack proceeds as arranged, only be made at times when the Infantry are believed to have reached the GREEN Line, and the final objective.

(b) When the Infantry consider it advisable to make known the position of their front line.

/RED FLARES.

- 3 -

RED FLARES will be used.

Contact Aeroplanes will be marked with a BLACK PLAQUE projecting behind the Right Lower Wing.

In addition to the above Contact Aeroplane, one Infantry Protection Machine will be in the air from ZERO hour until Dark. This machine will carry no distinctive marking.

9. Signal Instructions have been issued to all concerned.

10. A Staff Officer, XIX Corps, will visit Divisional and H.A. Headquarters between 11 a.m. and 1 p.m. daily, commencing on August 10th, to synchronise watches.

Watches will be synchronised again on the evening of 'Y' Day between the hours of 5 p.m. and 7 p.m.

11. ACKNOWLEDGE.

Hyon
Brigadier-General,

Issued at *9 p.m.*
General Staff, XIX Corps.

Copies to :-

No. 1. 15th Division.
    2. 16th Division.
    3. 36th Division.
    4. 55th Division.
    5. 61st Division.
    6. II Corps.
    7. XVIII Corps.
  8-9. No. 21 Squadron R.F.C.
10-12. 3rd Brigade Tank Corps.
   13. Adv. Tank Corps, Fifth Army.
   14. A.D.C. (for Corps Commander).
   15. G.O.C., R.A.
   16. B.G., H.A., XIX Corps.
   17. 'A' & 'Q'.
   18. C.E.
   19. A.D. Sigs.
   20. A.P.M.
   21. D.D.M.S.
   22. G.S. "I".
   23. File.
   24. War Diary.

SECRET.

XIX Corps No. O.O.79/1.

AMENDMENT TO XIX CORPS ORDER NO. 79, dated 8/8/17 :-

1. It has been laid down by the Army that the BLUE LINE as shown in Map 'B' will be known as the GREEN LINE, and the final objective, original GREEN LINE, as the DOTTED RED LINE.

   An amended map 'B' will be issued shortly.

2. The following amendments will be made :-

   (a) Para. 3 (a) line 2.   For "GREEN" substitute "DOTTED RED".
   (b) Para. 4 (a) Line 1.   For "BLUE" substitute "GREEN".
   (c) Para. 8 (a) Line 5.   For "BLUE" substitute "GREEN".

3. ACKNOWLEDGE.

9th August, 1917.

Brigadier-General,
General Staff, XIX Corps.

Addressed all recipients of XIX Corps Order No. 79.

Bibliography

Archival Sources

The National Archives, Kew (TNA)
WO 95 Series, Corps, Divisional, Brigade and Battalion war diaries
WO 153 Series, War Office Maps and Plans
WO 339 and 374 Series, Officer's personal records
CAB 23 & 24 Series, War Cabinet correspondence
CAB 45 Series, Committee of Imperial Defence. Official war histories correspondence

Imperial War Museum (IWM)
Doc. 7190 Private papers of Colonel Kenneth Charles Weldon DSO
Doc. 10995 Private papers of Captain Edwin Albert Godson MC
Doc 21037 Private papers of Captain Arthur Evanson Glanville
Doc. 22065 Private papers of Sergeant Robert McKay

Public Records Office Northern Ireland (PRONI)
D1973 2nd Lieutenant Jack Carrother's letters
D3835 Farren Connell papers – Major General Oliver Nugent letters
Londonderry Memorial Records

Liddell Hart Centre for Military Archives (KCLMA), King's College London
GB 99 KCLMA Beddington – Papers of Brigadier General Sir Henry Lionel Beddington
GB 99 KCLMA Edmonds – Papers of Brigadier General Sir James Edmonds

Liddle Collection, University of Leeds
Special Collections: Liddle/WW1/GE09. Papers of Lieutenant Colonel L Kalepky, *Das Fusilier Regiment, 'Konigin' Nr.86*.

Printed Sources

Christopher Thomas Atkinson, *The Seventh Division 1914-1918* (London: John Murray, 1927).
Christopher D'Arcy Baker-Carr, *From Chauffeur to Brigadier* (Driffield: Oakpast Ltd reprint of 1930 edition).

Robert Blake, *The Private Papers of Douglas Haig, 1914-1919* (London: Eyre & Spottiswoode, 1952).
Jonathan Boff, *Haig's Enemy, Crown Prince Rupprecht and Germany's War on the Western Front* (Oxford: Oxford University Press, 2020).
Timothy Bowman, William Butler & Michael Wheately, *The Disparity of Sacrifice: Irish Recruitment to the British Armed Forces, 1914-1918* (Liverpool: Liverpool University Press, 2020).
Frank Napier Broome, *Not the Whole Truth* (Pietermaritzburg: University of Natal Press, 1962).
Douglas Gordon Browne MC, *The Tank in Action* (Uckfield: Naval & Military Press reprint of 1920 edition).
Tom Burnell & Margaret Gilbert, *The Wexford War Dead: A History of Casualties of the World Wars* (Dublin: Nonsuch Publishing, 2009).
Tom Burnell, *The Waterford War Dead: A History of Casualties of the Great War* (Dublin: The History Press Ltd, 2010).
Tom Burnell, *The Clare War Dead: A History of Casualties of the Great War* (Dublin: The History Press Ltd, 2011).
Tom Burnell, *The Kilkenny War Dead* (Kilkenny: Privately published, 2014).
William Canning, *Ballyshannon, Belcoo, Bertincourt: The History of the 11th Battalion the Royal Inniskilling Fusiliers (Donegal & Fermanagh Volunteers) in World War One* (Antrim: Canning, 1996).
—— *A Wheen of Medals: The History of the 9th (Service) Bn. The Royal Inniskilling Fusiliers (The Tyrones) in World War One* (Antrim: Canning, 2006)
David Carrothers, *Memoirs of a Young Lieutenant 1898-1917* (Enniskillen: Privately published, n.d.).
Brigadier General John Charteris, *Field Marshal Earl Haig* (London: Cassell and Company Ltd, 1929).
Jim Condon, *Officers of the Royal Inniskilling Fusiliers in World War 1* (Droitwich Spa: Privately published, 1993).
Reverend James Ogden Coop DSO, *The Story of the 55th (West Lancashire) Division* (Liverpool: Daily Post Printers, 1919).
Hermann Cron, *The Imperial German Army 1914-18: Organisation, Structure, Orders of Battle* (Solihull: Helion & Company, 2002).
Dominiek Dendooven (ed.), *1917. The Passchendaele Year. The British Army in Flanders. The Diary of Achiel Van Walleghem* (Brighton: Edward Everett Root Publishing, 2017)
Terence Denman, *Ireland's Unknown Soldiers. The 16th (Irish) Division in the Great War, 1914-1918* (Dublin: Irish Academic Press, 1992).
George Albemarle Bertie Dewar & Lieutenant Colonel John Herbert Boraston, *Sir Douglas Haig's Command, December 19, 1915 to November 11, 1918* (London: Constable, 1922).
Brigadier-General Sir James Edward Edmonds. *Military Operations France and Belgium 1917*, Vol. II (London: HMSO, 1948).
John Ewing MC *The History of the 9th (Scottish) Division 1914-1919* (Uckfield: Naval & Military Press reprint of 1921 edition).
Cyril Falls, *The History of the 36th (Ulster) Division* (Belfast: McCaw, Stevenson & Orr, 1922).
Cyril Falls, *The History of the First Seven Battalions The Royal Irish Rifles in the Great War.* (Uckfield: Naval & Military Press reprint of 1925 edition).

General Sir Martin Farndale KCB, *History of the Royal Regiment of Artillery: Western Front 1914-1918.* (London: Royal Artillery Institution, 1986).

Anthony Farrar-Hockley, *Goughie: The Life of General Sir Hubert Gough* (St Albans: Hart-Davis, MacGibbon Ltd, 1975).

Sir Frank Fox, *The Royal Inniskilling Fusiliers in the World War* (Uckfield: Naval & Military Press reprint of 1928 edition).

Noel French, *The Meath War Dead: A History of the Casualties of the Great War* (Dublin: History Press Ireland, 2011).

Brigadier-General Stannus Geoghegan, *Royal Irish Regiment 1900-1922* (Uckfield: Naval & Military Press reprint of 1927 edition).

Phillip Gibbs, *Realities of War* (London: Heinemann, 1920).

Phillip Gibbs, *From Bapaume to Passchendaele 1917* (London: Heinemann, 1965).

General Sir Hubert Gough, *The Fifth Army* (London: Hodder and Stoughton, 1931).

—— *Soldiering On* (London: Arthur Barker, 1954).

Robert Graves, *Goodbye to All That* (London: Penguin Books, 1960).

Richard Grayson, (ed.), *At War with the 16th Irish Division 1914-1918: The Staniforth Letters* (Barnsley: Pen & Sword, 2012)

William Henry Archibald Groom, *Poor Bloody Infantry: The Truth Untold* (New Malden: Picardy Publishing, 1983)

Paul Ham, *Passchendaele: Requiem for Doomed Youth* (London: Penguin Random House UK, 2018).

Major Henry Edward Davis Harris, *The Irish Regiments in the First World War* (Cork: Mercier Press, 1968).

Thomas Hennessy, *The Great War 1914-1918: Bank of Ireland Staff Service Record* (Uckfield: Naval & Military Press, 1920, Reprint)

Trevor Henshaw, *The Sky Their Battlefield: Air Fighting and the Complete List of Allied Air Casualties from Enemy Action in the First World War* (London: Grub Street, 1995)

Richard Holmes, *Fatal Avenue. A Traveller's History of the Battlefields of Northern France and Flanders 1346-1945* (London: Random House, 2008)

Carole Hope, *Worshipper and Worshipped: Across the Divide – An Irish Padre of the Great War, Fr Willie Doyle Chaplain to the Forces 1915-1917* (Brighton: Reveille Press, 2013)

Laurence Housman (ed.), *War Letters of Fallen Englishmen* (Philadelphia, Pennsylvania: First Pine Street Books, 2002).

Gavin Hughes, *The Hounds of Ulster: A History of the Northern Irish Regiments in the Great War* (Bern: Peter Lang, 2012)

Intelligence Section of the General Staff, American Expeditionary Forces, *Histories of Two Hundred and Fifty-One Divisions of the German Army Which Participated in the War 1914-1918* (London: London Stamp Exchange 1989 reprint of 1920 edition)

John H Johnston, *Stalemate: The Real Story of Trench Warfare.* (London: Rigel Publications, 1995)

Tom Johnstone, *Orange, Green and Khaki: The Story of the Irish Regiments in the Great War 1914-1918* (Dublin: Gill & MacMillan, 1992)

Henry Albert Jones, *The War in the Air: Being the Story of the part played in the Great War by the Royal Air Force. Volume Four* (Uckfield: Naval & Military Press reprint of 1934 edition).

Nigel H Jones, *The War Walk: A Journey Along the Western Front* (London: Robert Hale, 1983).

Lieutenant Colonel Henry Francis Newdigate Jourdain & Edward Fraser, *The Connaught Rangers, Volume III* (Cork: Schull Books 1999 reprint of 1928 edition).
John Laffin, *British Butchers and Bunglers of World War One* (Godalming: Bramley Books, 1988).
Basil Henry Liddell Hart, *The Real War 1914-1918* (London: Faber & Faber, 1930).
Peter H Liddle (ed.) *Passchendaele in Perspective: The Third Battle of Ypres* (London: Leo Cooper, 1997).
Nick Lloyd, *Passchendaele: A New History* (London: Penguin Random House, 2017).
David Lloyd-George, *War Memoirs of David Lloyd George*, Vols I & 2 (London: Odhams Press Limited, 1934).
Paul Maze, *A Frenchman in Khaki* (London: Heinemann, 1934).
Nick Metcalfe, *Blacker's Boys: 9th (Service) Battalion, Princess Victoria's (Royal Irish Fusiliers) (County Armagh) & 9th (North Irish Horse) Battalion, Princess Victoria's (Royal Irish Fusiliers) 1914-1919* (Woodstock: Writer's World, 2012).
Catherine Minford, et al, *It wasn't all Sunshine. An Ordinary Man's Account of the First World War* (Larne: Larne Borough Council, 2012).
Gardiner S Mitchell, *'Three Cheers for the Derry's!' A History of the 10th Royal Inniskilling Fusiliers in the 1914-18 War* (Derry: YES Publications, 1991).
Stephen Moore, *The Chocolate Soldiers: The Story of the Young Citizen Volunteers and 14th Royal Irish Rifles during the Great War* (Newtownards: Colourpoint, 2016)
Lyn MacDonald, *They Called it Passchendaele: The Story of the Third Battle of Ypres 1917 and the Men Who Fought It* (London: Penguin, 1978).
Captain S McCance, *History of the Royal Munster Fusiliers 1861-1922* (Uckfield: Naval & Military Press reprint of 1927 edition).
Chris McCarthy, *The Third Ypres: Passchendaele, The Day-by-Day Account* (London: Arms and Armour Press, 1995).
Peter Oldham, *Pill Boxes on the Western Front: A Guide to the Design, Construction and Use of Concrete Pill Boxes 1914-1918*. (Barnsley: Pen & Sword Military, 2011)
David R Orr & David Truesdale, *'Ulster Will Fight' Volume 2: The 36th (Ulster) Division From Formation to the Armistice.* (Solihull: Helion & Company Ltd, 2016).
Ian Passingham, *All the Kaiser's Men: The Life and Death of the German Army on the Western Front 1915-1918* (Stroud: Sutton Publishing, 2005).
Nick Perry (ed.), *Major General Oliver Nugent and the Ulster Division 1915-1918.* (Stroud: Sutton Publishing, 2007).
Nick Perry, *Major General Oliver Nugent: The Irishman who led the Ulster Division in the Great War* (Belfast: Ulster Historical Foundation, 2020).
John Potter, *Scarce Heard Amidst the Guns* (Belfast: Northern Ireland War Memorial, 2013).
Geoffrey Powell, *Plumer: The Soldier's General* (London: Leo Cooper, 1990).
John Powell, *Haig's Tower of Strength: General Sir Edward Bulfin. Ireland's Forgotten General* (Barnsley: Pen & Sword, 2018).
Robin Prior & Trevor Wilson, *Passchendaele: The Untold Story* (New Haven & London: Yale University Press, 1996).
Andrew Rawson, *The Passchendaele Campaign 1917* (Barnsley: Pen & Sword, 2017).
Neil Richardson, *A Coward if I Return, A Hero if I Fall: Stories of Irishmen in World War 1.* (Dublin: The O'Brien Press, 2010).

Gary Sheffield & John Bourne, *Douglas Haig: War Diaries and Letters 1914-1918*.(London: Weidenfeld and Nicolson, 2005).

Jack Sheldon, *The German Army at Passchendaele* (Barnsley: Pen and Sword, 2007)

Peter Simkins, Geoffrey Jukes & Michael Hickey, *The First World War: The War to end all Wars* (Oxford: Osprey Publishing, 2003).

Edward Louis Spears, *Prelude to Victory* (London: Jonathan Cape, 1939).

Nigel Steel and Peter Hart, *Passchendaele. The Sacrificial Ground*. (London: Cassell & Co, 2000).

Lieutenant-Colonel J. Stewart & John Buchan, *The Fifteenth (Scottish) Division 1914-1919* (Edinburgh: Blackwood & Sons, 1926).

Paul Strong & Sanders Marble, *Artillery in the Great War* (Barnsley: Pen & Sword, 2013).

James W Taylor, *The 1st Royal Irish Rifles in the Great War* (Dublin: Four Courts Press, 2002).

—— *The 2nd Royal Irish Rifles in the Great War* (Dublin: Four Courts Press, 2005).

—— *Guilty but Insane: J.C. Bowen-Colthurst: Villain or Victim* (Dublin: Mercier Press, 2016).

John Terraine, *Douglas Haig: The Educated Soldier* (London: Hutchinson & Co, 1963).

Colonel Edward G L Thurlow, DSO, *The Pill-Boxes of Flanders* (Uckfield: Naval & Military Press reprint of 1932 edition).

Tim Travers, *How the War was Won: Command and Technology in the British Army on the Western Front 1917-1918* (London: Routledge, 1992).

Jan Vancoillie & Kristof Blieck, *Defending the Ypres Front 1914-1918. Trenches, Shelters and Bunkers of the German Army* (Barnsley: Pen & Sword, 2018).

Edwin Campion Vaughan, *Some Desperate Glory: The Diary of a Young Officer, 1917* (Barnsley: Pen & Sword, 2011).

Garrett Alexander Cooper Walker MC, *The Book of the 7th (S) Battalion Royal Inniskilling Fusiliers* (Dublin: Privately published, 1920).

Philip Warner, *Passchendaele* (Barnsley: Pen & Sword, 2005).

Stuart N White, *The Terrors: 16th (Pioneer) Battalion Royal Irish Rifles* (Belfast: Somme Association, 1996).

Lieutenant-Colonel Frederick Ernest Whitton, *The History of the Prince of Wales's Leinster Regiment (Royal Canadians) Part II* (Uckfield: Naval & Military Press reprint of 1924 edition).

Denis Winter, *Haig's Command: A Reassessment* (London: Penguin, 1991).

Leon Wolff, *In Flanders Fields: The 1917 Campaign* (London: Longmans, Green and Company Ltd, 1959).

Colonel Harold Carmichael Wylly, *Crown and Company 1911-1922: The Historical Records of the 2nd Battalion Royal Dublin Fusiliers formerly the 1st Bombay European Regiment* (Uckfield & London: Naval & Military Press reprint).

Captain G.C. Wynne, *If Germany Attacks: The Battle in Depth in the West* (London: Faber and Faber Ltd, 1940).

Major General David T Zabecki, & Lieutenant Colonel Dieter J Biedekarken (eds.) *Lossberg's War: The World War I Memoirs of a German Chief of Staff Fritz von Lossberg* (Lexington, Kentucky: University Press of Kentucky, 2017).

Local History Publications

6th Connaught Rangers Research Project, *The 6th Connaught Rangers. Belfast Nationalists and the Great War.* (Belfast: Ulster Historical Foundation, 2011).
Fiona Berry, *Names Carved in Stone* (Armagh: The Mall Presbyterian Church, Armagh, 2016)
Andrew Henry, *From Hilltop to Over the Top.* (Rathfriland: Privately Published, 2018).
The Inniskillings Museum, *The Fermanagh War Memorial Book of Honour 1914-1921* (Enniskillen: The Inniskillings Museum, 2014).

German Regimental Histories

Oberleutnant Hans Jager, *Das K.B.19 Infanterie-Regiment Konig Viktor Emanuel III. Von Italien* (Munchen: Schick, 1930).
Generalmajor Karl Reber, *Das K.B. 21 Infanterie-Regiment Grossherzog Friedrich Franz IV. Von Mecklenberg-Schwerin* (Munchen: Max Schick, 1929).
Hauptmann Otto Schaidler, *Das K.B.7. Infanterie-Regiment Prinz Leopold* (Munchen: Selbstverlag des Bayerischen Kriegsarchivs, 1922).

Chapters in Edited Volumes

Ian F W Beckett, *Hubert Gough, Neill Malcolm, and Command on the Western Front* in Brian Bond, et al, *Look to Your Front: Studies in the First World War by the British Commission for Military History* (Staplehurst: Spellmount, 1999).
Gary Sheffield & Helen McCartney, *Hubert Gough, Fifth Army, 1916-1918* in Ian F W Beckett and Steven J Corvi, (eds.) *Haig's Generals* (Barnsley: Pen & Sword, 2006).

Journal Articles

Lynn Speer Lemisko, A Dubious Reputation? The Performance of 16th (Irish) Division, 1916-20 March 1918, *The Irish Sword. The Journal of the Military History Society of Ireland*, Vol XXII, No 87, 2000.
Glyn Taylor, 'The Pill-Box Problem': The Tactical Importance of German Concrete Fortifications at the Third Battle of Ypres, *Stand To! The Journal of the Western Front Association*, No. 119, 2020.

Newspapers

The Ballymena Observer
The Belfast News Letter
The Belfast Weekly Telegraph
The Carlow Sentinel

The Dublin Daily Express
The Irish Times
The London Gazette
The Londonderry Sentinel
The Portadown News
The Sligo Champion
The Northern Whig

Electronic Sources

Letter to the Editor of *The Spectator* by JFC Fuller, late Tank Corps, 10 January 1958 available online at: *The Spectator* <http://archive.spectator.co.uk/article/10th-january-1958/19/euston-3221>

Letter to the Editor of *The Spectator* by G. Gold, late Meteorological Section Royal Engineers, 17 January 1958, available online at: The Spectator, <http://archive.spectator.co.uk/article/17th-january-1958/14/sirin-his-letter-about-passchendaele-spectator-dec>

Index

PEOPLE

Armin, General Friedrich Sixt von, 47, 92

Baker-Carr, Brigadier General C., 91, 102
Beddington, Brigadier General E.H.L., 195–96

Charteris, Brigadier General J., 36, 43, 57, 223
Chavasse, Captain Noel, 61–62

Davidson, Brigadier General J., 32
Doyle, Chaplain Father W., 66, 105-6

Gibbs, Philip, 134, 200, 202, 206
Gough, General Sir Hubert, 27–32, 37, 43–44, 63–65, 69, 87, 89–90, 189, 192–95, 197–98, 202, 204–6

Haig, Field Marshal Sir Douglas, 21–22, 24–32, 36–37, 40–41, 43, 56–58, 64, 87, 90, 189, 192–94, 198, 204-5
Hickie, Major General W. 30, 76, 183, 193

Lloyd George, David, 24–26, 30–31, 37, 204

Lossberg, Colonel Fritz von, 47–49, 208, 226

Macdonogh, Brigadier General G.M.W., 36
Malcolm, Brigadier General N., 64, 195–98, 206

Nivelle, General Robert, 21-22, 24–26
Nugent, Major General O., 30, 38, 56, 70–71, 86, 91, 167, 173, 191-93, 194, 207, 222, 225

Plumer, General Sir Herbert, 21–22, 24, 27, 28–30, 32, 205, 225

Rawlinson, General Sir Henry, 21–22, 27
Rupprecht, Crown Prince, 45, 223

Uniacke, Major General H.C.C., 38, 196

Vaughan, Second Lieutenant E.C., 95, 178
Watts, Lieutenant General H.E., 64, 135, 193–94, 207

PLACES

Albrecht Stellung, 48

Beck House/Kaminhof, 78, 103, 116, 119–20, 125–26, 128, 130, 201
Belgian coast, 22, 24, 32, 37, 45, 55
Black Line, 61, 64, 69, 71, 107, 109–11, 125–26, 141–42, 152–53, 156, 165–66, 174, 176, 183–85, 189

Border House, 63, 152, 169–71, 173–74, 176, 178–79
Borry Farm, 103, 107, 109–10, 115–16, 118, 120, 125, 130, 134, 201, 205
Brandhoek, 65, 75, 147

Corn Hill, 165, 167, 169

Delva Farm, 79, 119, 121–25
Dotted Green Line, 160

Frezenberg, 56, 64, 66, 71, 79–80, 93, 121

Gallipoli, 79, 112
Gallipoli Farm, 61, 136, 140–44, 148, 179–80, 187, 195, 201
Gheluvelt Plateau, 22, 24, 29, 51, 56, 59, 69, 87, 89–91, 102, 189, 205, 207
Green Line, 32, 61, 64–65, 102–5, 115–16, 136, 138, 167

Hindu Cottage, 148, 158, 169–70

Iberia, 120, 123–24

Low Farm, 115–16

Menin Gate, 66, 72, 79, 83, 90, 103, 187
Messines, 29, 48, 117, 178, 192

Passchendaele, 25, 45, 57, 92, 106, 201, 206, 224–26
Pilckem Ridge, 60, 187

Pommern Castle, 79, 120, 122, 138
Pommern Redoubt, 201
Pond Farm, 97, 148, 151, 158–59, 163, 166–67, 169–70, 176, 201
Potsdam, 103–5, 107, 109–10, 183

Red Farm, 74, 87, 180

Spree Farm, 61, 95, 158–59, 162, 174, 176–77, 179, 183
Square Farm, 61, 71, 78–79, 117, 121, 123
Steenbeek, 42, 47, 56, 97, 138, 178
St Jean, 74, 87
St Julien, 42, 56, 92, 95, 100, 102, 183, 187

Uhlan Farm, 83–85, 152, 156

Vampir, 103, 108–10, 183
Vlamertinghe, 66, 75, 79, 83, 134

Westhoek, 51, 88–89
Wieltje, 71, 74, 87, 95, 166, 176, 179–80
Wieltje Dugouts, 39, 167, 179
Wytschaete, 28, 31, 43, 208

FORMATIONS/UNITS

Armies
Second Army, 21, 30, 31, 205
Third Army, 191
Fourth Army, 21, 22
Fifth Army, 27, 29-34, 38, 40, 41, 47, 64, 65, 75, 83, 90, 100, 134, 135, 182, 188, 190-192, 194-199, 205-208, 224, 227

Corps
II Corps, 29, 30, 69, 90, 102, 103, 182, 206
VIII Corps, 29, 30, 183
XVII Corps, 193
XVIII Corps, 65
XIX Corps, 68, 70, 74, 98, 100, 102, 107, 116, 123, 135, 179, 182-83, 187, 190-195, 197-199, 208

Divisions
7th Division, 30, 194,
8th Division, 63, 93, 100, 186, 196, 206
11th Division, 193

15th Division, 35, 59, 63, 64, 69-72, 75, 116, 206
16th Division, 13, 14, 30, 34-35, 38, 59, 66, 70-71, 75, 83, 89, 92, 100, 102, 106, 134, 136, 138, 141, 183-184, 186-189, 192, 198, 200, 206
25th Division, 30, 89
28th Division, 193
36th Division, 8, 14-5, 30, 34, 38-9, 56, 68, 70, 74-75, 92, 97, 100, 102, 118, 122, 134-136, 138, 154, 178-179, 183, 186-188, 191-192, 200, 208
38th Division, 194
39th Division, 59, 61
48th Division, 52, 95, 100, 167, 178, 187
55th Division, 31, 34, 59, 61, 63-64, 68-69, 70-71, 74-75, 83, 85, 206

Brigades
21st Brigade, 30, 194
23rd Brigade, 102, 189, 190, 193

47th Brigade, 66
48th Brigade, 35, 36, 66, 93, 102, 113, 115, 183, 189
49th Brigade, 66, 78-79, 92, 95, 115, 124-126, 186, 190, 209
107th Brigade, 15, 70-71, 83, 85, 92, 183, 209
108th Brigade, 5, 84, 95, 115, 136, 140, 142, 148, 149, 152, 156, 186, 190, 210
109th Brigade, 15, 83, 95, 158-160, 167, 169, 176, 179, 182, 187, 210
143rd Brigade, 52, 95, 178
145th Brigade, 167, 187
164th Brigade, 59, 66, 70
165th Brigade, 59, 70
166th Brigade, 59, 61, 70

Battalions
6th Connaught Rangers, 69, 70, 75, 80, 116, 125, 126, 227
11th Hampshire Regiment, 35, 52, 69
7th Leinster Regiment, 15, 30, 34, 65, 72, 74-76
2nd Middlesex Regiment, 93, 102, 104-107
2nd Royal Dublin Fusiliers, 69, 93, 98, 102, 104, 107, 109, 112, 209
8th Royal Dublin Fusiliers, 66, 76, 78, 93, 95, 102, 105, 106, 107, 109
9th Royal Dublin Fusiliers, 66, 76, 78, 93, 102, 105, 108, 110, 111, 113
10th Royal Dublin Fusiliers, 35
7th Royal Inniskilling Fusiliers, 66, 68, 78, 79, 95, 115, 118, 119, 125, 128, 138, 200
8th Royal Inniskilling Fusiliers, 17, 72, 77, 80, 95, 115, 181, 186
9th Royal Inniskilling Fusiliers, 95, 106, 158, 166, 167, 170, 173, 174, 176
10th Royal Inniskilling Fusiliers, 95, 158, 174, 176, 177
11th Royal Inniskilling Fusiliers, 95, 158, 169, 188, 203, 208
1st Royal Irish Fusiliers, 15, 111
7/8th Royal Irish Fusiliers, 52, 80, 92, 115-116, 118-119, 124, 125, 127-128, 130, 141, 187, 191, 209
9th Royal Irish Fusiliers, 71, 95, 115, 118, 136, 138, 140-141, 144, 147-150, 152, 155, 166-167, 178, 186, 190-191, 207
2nd Royal Irish Regiment, 80, 95, 111, 115, 125, 130, 132, 209
6th Royal Irish Regiment, 71-72
2nd Royal Irish Rifles, 89
7th Royal Irish Rifles, 66, 93, 98, 102-105, 107-108, 111, 113
8th Royal Irish Rifles, 84, 86
9th Royal Irish Rifles, 38, 83
10th Royal Irish Rifles, 84, 87
11th Royal Irish Rifles, 95, 136, 140, 156, 158
12th Royal Irish Rifles, 95, 123, 136, 140, 152-154, 156, 182
13th Royal Irish Rifles, 71, 95, 123, 136, 147, 150-152, 178, 180, 186, 190
14th Royal Irish Rifles, 15, 71, 83, 95, 152, 158-159, 163, 165-167, 171, 173, 176, 178
15th Royal Irish Rifles, 38, 48, 85, 112
16th Royal Irish Rifles, 68, 97, 166, 178
1st Royal Munster Fusiliers, 66, 76, 209
1/8th Royal Warwickshire Regiment, 178, 182, 95
2nd West Yorkshire Regiment, 102

Miscellaneous
3rd Brigade Tank Corps, 102
48th Brigade Machine Gun Company, 113
107th Brigade Machine Gun Company, 85
108th Brigade Machine Gun Company, 140, 148
109th Brigade Machine Gun Company, 167, 169
108th Field Ambulance RAMC, 152, 180
109th Field Ambulance RAMC, 68, 74, 87, 97, 180, 181
110th Field Ambulance RAMC, 74
112th Field Ambulance RAMC, 75, 83, 134
122nd Field Company Royal Engineers, 97
150th Field Company Royal Engineers, 97, 179
153rd Brigade Royal Field Artillery, 8, 39, 74, 179
173rd Brigade Royal Field Artillery, 39
48th Trench Mortar Battery, 113
108th Trench Mortar Battery, 150
109th Trench Mortar Battery, 159

21 Squadron RFC, 190, 208
32 Squadron RFC, 66
57 Squadron RFC, 112
100 Squadron RFC, 40

Church Lad's Brigade, 132

Loyal Dublin Volunteers, 170
Ulster Volunteer Force, 38, 142, 163, 170, 181

German Army
Fourth Army, 45, 47, 48, 92, App II
Group Ypres, 47, 92, 211, App II

Divisions
3rd Reserve Division, 110
5th Bavarian Division, 92, 141, 187, App II
12th Reserve Division, 106
54th Division, 110

Regiments
Bavarian Infanterie Regiment Nr. 19, 92, 93, 115, 116, 120, 123, 138, 147, 148
Bavarian Infanterie Regiment Nr. 21, 93, 123, 124, 141, 142, 154
Fusilier Regiment Nr. 34, 93
Fusilier Regiment Nr. 86, 41, 51
Infanterie Regiment Nr. 84, 110
Reserve Infanterie Regiment Nr. 2, 93
Reserve Infanterie Regiment Nr. 49, 93